PUZZLED
100 Pieces of Autism

For Lee

Nilla Childs

Nilla Childs

Fifth Generation Publishing
3320 Robinhood Road #305
Winston-Salem, NC 27106

Some names and identifying details of individuals and organizations
have been changed to protect their privacy.

Cover photo of Daniel Childs, age 15, by Nilla Childs.
Back cover photo of Nilla Childs by Steve Childs.
Cover design by Nadine Buckinger.

ISBN: 1469956721
ISBN-13: 978-1469956725

For my three loves: Steve, Daniel and David.

"The riddles of God
are more satisfying than the solutions of man."

—G. K. Chesterton

CONTENTS: 100 PIECES

PREFACE

When I finished writing this book, I gave the manuscript first to my husband Steve to read. I felt very anxious because I didn't know what he would think. For the four and a half years I had been writing, he hadn't read any part of it.

One Saturday afternoon, I was out shopping for groceries. My cell phone rang as I stood on the concrete floor in the freezer section of Costco. When I answered it I heard Steve giggling, "I love your book. This is so funny. I am laughing and I am getting choked up and then I'm laughing again. You are a great writer."

I was surprised by his positive response. I was relieved that he liked it. While I was loading the groceries into the car, the phone rang again. "I'm laughing so hard I'm about to vomit!" Well, wasn't that the highest compliment?

Once Steve approved, I planned to give the manuscript to Daniel. I was even more nervous about having him read it. I didn't know how to anticipate his reaction. I didn't want him to be hurt. There is nothing in the world worth hurting my son in any way.

I invited Daniel to have lunch with me at our favorite Indian restaurant. I prefaced handing the three-ring binder to him by saying, "I want you to know how much I love you. I hope this will help people, but if you don't want me to publish this, I won't. If you don't want me to give this to anyone else, I won't. I wish you had someone you could talk this over with. Some of it is hard stuff. Some of it was hard to write. Please let me know what you think."

That night, as I reviewed the day, Steve warned me NOT to ask Daniel about the book while he read it. He reminded me to be patient and to wait until Daniel brought it up to me.

Several days went by. I knew that Daniel didn't have anything on his schedule. I knew he was dog sitting which literally meant sitting most of the day. I knew he didn't have anything else to do and would have plenty of time to read. He didn't mention the book. I couldn't help myself. I couldn't stand the suspense. "Have you started reading?"

"No."

Several more days passed. Each day, I discussed with Steve what I would do if Daniel never read it or never gave me his approval. I knew that if either Steve or Daniel responded negatively I would stop the process; but if Daniel didn't respond at all what would I do? I predicted that, in a void, I would have to choose to move forward.

When I saw Daniel again, he didn't say a word. I tried to hold my tongue; but impulsively, it slipped out, "Have you started reading?"

"No."

The next night, Daniel came over to eat dinner with us. While we were waiting for David and Andrea to arrive, he sat on the kitchen floor playing with the dogs as I finished cooking. I tried to ask him about his day. He wasn't saying anything. Finally, about to burst, I said, "If you're not going to read the book now, will you please give it back to me so I can let someone else read it?"

He responded with a snap in his voice, "Well, I'm on page 150!" as if he was indignant that I would question his competence.

"Oh, okay, good." I paused, hoping he would say something about it, any comment at all. "Do you have anything you want to tell me at this point?" He shook his head no. Why do I continue to expect something that I know is not going to happen?

One evening the next week, I noticed a white three-ring binder on the foyer table. I picked it up and realized it was the copy Daniel had been reading. When I saw him again, I invited, "Whenever someone agrees to read my book for me, I take them out to lunch to go over their feedback. Do you want to go to lunch with me tomorrow? We can go to our same Indian buffet."

"That should work."

"I'll pick you up tomorrow at 11:30."

Instead of our favorite, tried-and-true, we tried a new Indian place, at Daniel's suggestion. We went through the buffet. I asked the waiter to bring us some naan to go with our meal. I tried to get Daniel talking about the book. "Did it hurt your feelings? Is there anything you want me to take out?"

"No. There is some unflattering stuff, but that doesn't mean you should take it out."

"Oh."

As I tried to pull comments out of him, I became increasingly astounded by his insight. I told him how significant his perspective was. I asked him if he would be willing to give me comments "chapter by chapter." He agreed. I wanted to get this from him while it was fresh on his mind and while he was willing. I drove us straight from the restaurant to my office. "Do you want to sit at the computer and type, or do you want to dictate to me and I'll take notes?"

"You write."

I flipped through the manuscript, page by page, asking him about each "piece." You could never imagine how grateful I felt for Daniel's willingness to share. For me, this was like a dream come true, to be able to hear my son's thoughts; healing the past ten years of silence.

Throughout the book, at the end of each "piece," you will see in italics: my questions in [brackets] and Daniel's words in "quotation marks."

INTRODUCTION — PIECE BY PIECE

I am an obsessed mother.

I live my life trying to prevent others from experiencing pain. My efforts are magnified when it comes to my children: I would do anything to protect them. My motherly antennae are perpetually focused, quivering, anticipating any potential harm. If I detect danger, I begin squealing alarms of warning. Further terrifying me, it seems no sound comes out of my mouth, or at least, no one else hears. The way I try to control others feels like I am trying to steer a rhinoceros through a maze with a drinking straw—utterly impossible. I am learning to stop this insanity. I am practicing letting people live their own lives without my help.

I still try to control my own little world by keeping things in order. I alphabetize my kitchen spices so that I know basil is on the back row, left, while turmeric is on the front row, right. When I unload the dishwasher, I put away my dishes in alternating stacks of blue, green, purple, etc., so that identical colors do not touch. I try to stay organized. I love lists, plans and systems. I follow a set process, even with leisurely activities like assembling a jigsaw puzzle.

Nilla's Method for Completing a Jigsaw Puzzle
1. First, I turn all the pieces out of the box.
2. I plop the pieces onto the table into a big jumbled pile.

3. Turning over each upside-down piece right-side up, I begin to see what I have.
4. Next is finding edges—pieces with straight edges form the outer border.
5. I look for matching details like fragments of words, faces or shapes.
6. I start fitting together complementary pieces to form the central design.
7. Nearing the end, I focus on solidly colored pieces, linking the background.
8. Seeing the completed image, I admire my work and pat myself on the back.

Assembling a jigsaw puzzle is the perfect metaphor for the way I have tried to figure out how to help my son Daniel. I can only pick up one "piece" at a time, just as twelve-step programs recommend taking life "one day at a time." Piece by piece, I keep trying, turning in different directions, to see what fits. Similarly, in life, I tried strategy after strategy, searching for ways to help my sons Daniel and David, or for ways I could get along with my husband Steve.

You will read one "piece" of my story at a time. The first two sections are not chronological; they skip around, jumping through time from Daniel's life as an adult to back to the time Steve and I met, forward to when Daniel was a baby, and so on. The chaotic fragmentation is meant to represent the way my mind tumbled backward through my bewilderment as I tried to figure out what was going on. Although you may feel as confused and frustrated as I did in my life, please keep reading. Slowly, the pieces begin to fit together. Each subsequent section becomes more orderly, just as jigsaw puzzles begin to take shape and ultimately reveal a cohesive image.

STEP ONE
OUT OF THE BOX

Nilla's Method for Completing a Jigsaw Puzzle
1.   First, I turn all the pieces out of the box.

Imagine a jigsaw puzzle box which pictures a perfect family. Mom's and Dad's arms encircle two smiling children standing on a grassy green lawn in front of a quaint cottage. A clear blue sky welcomes one fluffy white cloud and the sun is shining.

One hundred carved cardboard pieces, clustered safely together on the box bottom, are protected within the dark, quiet interior. With an earthquake shake, the box is lifted into the air; pieces collide into one corner. A long fingernail slices the seal on all four sides. Light announces the inevitable Titanic slide out of the box. Like the pieces fall into space, my memory scatters to random, disordered moments.

I wonder…when did this all begin? At what point did our son's life become unmanageable? Was it when he left the structure of high school? Was it when we forced him out of the shelter of our home? Did his brain change at puberty, influenced by surging hormones? Was he damaged emotionally by high school bullying? Did his brain mutate, constantly influenced by computer radiation? Was his mind slowly starved of proper nutrients due to his faulty digestive system? Was his brain injured when he fell snow-skiing as a teen, or when as an infant, still strapped into his car seat, he landed head-first onto our

3

gravel driveway? Is his condition a result of genetics? Are environmental toxins to blame? Has my simmering anxiety poisoned his well-being? Were we, as parents, too slack as disciplinarians? Or is he simply just like his dad, a creative "genius" who doesn't adhere to common social conventions?

PIECE 1—COLLAPSE

D aniel had no idea where he was going. We had no idea where he was going. He didn't have a cell phone, so Steve and I had no way to check up on him, to make sure he was all right. As I watched Daniel's car pull away, I feared the worst deep down in my gut. Daniel had seemed desperate, depressed. But what else could we have done? His dad and I were exasperated. For years, we had argued and pleaded, "If you're not in school, you need to work and find your own place to live…or get treatment."

This week had been the last straw. When Steve and I returned home from the beach, our expensive new trees were dried out and dead. Daniel had not watered them, as we had asked. He had never even left the house. The whole week he had been playing online poker, sleeping all day, eating crackers, and drinking soda. Steve and I could not allow Daniel to continue to live at home. We couldn't stand any longer to watch the precious life we had nurtured and loved, disintegrating before our eyes. We gave Daniel an ultimatum: agree to look at the treatment program in Florida or leave the house, tonight.

Once Daniel's silver car was out of sight, I burst into tears. Steve and I hugged each other as if to keep from collapsing in the hallway. Heavy sadness gripped me. My head was throbbing. Exhausted from grief and unbearable anxiety, I took a Xanax and crumpled into bed.

I woke several hours later, still aching with sadness, feeling like I was missing a limb. I didn't know what to do. It was Sunday night—that meant recycling pickup tomorrow. Grateful for the relief of a menial, mindless chore, I carried the green plastic bin of aluminum cans, glass jars, and newspapers around the side of our one-level stucco house, to the street.

What on earth? There was Daniel's car back in our driveway. After bracing myself from the shock, I ordered my legs to keep moving toward the curb. I placed the bin down on the wet asphalt. Out of the side of my eye, I saw Daniel sitting in his five-year-old Toyota, thumbing through the AAA book. I went over to him. Tears, matching the texture and the intensity of the pouring rain, were streaming down his face. Something had broken in him.

"I can't find a hotel." I knew there were dozens of hotels in our area listed in black ink on the flimsy pages in his hands. "I went to the Wal-Mart parking lot. I thought about sleeping in my car, but it was raining so hard I couldn't crack the windows for air."

I shrugged my shoulders, trying to maintain my "tough love" stance. I was wary that this was another effort to postpone action. Steve must have glanced outside because he came out through the front door down the brick sidewalk and seemed as confused as I was. He motioned for Daniel and me to come inside.

As Daniel walked through the door, his body was limp, but weakly he allowed me to hug him tight as I tried to balance my "Oh, honey" assurances with my artificially-induced no-nonsense position. Steve's cell phone rang, and he walked out of the room to carry on his conversation. I motioned for Daniel to sit on the living room sofa. I eased myself down next to him. Daniel began quietly, "I don't know what to do. I don't know where to go." Then he broke down, bawling, sobbing.

I tried to comfort him by rubbing his back, my flat palm circling from one shoulder to the other. "It's OK, go ahead and cry." I was relieved to see signs of life in his stone cold face, even if it was anguished.

After a while, he mumbled, "Is it too late to go to Florida?"

"We can go to Florida. It's too late tonight, but we can leave tomorrow morning. Go ahead and pack tonight."

PIECE 2 — ORANGE BLOSSOM

In spite of the somber mood fogging the silver sedan that miserable August drive south, I tried to engage Daniel in lighter conversation. Summoning more cheerful memories, I sang the Orange Blossom Song that my mother had taught me, age 13, and my three little sisters, 11, 7, and 3, on our Christmas vacation to Florida thirty years earlier. "I want to wake up in the morning where the orange blossoms grow. Where the sun comes peeping into where I'm sleeping and the songbirds sing hello. I love the fresh air and the sunshine it's so good for us you know. So I'll make my home in Florida where the orange blossoms grow."

My mother had grown up in Florida, and she proudly sang the Orange Blossom Song with the fervent enthusiasm of a sports fanatic belting out her college team's fight song. She sang allegiance to her tropical inheritance as if cheerleading against the opposing team, as if it were my father's northern climes. She sang as if cheering for Southern sunshine and against icy accumulations of the latitudes my father's medical school and career had taken the two of them, starting their marriage in frigid Pennsylvania, to the miserably cold winters of Wisconsin, and now, to North Carolina.

My mother had a beautiful alto voice. She loved to harmonize. I loved it when she sang lullabies to me, from the time I was a baby, and for each of my younger sisters. Everything about my mother was the essence of beautiful, from her stylish fashion, her neatly trimmed blonde hair, her sculpted cheeks and symmetrical facial features, to her slim figure, down to her delicate ankles. Everything—her appearance, her poise, her broad smile, her lyrical laugh—seemed almost too perfect. She was a social queen. It always seemed to me that everyone loved her.

I tried to entertain Daniel out of his gloom by telling him about my childhood Florida trip. "My mom had the station wagon all packed, and we four girls—Sally was still a baby— waited restlessly for my dad to get home from work so we could all drive south to our grandparents' home in Florida. Dad surprised us all by pulling into our driveway in a huge motor home he had borrowed from a colleague! We just about flipped! Screaming with joy, we raced around, inspecting all the cool stuff, from the compact kitchen to the bathroom with shower. Mom heated up Chunky Beef soup for us while we were buzzing down the highway. Mom took over driving while Dad set up the beds, and we slept until morning, when Dad surprised us again by announcing we were at Disney World! This was back in 1971, when the park had only been open a few weeks. We girls were energized from a full night's sleep, but Dad was so tired that we left after only one hour. We had the monorail to ourselves, because no one else was leaving that early! Several hours later, we arrived at Granny and Big Dave's house, in time for lunch."

I glanced to my right, hoping my reminiscence might have sparked some slight sign of life. Daniel stared straight ahead, eyes glazed, showing zero recognition that I existed. I re-focused my eyes above the steering wheel, back to the asphalt pavement with white lines flashing quickly past.

PIECE 3 — STOPPED UP

My baby did not want to leave my womb. Maybe that was a sign of things to come: a lifetime of transition-intolerance. I was two weeks overdue, huge, and miserable. I had gained more than forty pounds with this pregnancy. The weight gain had started with my eating to overcome morning sickness. I was tired and impatient and anxious. My obstetrician brought me in to the hospital to induce labor. Even after twelve hours of increasing levels of Pitocin, the baby still refused to enter this world. I went home to get some rest. I woke several hours later to contractions, and my water breaking. Steve rushed me to the hospital where I labored for seven more hours, screamed for an epidural, and, finally, pushed the baby out!

He was a big boy: 9 pounds, 5 ounces. All was normal. Of course, Steve and I were beyond thrilled by this long-anticipated, precious little miracle of life. My parents and sisters came to "ooh" and "aah" and take turns cuddling the newest, tiniest family member.

During the night, the nurse brought Daniel to me and showed me how to breastfeed him. Coincidentally, the nurse was my friend from high school: tall, friendly Patricia, whom I hadn't seen or talked to in four years. In between feedings, she took him back to the baby nursery so I could get some sleep. I could hardly stand to see her taking him from the room. Now that he was outside of me, I wanted to keep him close to me constantly.

The next morning in the hospital room, I was startled to find my pediatrician waking me to say my baby boy had been taken to intensive care. His intestines were stopped up, probably by a "meconium plug," he called it, and he assured me this was common. It didn't seem common to me as I walked down the hall and cried and cried at the sight of my baby attached to all kinds of tubes and monitors, lying in a little incubator. After a day and another night of observation, they said he was fine, and sent us home.

I guess I was like any typical first-time mother. Elation, exhaustion, and ecstasy all overlapped in this overwhelming, tiny miracle in my arms. I held him, fed him, and adored him. I stared at him, amazed at the beauty of his soft skin, his miniature fingers and toes. I smiled at him, bathed him, and dressed him. He slept next to our bed in a bassinet. Down the hall in his crib in the nursery would have seemed too far away.

All babies spit up occasionally, but this wasn't a typical newborn baby. This baby spit up all the time, but you really couldn't even call it spit up. It was "projectile vomiting," more like an eruption of soured milk. One Sunday after church, a family invited us to their home for lunch and Daniel sprayed vomit across their neatly set table of food, like a fire hydrant opened on a hot summer day.

Many times the baby was constipated, his belly swollen and hard. Sometimes days passed between dirty diapers. The pediatrician prescribed suppositories. Steve and I held Daniel down to insert the waxy capsule and instantly feces erupted, spraying over us and across the room.

Day after day, week after week, this cycle of bloating, vomiting, constipation, and diarrhea continued. It seemed Daniel's stomach swelled only on nights and weekends, because whenever I took him to the pediatrician, he looked fine, his belly normal. I remember the pediatrician disguising a slight smirk mixed with a touch of pity as he told me Daniel looked normal. I could read in his eyes he thought I was nothing more than the stereotypical over-anxious first-time mother.

Three days, four, five, then six. One week, two, three, four, then five weeks of this constant concern. Daniel's belly was bloated and swollen again—this time during office hours. The pediatrician realized the seriousness and sent us straight to the children's hospital. After a day of X-rays and other exams, they diagnosed his condition: Hirshsprung's Disease, also called congenital mega colon. The nerve endings in a portion of his intestines were not functioning. He was immediately admitted to the hospital for surgery to treat his life-threatening condition.

I had to stop breastfeeding Daniel so they could administer anesthesia. My breasts continued filling up with milk that had nowhere to go. They swelled to painful fullness that felt like they would burst. The worst of it was that the baby must have thought I was teasing him. When I held him in my arms to comfort him the night before surgery, he could smell the milk, but I wouldn't feed him.

Daniel was so little that the nurses and residents had a difficult time finding his veins for intravenous fluid, so the veins would collapse, and the fluids would build up in his flesh, making his arm or leg swell to three times normal size. The alternative was for them to do "cut downs," where they made small incisions in his ankle to have easier, more reliable access to his veins.

After surgery, my little baby had a colostomy. It was a gruesome and frightening sight, like a scene I would imagine from a horror movie, or from some Halloween prank. Green goo squirted from the red fleshy stoma (raw end of intestine) pulled through a hole cut in his belly.

The nurses taught me how to empty and change the little plastic bags adhered to his tummy with adhesive putty. The bags had to be cut down to size for such a tiny fellow. It took practice until I could learn to remove the bag, clean the area, have another bag ready quickly before another greenness exuded. I had to make sure no air was caught, so it wouldn't be too puffy, and the adhesive irritated his skin, causing red rashes. Sometimes the bags leaked—yechh! The bags filled with gas, and puffed out his clothing on the left side. But no more dirty diapers until his other two surgeries were completed at 7 months and 9 months of age to reverse the colostomy.

During each hospitalization, I had to stop the breastfeeding, and tried to compress my breasts to reduce the flow of milk. I was able to pump some milk and freeze it for later use. I didn't mind the pain and inconvenience, compared to the horrific pain I knew my tiny little one was feeling. I would have given anything to take his place, to go through the surgery for him so he wouldn't have to endure the awful pain.

PIECE 4 — WALTZ

It was a sunny Saturday morning in March. I was a senior at Salem Academy, an all-female, college-preparatory boarding school. My head was still spinning from taking a three-hour long exam in French, for advanced placement credit, at the local college, Wake Forest University. As I was walking down the stairs, I heard what sounded like my friend Jim playing the piano in the girl's dorm next door to the academic building where my exam had taken place.

I crossed the grassy quad, pulled open the heavy oak doors, and walked past the receptionist into the spacious lobby with cathedral ceiling. Jim was playing my favorite song, his original composition, "The Waltz of the Spirit," as a group clustered around the baby grand piano, singing together. I recognized Rich, and almost everyone else looked familiar to me from the Inter-Varsity Christian fellowship group.

Who was this strange man in denim overalls with dark hair, thick eyebrows, and a heavy mustache, suddenly running toward me in slow motion? His arms were extended as if he was mimicking the corny television commercial—advertising soap or shampoo—of two lovers approaching each other in a field of flowers. The stranger wore a huge grin from ear to ear and ended his approach with a big bear hug. I had never seen this guy before in my life. What did he think he was doing, running up and hugging me? The room erupted in laughter. Jim stopped playing and turned toward the commotion.

My face must have turned a bright red! It was embarrassing enough to be the center of attention, but I felt totally uncomfortable as unwilling participant in this bizarre, socially inappropriate display. Ha, ha, I smiled reflexively, pretending I thought it was funny too.

Trying to regain my composure, I formally introduced myself to the stranger, extending a culturally acceptable handshake. "Hello, my name is Nilla Dudley. Who are you?"

"Steve," he returned in three distinctly southern syllables, his giant grin swallowing all other features.

Later I learned that Rich had whispered to Steve, "It's Nilla! Do something!" Apparently, for months Rich had told Steve "all about me," trying to convince his childhood pal Steve to drive six hours to visit him for the weekend, with the "carrot on the stick" being that he would set him up with a cute girl with a funny name, "Nilla Dudley." But Rich had neglected one important task: to fill me in on the plans. He had never told me the first thing about Steve. He had never even mentioned Steve to me during the year I had known him. So, it was an awkward first meeting. Humorous, yes. Memorable, yes. Weird, yes.

Attending an all-girls school rendered me desperate for a date. Boys were few and far between and finding someone to take me to the prom was like finding a needle in a haystack. One or two of my friends had steady boyfriends, so their chore was done. Most of my other friends had, by this late month, located a friend's cousin or brother who agreed to attend. I had less than three weeks to find a date, and one of those weeks I would be on spring break snow skiing in Colorado. My mind couldn't focus on math or science or Modern European classes. I had to find a prom date!

When I went to church the next day and saw Steve and Rich sitting two pews in front of me, I did what I had to do. I pretended to be a member of the church, so I could go up to the "visitors," Steve and Rich, to shake their hands, as was the church's custom to welcome newcomers. After church, I went out to lunch with the usual group of college kids. Steve slyly slipped his car keys to Rich and pretended he needed a ride to the restaurant, so I gave him a lift. Later that afternoon four of us met up to play tennis.

We exchanged phone numbers and addresses, and I called him later that week to invite him to the Senior Prom. He didn't know if he could afford the cost of gas, but he would see what he could do.

For the next few weeks, Steve worked extra hours mowing lawns and raking to earn the dough from his dad.

PIECE 5 — WISDOM, EXTRACTED

In the 10th grade, Daniel had all four wisdom teeth extracted at once and had the usual pain and swelling. As the dental surgeon instructed, Daniel took antibiotics and pain medication and rested at home for a few days, putting ice on his swollen jaw twice an hour, and gargling with warm salt water solution.

Steve was the "stay-at-home-dad" in charge of Daniel and David while I was at work. He invented an ingenious way of tying a bag of frozen peas to each side of Daniel's puffy face using a pair of pantyhose (new and unused!) After a few days, the swelling decreased, so Daniel stopped taking the pain medication. He returned to his normal school schedule. A week or two later, Daniel mentioned his teeth ached.

"Really?" I looked at him, wondering what could be the cause. He should have healed up by now. "Oh, honey, I'm sorry, I wonder what the matter is. Are you still taking your antibiotics?"

"No."

"You're not? When did you finish them?"

"I stopped taking them."

"What? You're supposed to take *all* of them."

"Oh. I thought I could stop taking them when I stopped taking the pain pills."

"You're *always* supposed to finish antibiotic prescriptions, or you can get an infection."

"Oh."

"Where's the bottle? Go get it for me. Let me see how many you took, so we can figure out when you stopped taking them. I'll call the dentist's office tomorrow morning to make an appointment for you and we'll have him take a look."

The dentist said he had never seen an infection like this. The infection, raging in the hollow sockets where his wisdom teeth had been, had spread to his jaw bone.

The dentist had to place tubes in the sockets and scrape out the infected tissue and bone. It was extremely painful, and Daniel cried so hard his body shook uncontrollably, as he gasped for breath, convulsing. He was embarrassed that he was crying so hard, but he couldn't help it, and they wouldn't let him leave the dentist's office until he could stand on his own and walk.

The dentist prescribed an even more powerful antibiotic and made sure that all of us knew that Daniel had to take every last pill. As the dentist talked to Steve and me and explained the process, he warned us it was a severe, dangerous infection, and had it gone untreated, it could have been fatal. At every visit, the dentist repeated his concerns, and said he could not guarantee us that the infection would clear up, but that he would do everything he could.

Daniel had to return to the dentist four or five more times for nightmarish torture sessions with shots of Novocain, more holes drilled, and more digging and scraping. It was like Daniel had to have multiple surgeries with no general anesthesia. The dentist himself seemed to experience Daniel's pain vicariously as he performed the procedure on Daniel. Daniel had to return daily for two weeks for treatments, and consequently fell behind in school.

The infection did eventually clear up, but to this day, thirteen years later, Daniel has remained anxious and comes close to a panic attack any time he goes into a dentist's office, even for a routine cleaning.

PIECE 6 — PROM-ISED

Ah, awkward memories of our first date, my senior prom. After his day-long 300+ mile drive from Atlanta, Steve didn't think ahead to clean the trash and food out of his car, so when I was trying to sit on the passenger seat in my formal gown, balancing on my high-heeled shoes, I had to wait for him to throw the McDonald's wrappers and empty paper cups into the back. He felt uncomfortable dancing seventies-style at the prom, so he enthusiastically broke into a square-dance do-si-do around me while my friends stared and smirked. The next day we played tennis.

We wrote letters daily. We phoned weekly. We arranged weekends we could get together. Steve drove up to attend my high school graduation and to see me star in the play, *The Boyfriend*. Oddly, I played the character of Pierrot, the male lead (it was an all-girls school.) We both attended our friend Jim's wedding in Florida that summer. Steve's family invited me to join them on their vacation to Hilton Head.

In September, my father drove me and all my dorm room paraphernalia north in the family station wagon. It was a two day drive, to Mount Holyoke College in South Hadley, Massachusetts, one of the "Seven Sisters" all-female colleges. I met my roommate, unpacked my clothes, attended orientation, purchased my textbooks, and went to my first week of classes. There was only one pay phone on the entire hall, so women lined up every night by 11 p.m., when the long-distance rates dropped dramatically.

I couldn't imagine spending an empty weekend, especially a long weekend, like Labor Day, without Steve. I made a flight reservation to Atlanta and took the local bus to the airport an hour away. I didn't think it necessary to inform my parents of my plans. Being away at college, I was independent now, and I didn't think I needed to report my whereabouts to them.

Trouble is, my mother called that weekend. When she couldn't get in touch with me, she asked to speak to my roommate, who must have thought she had to lie for me, because she kept saying she "didn't know where I was." When I returned to campus Monday night, I found dozens of "While You Were Out" messages stuck to my door. I called home, confused about the panic. "What's the matter?" I got an earful. After several days of calling many times a day, my mother had become hysterical. She had imagined that I was pregnant and had eloped with Steve.

I apologized. I was sorry I hadn't called to tell them my plans. I hadn't intended to be sneaky or to trick my parents, but I couldn't deal with my mother's overreaction over the phone. I dissolved into tears that my mother didn't trust me, didn't know me. Steve and I had never even had sex! I was completely innocent of her imagined charges. Previously, Mom had recommended birth control pills to me. It had been an awkward conversation, where I had tried to explain that Steve and I had agreed to wait until marriage, so abstinence was our choice.

I felt devastated that my own mother didn't understand me at all. My sister had to play mediator of our heated discussions and the eventual outcome was that I agreed to finish my entire freshman year at Mount Holyoke before I considered transferring to be closer to Steve. That seemed to calm my poor mother's nerves.

I tried to convince Steve to transfer to Hampshire College, an arts school near Mount Holyoke. He said he couldn't afford to. I applied to transfer to Emory University so I would be living in the same town as Steve, and I was accepted.

In June, at my mother's suggestion (go figure), Steve and I drove out west for the summer in his clunky golden Ford Falcon. We camped out, hiked at Estes Park, and looked for work at National Parks all over the western U.S.

Finally, we found work as "maids" at a small motel, the Tyrolean Lodge, in Sun Valley, Idaho. The owners provided two tiny rooms for us, one under each eave, on opposite ends of the Lodge. At first, they looked puzzled when we said we needed two rooms but agreed when they read our sincere expressions.

We washed and dried sheets and towels in the huge commercial machines. We figured out how to cooperate enough to fold sheets in the same direction. We cleaned motel rooms each morning and went swimming or hiking in the afternoons. We had a sweet deal for a while, until Steve realized he hadn't registered for college that fall at Georgia State. For some reason, he couldn't take care of it from a distance, and his mother couldn't do it for him, so we had to quit our motel work almost as soon as we had begun, and head back east.

That fall, I moved into my dorm room at Emory, met my roommate Kathy, unpacked my clothes, and on the first night I took the city bus to Steve's house for dinner. His mother was a good cook! I kept up with my classes and did my homework, but I never felt connected socially on campus. I worked part time and spent most of my free time with Steve, going to church, walking up Stone Mountain, and hanging out at his house.

Steve and I were in love. We had fun together. We laughed together. We could imagine growing old together. We missed each other when we were apart. We wanted to be together all the time. We couldn't imagine waiting to be married, even a few more years until I finished college.

We became engaged in October and set the wedding date. We asked the minister at the church in my home town to marry us. During our pre-marital counseling sessions, the minister listened, questioned, and considered our story. At our final session, he advised against our marrying, saying we had too many differences in our backgrounds, that our marriage would be difficult. He explained his opinion: that we come from different social backgrounds, different economic backgrounds, and different educational backgrounds.

We considered his advice, but continued with our plans to marry in June.

PIECE 7 — BITTEN

My part-time job was to babysit two school-aged children, a boy and a girl. I was to meet them as they got off the bus each afternoon, make sure they did their homework and practiced their music lessons. Then I was to start dinner for their working single mother. She encouraged me to bring my baby with me and allowed me to keep Daniel's playpen and highchair in her living room.

One clear autumn afternoon, I was sitting on the swinging bench on the porch of the Victorian home in the West End area of Winston-Salem. It was three o'clock, time to breastfeed Daniel. I arranged myself and my shirt in my usual, modest position, with a blanket draped over one shoulder.

The process of breastfeeding seemed a miracle to me, a continuation of the mystery of pregnancy. Breastfeeding was an ongoing, quiet, soft, tender, life-giving, stunning revelation of God's wonderful creation. I was pleased to be able to comfort and soothe my crying, hungry, child with milk that was created uniquely for him.

Slowly, I rocked the porch swing back and forth. I heard Sally playing the piano and Ross playing the violin from inside the house. I heard the birds below, as they hopped along the sidewalk, between neighbors strolling by. Everything was peaceful. Milk flowed and life was good. "Yaaaah!" Suddenly, that little baby BIT DOWN HARD! As I jumped up and screamed in pain, he looked up and smiled, showing off his newly budding teeth. When I recovered my wits, I said "NO!" firmly and pulled him away. A few minutes later, thinking he would respond to my correction, I tried breastfeeding again, with the same results. "OUCH!" I yelled sharply, "THAT HURTS!" I was not only hurt, I was MAD!

This naughty little imp was grinning. I knew from reading La Leche League educational materials that biting could be common, that teething babies have to learn not to "bite the boob that feeds them."

Years later, my second child did this same thing. But the difference was in the baby's facial expression. David looked afraid when I shouted "NO!" and changed his behavior. But there was something different about Daniel's mischievous smile that lingers in my memory. Maybe that incident was irrelevant, or maybe it was a foreshadowing of a lifetime of acting upon people as if they were concrete objects. Now that I know more about the patterns of the rest of his life, I interpret that grin in hindsight as his delight that he had made the "object" squeak like a toy.

Nilla's Diary April 29 (Daniel Age 4)
Daddy and I are seeing a counselor because you are so aggressive and wild and too rough with playmates. Maybe she will give us some guidelines to help you.
Nilla's Diary May 3 (Daniel Age 4)
You bit your friend Gabriel today on his shoulder. It broke the skin. I am really worried about your behavior."

PIECE 8 — HEARTS GROW FONDER

Steve's love letters to me, although I treasured them for the ebullient affection they contained, were atrociously composed. His handwriting was barely legible, scribbled and marked through, the writing of a child in elementary school just learning to write. He couldn't spell worth a darn! He wrote "can" when he meant "cannot" and vice versa. He wrote to me on wrinkled lined paper, with ragged edges, freshly ripped from a spiral notebook:

(Steve Age 19, Nilla Age 17)

Howdy Nilla,

How you doin? I'm back, studin more than ever and playin guitar more than ever. i need to learn a bunch of songs. So I bought the same John Denver song Book that you got. I like it.

i wanna thank you for a really nice weekend. Thank you're parents, (for me), for having me over Sunday afternoon. That was nice of them. Nilla, even though i might not have acted to much like it, really, i did enjoy Saturday night. i [smudge] figured out i probably kidded you to much about it, but i enjoyed it. Thanks for askin me to go. i also like the eatin place Friday nite, when all 4 of us went, then walk around the lake and were chased by a big bad black brown buschy beautiful bear. i hope his feelings weren't to hurt when we said he was pregnant. By the time you get this letter i reckon you'll know where you got accepted. i hope you go were You want to. i mean i hope that you [smudge] get accepted to the main one you wanted to go to. [crossed out] They all are so far away. i wish they were closer. i guess after this summer i want be seening you for a while. i enjoy being with you. i guess guys even have to be gunky sometimes. But, i really do like being with you. i talked to Rich and Elaine just before I left and they said [smudge] i could meet them at Carowind (or whatever its called) the amusement park [crossed out] They said probly the weekend of the 24th (in a week and ½). But that would be a long round trip for one day. i wish they new of a camping place or something near there, to stay. i'll write Rich and ask him more about it. It would be neato-spegittioooooo if you could come down with em. Maybe you can talk to them about it. i was sad to leave ya'll (you, Rich, Elaine) this passed weekend. That [smudge] feeling can sure make the drive home a long one.

i found out my final exams are June 7, 8, 9 and Rich & Elaines wedding is June 8th. He wanted me to be in it. i guess i might have to tell him i can't. i don't wanna miss his wedding for anything cause if i don't see it with my own eye i probly wont believe it. i gotta go beddy bye. i've had a long day. Goodnite.

Love, Steve   Hebrews 4:12-16

Three months later, I wrote to Steve in French. I also wrote on notebook paper, but without ragged edges. I wrote two and a half pages in neat cursive; then translated it into English.

(Nilla Age 17, Steve Age 19)
Ce poème, qui n'est pas vraiment un poème, mais plutôt une lettre, écrite spécialement pour toi, mon amour. Je ne peux pas composer une chanson à la guitare ou de piano, mais j'aime écris en français. Peut-être que tu comprendras:Les rêves d'un amant, en l'absence sont comme le parfum s'attarder un chèvrefeuille. Les pensées de nager dans les joies et les peurs. Toute la force de l'opinion est concentrée dans l'amour;pour les différentes choses que tu ne peut pas le croire. Moi, je suis accablé par toi. Je compte chaque seule seconde jusqu'à notre prochaine réunion. Les difficultees d'une séparation me froisser. L'endurance. L'endurance est nécessaire. Je prie Dieu de me donner la paix afin que je puisse avoir de la patience. Cependant, chaque mile est triste, c'est aussi une benediction parce que Dieu a un plan précis de notre relation. Dieu nous dirige et qui contrôle notre temps.

Jamais dans ma vie j'ai été ébloui par l'amour. Avant, j'ai eu un engouement pour quelqu'un, mais c'est seulement une phase immature. Quand j'étais une jeune fille sotte, je rêvais d'un homme idéal. Souvent, j'ai essayé de découvrir l'homme de mes rêves, mais sans succès. Je n'ai jamais été convaincu, et bien, jusqu'à ce que tu es entré dans ma vie. Quand j'avais renoncé à mes propres mauvais choix, après mes efforts constants inutile et futile, Dieu m'a envoyé une personne special pour que je puisse l'aimer.

Chaque fois que je vois quelque chose de special une montagne majestueuse, une jolie petite fleur, un enfant mignon, ou une personne gentille, je pense à toi, parce que je veux tout partager avec toi. Mais peut-être je suis trop sentimentale; peut-être que je dois essayer de tu oublier, je dis. Mais il ne sert à rien, je suis amoureuse. Je sais que je devrais me résigner pour notre séparation, cet automne, parce qu'elle est inévitable. Mais les nuits d'hiver sera froid et solitaire, et je te manquerai tellement.

21

Translation:

This poem, which is not really a poem, but rather a letter, is written especially for you, my love. I cannot compose a song on guitar or piano, but I like to write in French. Maybe you'll understand:

The dreams of a lover in the absence are like the lingering scent of honeysuckle. Thoughts swim in joys and fears. All of the mind's force is concentrated on love; on anything else one cannot think. Me, I am overwhelmed by you. I count every single lonely second until our next meeting. Difficulties of separation crumple me. Endurance. Endurance is necessary. I pray to God that He give me peace that I may be patient. However, every sad mile is also a blessing because God has an exact plan for our relationship. God directs us and controls our time.

Never before in my life have I been so dazzled by love. Before, I've had an infatuation for someone, but it was only an immature phase. When I was a silly young girl, I dreamed of an ideal man. Often I tried to discover the man of my dreams, but without success. I was never satisfied, well, until you came into my life. When I had renounced my own poor choices, after my constant useless and futile efforts, God sent me a special person so that I could love him.

Whenever I see something special, a majestic mountain, a pretty little flower, a cute child, or a kind person, I think about you, because I want to share everything with you. But perhaps I am too sentimental; perhaps I must try to forget you, I say. But it is of no use; I'm in love. I know I ought to resign myself to our separation this fall, because it is inevitable. But the wintry nights will be so cold and lonely, and I will miss you so much.

PIECE 9 — ZERO TRANSMISSION

June (Daniel Age 17)

Daniel lived with his aunt and uncle and worked in Atlanta. Several times a week, I called to check in on him to see how he was doing. My greatest worry for him was the rush hour commute. It seemed like too much to expect a 17-year-old to face that daily stress. I had hoped he could ride with his uncle, but their schedules were too different.

Steve and I shared a car that summer so Daniel could borrow my car. I took the bus to work most days, an hour each way. Regularly, I reminded Daniel to take good care of the Subaru station wagon I had lent to him: "Get the oil and filter changed, check fluid levels, check tire pressure... is it running okay? Is the air conditioning cool enough?" Steve's brother Mike is mechanically inclined, so I told Daniel to ask him for help maintaining the car, to keep it in good condition.

August (Daniel Age 17)

I took a week of vacation from my full time job to take Daniel and David to orientation at their boarding school McCallie. David and I flew into the Atlanta airport; Daniel was supposed to pick us up, but he was not there. None of us had cell phones, so it took some time to find out that the Subaru had broken down. We took MARTA rapid transit from the airport, and my brother-in-law Kirk picked us up after work.

In between meetings at the orientation, in Chattanooga, Tennessee, a town unfamiliar to me, I had to find an auto repair shop and call AAA to have the car towed there. The shop discovered there was ZERO transmission fluid in the engine. The transmission was destroyed. As you can imagine, I was not in a perky frame of mind. The Subaru dealer estimated it would cost around a thousand dollars to fix it, and at least a week to order the parts and repair it. I had to find a rental car to use for the week, and asked them to come pick me up at the school.

After orientation, we planned to spend a few days at a rustic mountain cabin in Maggie Valley, North Carolina, which my great-grandmother Dorothy had built the year after Great Smoky Mountains National Park was established. The cabin was only a few miles from the park boundaries. My aunt and uncle owned the cabin now, and had graciously agreed to let us stay there.

The drive seemed to take forever. David and Daniel were loud, complaining, and disagreeable about a place to eat. There were few choices on the mountain roads, and I was so hungry that I stopped at the next restaurant I saw. The whining continued. I was angry, I was tired, and I was frustrated. I had a headache. Both boys were being so goofy and so rude. I couldn't wait to get where we were going, to lie down and take a nap, to get some peace and quiet!

After dinner we drove hours and hours more and finally arrived at the cabin. The car bumped along the rough gravel road, between barns and shacks and trailers, past cows and barking dogs and chickens and pigs. I turned up onto the steep driveway to the cabin and stopped. I engaged the emergency brake and got out to unlock the large metal gate. As we wound up the twisty gravel drive, I asked them in advance to help bring things in from the car.

I pulled up next to the cabin, parked, turned off the ignition, and sighed in relief. I eased out of the car, and stood for a moment, breathing deeply, stretching my arms into the fresh air, bending my stiff back.

Both guys bolted out of the car as if racing to be the first one inside. One of them grabbed the key out of my hand, unlocked the screened porch door, ran in and slammed it behind him, then unlocked the wooden cabin door, throwing it open. They ran around inside, room to room, looking at everything.

"Cool!" Daniel climbed the ladder to the loft. He found a TV in the attic and handed it down to David. I asked him to put it back. The LAST thing I wanted in this hideaway from civilization was the noise and sensory overload of television! He wouldn't put it back. He found the satellite cable cord and connected us to the stimulation of the outside world. He and David sat there, eyes glazed, staring at the noise box, and flipping channels with the remote.

"I need you both to come to the car and help bring in our suitcases."

[Nothing.]

"Come on, David. Come on, Daniel, right now!"

[Nothing.]

My begging escalated. Voice volume increased, tone intensified, cursing thrown in for effect.

[Nothing.]

Exasperated, huffing, sighing, I stomped out to the car, jerked the bags out, lugged them up the moss-covered stone steps, flung open the screen door to the porch, bumped open the heavy wooden cabin door, and threw the duffels, backpacks and suitcases into the cabin.

I returned to the car many times, returning arms full of brown paper grocery bags stuffed with food I would cook for the next few days. With every trip in, I repeated, "Come on, I need your help!" knowing my requests were useless.

After everything was in from the car, I started to unload the grocery bags onto the kitchen counter. First out: flour, sugar, butter for cobbler—we would pick the blackberries ourselves.

Daniel walked past me through the kitchen, back to his spot on the couch. I heard a noise, a gurgling sound. It sounded like the toilet was still running. I turned around, and saw a tide of brownish liquid flowing onto the kitchen floor.

"Daniel. Daniel! You stopped up the toilet! It's overflowing!" I raced into the little bathroom, frantically jiggling the handle, simultaneously searching for a plunger. I grabbed the monogrammed bath towels off the racks to keep the sewage contained. I took the lid off the back of the toilet. Somehow, I got it to stop running.

"Daniel! Come in here! NOW!" He sat motionless on the couch, watching TV. David sat next to him. Neither one of them budged. Neither one of them so much as turned their head toward me.

For the next hour I mopped up poop. There was no mop, no bucket, so I improvised with rags and towels I found. I was ashamed that I had to use the beautiful, fluffy, fine, first-quality, terrycloth towels. I was embarrassed, hoping my aunt and uncle would never know what had happened here. I already felt I owed them so much, I could never repay their generosity, and now we were destroying the serenity of their getaway. I stuffed the dirty towels into heavy duty trash bags.

As I scrubbed my hands with soap and hot water, I was furious at Daniel. I couldn't understand his oblivion. I kept muttering in disgust, even though no one was listening to me, "Didn't you realize the toilet didn't stop flushing? Didn't you know it was overflowing? Why didn't you call me? Why didn't you try to do anything to stop it?"

[No response.]

I hauled the big black biohazard-filled trash bags to the car. I told Daniel and David "Get in the car. We're going to the Laundromat." I don't know how I got those ungrateful trolls to get in the car. I probably bribed them with dinner out, or maybe they wanted to rent a video game in town that they could play on this wretched TV. In between chauffeuring them around the grimy little tourist-trap town, I spent the evening with the local working poor, washing and re-washing, drying and folding.

(Steve Age 17)

When Steve owned his first car, he couldn't afford to take it to a shop to have the oil changed. He didn't want to pay his brother Mike or his brother's friend, a car mechanic by hobby. Steve asked Mike how to change the oil in his car.

"Simple. Buy four quarts of oil. Drain the oil, and pour the new oil in." Mike described to him how to go up under the car and find the oil tank and how to loosen the screws, or bolts, or whatever.

Steve followed Mike's instructions and drained the oil out, but was puzzled that only one quart of oil fit before it overflowed. He put the other three quarts in the garage for the next time. He got in his car, satisfied that he had accomplished a new task, until the engine started smoking. He asked Mike's advice. Mike looked at the car and asked Steve to show him what he had done. "You idiot! You drained out all the oil, but put the new oil into the transmission!"

PIECE 10—OXYMORON

Honeymoon social—isn't that an oxymoron? For that one week, after we had waited what seemed an eternity to be married, we wanted to be alone together, just the two of us, learning to become "one."

The week we honeymooned at the Cloister at Sea Island, Georgia, the fancy beach resort was welcoming their 24,000th honeymoon couple, which would receive their (very expensive—and all-inclusive) week's honeymoon for free! Steve and I were cornered into attending a cocktail party and dinner, along with two dozen other newlywed couples, to celebrate this milestone and for the announcement of the prize winning pair. Most couples were wealthy young professionals—doctors, lawyers, executives, etc. We sat at the head table with the Master of Ceremonies, who reminded me of Bob Barker.

The resort required formal attire for dinner—coat and tie for the gentlemen and long dresses for the ladies. At least eight courses were served at dinner. Our table alone had a waitress, an assistant, a woman who served bread, another who served jelly, jam and butter, another who served relish, and another who served vegetables. After each course, a waiter offered a bowl of warm water for each person to clean their fingers. Every honeymoon couple was photographed professionally and their photos were displayed in albums for review for decades, assuming the couples would return regularly for anniversaries and look back at earlier photos.

One of the hostesses graciously introduced herself to us and asked Steve what he did for a living. She probably expected an answer like "I finished med school and will begin my internship at X hospital in X city," or, "I'm in training to become Vice President of my wife's family's business, X corporation."

His stark reply to the high-society matron was "I BAG GROCERIES."

She seemed flustered, as if she was searching her mind's card catalog for any connection with the lower classes. Her cheeks reddened as she muttered some non-sense response like, "I once knew a yard man." It was literally as ridiculous as that.

Over the years, we have laughed and laughed at the way that poor little rich woman was caught off guard that night, the way Steve had yanked her right out of her upper class world. Of course I expected Steve to answer honestly that he worked in a grocery store, but it was the way he said it, with his deep redneck accent and blunt intonation, that made his reply sound as if he was trying to shock her. He doesn't know how to finesse, how to bluff an answer. He is unable to be pretentious. He tells it like it is.

PIECE 11 — SHOCKED SITTER

I found only one babysitter I could trust to manage the colostomy care, so I could not leave Daniel very often. I remember one time I went to the YMCA to exercise class and dropped Daniel off at the nursery. I don't know what was going through my mind, or maybe I should say what *wasn't* going through my mind. Maybe stress had shut down all my responsible neurons. I hadn't planned to leave him there long. I didn't think he would need a diaper change, or maybe I was so used to the colostomy that I forgot to warn the sitters there that morning.

Bless her heart, the nursery worker took Daniel's outfit off to change his diaper and was startled half to death to see this horrible, monstrous appliance adhered to his belly.

When I came back to pick up Daniel, I could tell she was trying to stay composed, and to be polite, as she scolded me that I should have told her about it, but I could tell she was shaken up. I felt embarrassed and guilty that I had caused her to be uncomfortable.

Then I started to feel sorry for myself. Why couldn't I have time away from my child to exercise? Why wasn't there anyone to support me? Why couldn't I find a babysitter who could stomach what I had to do every day, many times a day? Why did I have to bear all this responsibility and emotion on my own?

My own mother wouldn't even visit me and baby Daniel in the hospital the three different weeks when he had surgery. Not because she wasn't sympathetic, but because she was too empathetic. It tore up her sensitive heart to know that her grandson was in pain. She simply couldn't bear it.

As I recall, my father visited us in the hospital every day and gave me time to walk down the street to eat some dinner. Steve came to the hospital when he wasn't working or sleeping.

Beyond my self-pity was a deeper sadness that I could do nothing about: my baby was in excruciating physical pain. I guess that is why, at the time, I did not dwell on my own needs. There was a more important issue of comforting my baby and doing everything I could do to alleviate his pain and moving him along toward improving health.

PIECE 12 — PLOPPED

In June, Daniel graduated from McCallie, a college-preparatory boarding school in Chattanooga, Tennessee. He registered to attend University of North Carolina at Asheville. Our mailbox was inundated by the usual flurry of information for incoming freshmen. We ordered extra long twin bed linens and towel sets. Daniel was assigned a dorm room and a roommate. He received a list of his classes and professors, his registration was complete, tuition paid, and everything was packed.

One hot, sweaty August evening, Steve and I sat on the screened porch with the ceiling fan rotating on the highest speed, and read the Sunday paper. It was one week before Daniel's classes were scheduled to begin. Daniel quietly walked out on the porch, stood until we looked up, and said, "I'm not going to UNCA."

We were both shocked. Neither of us could speak. We had not expected this. We hadn't seen any hints that this bombshell was coming. Slowly, one of us found our words again and began to question him. "What? Why? What brought this on?" We tried to persuade him to reconsider. It may have come across more as begging. "What will you do instead?" Steve asked.

[Shoulder shrug]

Beyond the concern for my son, I admit feeling my own personal freedom slipping away, as if my world had just been yanked askew. One minute I had one son going away to boarding school and another son going away to college, preparing myself for the metaphorical empty nest. The next minute, I was trapped. We floundered a while, flustered. Then gradually, we recovered our parental bearings. "If you don't go to college, you'll have to find a job or get an internship."

[Nod]

No job or internship materialized. Daniel stayed at home and disrupted our household by sleeping all day, making me feel like I had to tip-toe around my own house, and staying awake all night playing games on the internet. Of course, he didn't tip-toe, so I couldn't get a good night's sleep. He stunk up the den with his toxic farts, and the foul odors permeated sofa, carpet, and curtain fabrics. He watched loud, car-chase action television shows with the volume turned up to the max, and eating all our food, but never going grocery shopping to replace it.

We took Daniel to a psychologist for an evaluation. We had to beg him to get in the car to go to the appointment. The fact that he was unshowered, greasy, and smelly, with scraggly hair and beard, wearing a t-shirt inside-out, seemed like punishment designed specifically to hurt me.

After the meeting with the psychologist, Steve and I made Daniel sign this contract to be allowed to stay in our home:

CONTRACT September 20 (Daniel Age 18)

Daniel agrees to:

1) Wake self up and be out of the house to work or volunteer M-F 9-5 effective immediately, until further notice (in addition to starting own business)

2) Use respectful language (NOT chum, insane, retarded, weird, stupid, etc.) and use respectful attitude toward parents

3) "Limit" computer/TV use to M-F 6-10 pm and flexible 4 hours Sat & Sun (set timer)

4) Attend fellowship group once/week, either Thursday night or Sunday morning

5) Assist with household chores (same day service) example: Mow Saturday; daily chores: take out trash, wash dishes, fold clothes

6) List of Consequences:
   a. Language "Slippage" =-$1.fine
   b. Chore/Obey Refusal=-2hr.computer time penalty

    c.   Fellowship "Missage"=-4hr. (1 night) computer penalty (2 Fellowship Groups in One Week=Buys Extra+4hr.)

    d.   Late Leaving House =-2hr. that night

    e.   Contract Excessive "Breakage"=moveout of home

7)   Additional Consequences will be determined by parents

Signed,   Daniel   Dad   Mom

His behavior improved some, but he did not follow most of the rules and I felt like all I was doing was nagging him to comply. After five or six weeks of stagnation, I was tired from not sleeping well and tired of having him hanging around the house. One day while trying to get him to identify his dreams, I asked him, "Daniel, if you could do anything, anything at all, what would you want to do today?"

"Go to Montana."

"Oh. Hmmm. Yes, that is a beautiful part of the country. Mountains, canyons, rivers, big open skies! Let's go there, you and me. Do you want to? I will look into flights out west." For several days, I searched travel sites for airline flights, but domestic fares were expensive to the western part of the U.S. during the summer peak season.

In my internet searches of the best travel deals, I found a doozy. "Oh my gosh! Look! Here's a flight for $188 round trip to London. That's unbelievable! How about if we take a trip to Europe? We could travel by train, carry all our stuff in backpacks, and sleep in hostels." He agreed. I booked the flights. I purchased two 30 day Eurail passes. We rushed his passport renewal through the system. Within a few weeks, Daniel and I were on our way to tour 17 countries around Europe from Greece to Spain to Scandinavia.

Email Excerpts, Daniel to Steve (Daniel Age 18)

Dad, we had a great day yesterday at Stonehenge, I pictured being there 4,000 years ago. Green fields as far as the eye could see, wind in your face, Stonehenge completely constructed and burial mounds all around. It reminded me of the beginning of the movie "Braveheart.

Hey peeps, I am writing from a youth hostel in Brindisi, Italy. We took a boat from Patras, Greece, that took 18 hours. On the way we stopped at a city in Greece. We didn't get off there but we watched the sun rising behind the mountains. The ship was different than I had imagined. I thought it would be a small boat, with a covered plastic area shielding us from wind and rain. Instead, it was more like Titanic, and we were out on the deck. It got cold fast and we put on every layer of clothing we had. We also found benches up against a wall to shield us from wind as much as possible. We didn't get much sleep because of the cold. But the stars were incredible! And we were some of the only ones sitting out there. The next day we started up a conversation with a German woman who said she walked into a room and slept there.

Last night I had the worst stomach pain I've ever had. Besides the pain, I also threw up a lot. They called a doctor and she came to our hostel, examined me, and gave me a shot to stop the vomiting and help the pain. She said I should go to a hospital. This was when we were in a little tiny town on the coast of Italy that's only reachable by train. I was transported in an ambulance at 22.00 (that's 10 p.m.) on dark, windy roads in the rain… that would have made any normal person sick. After exam in the emergency room, they took me in another ambulance to go to the other end of the hospital for x-rays. Of course, no one spoke a word of English. Mom was afraid they were wheeling me straight into surgery when she saw the sign, "chirurgie" in Italian. I missed out on breakfast—they brought every patient only giant bowls of coffee.

Email, Nilla to Steve
Daniel is resting well and beginning to eat again. I think it was food poisoning. Daniel appreciates my sticking with him through the hospital. Says he doesn't know what he would have done without me. I think the doctors panicked when they saw his scars and assumed this problem was due to that. But this has not been a slow buildup. It was quite sudden. So, I don't think it is a return of his Hirshsprung's disease.

PIECE 13—MEAT LOAF

When Steve and I returned from our honeymoon, I was sunburned to a crisp after a week of sunbathing, intensified by the birth control pills I was now taking. My skin was so raw I had to soak in a cold bathtub. I couldn't wear normal clothes and I had to ride home in a terrycloth bath set. Fine except for when we stopped on the way home to visit Steve's sweet grandmother, and I felt embarrassed by the way I was dressed.

We moved into our little one-story, two-bedroom apartment in Decatur, a quiet suburb of Atlanta, surrounded by leafy sycamore trees, a block from a park. Steve's brother Kirk and his wife Sharon had moved the rest of our belongings in for us while we were away. They had made up our bed and put a few essentials in the refrigerator to welcome us to our new home.

Steve and I learned to live together; how to share a bathroom, how to compromise on radio stations, how to make space for studying. He learned how to pick up his dirty clothes. I learned how to cook. I went back to school and Steve went back to work at Kroger.

After work one night, he picked up our honeymoon photos, and stopped by his parents' house for a quick visit on his way home. When he walked in the back door of our little apartment he put the photo envelope on the kitchen counter. "Hey, Nilla!"

I had been making dinner for the two of us from a recipe in my cookbook for newlyweds. I had set the table, and was pulling the meatloaf out of the oven. "Hey, Steve!" I noticed the photos on the counter. "Oh! Our pictures! I can't wait to see them!"

"Yeah, they turned out great. Mom and Dad loved them too." He put his keys down and took off his shoes.

I was carrying the scalding meatloaf to the table with my oven gloves. "What?" I paused to glare at him.

"I stopped by their house on the way home and showed them the photos." Steve threw his shoes "Clonk!" one at a time "Clonk!" into our bedroom.

"You showed them our honeymoon photos?" I reached for a knife to slice the meatloaf.

"Yeah, what's wrong with that?" He walked in from the bathroom.

Before he showed our honeymoon photos to me, he showed them to his mother! Including the photos of me wrapped in nothing but a bath towel, in a "sexy" pose at sunset on our private hotel room balcony. "I would like to have seen them first." I chopped at the meatloaf, remembering only a week ago—standing, hip tilted against the balcony railing on that romantic night under a full moon, giving my photographer/husband the eyelash-batting, flirty "look" that was intended only for him. Steve could not comprehend what he had done wrong. He could not understand my point of view.

"Well, what's the big deal?"

"What do you MEAN, what's the big deal?" I shouted. "HOW COULD YOU? I CAN'T BELIEVE YOU SHOWED THOSE PHOTOS TO YOUR MOM!!!" Then the meatloaf started flying. The angrier I got, the more out of control my arm became. I chopped and chopped and flailed with a vengeance. I raged, I yelled! With every scream, a chunk of oily ground beef, bathed in crimson ketchup, flung onto the ceiling, on the floor, all across the room.

"What is the matter with you? What are you doing? Stop that! You're crazy!"

His words made me chop all the more. "Fwing! Clank! Zing!" ...went the knife on the metal pan. For the first time in my life I was completely out of control. I had never been so angry. I had never in my life not known what to do. When, at the age of nine, my little sister jabbed a sharp metal dart in my knee, I had gone crying to my mother. When that same bratty sister drank straight out of the milk carton, though I, a germ-o-phobe, begged her not to, I complained to my father. Now, there was no one to go to. Maybe it was that time of the month. Maybe I could blame the hormones in my new birth control pills for influencing my behavior. Maybe I had no clue how to understand a man's point of view. I couldn't help myself, I couldn't contain myself. I was weeping, furious. This was SO not what I expected marriage to be like.

The more Steve told me to stop, the more I raged. I tossed the knife down on the table, turned to him, and started flailing my fists against his chest. He grabbed my arms and held me tight to try to get me to calm down. "Leave me alone!" I pulled away from him and ran into the bedroom, locked the door, and flopped on the bed, sobbing.

I don't know if either of us ate dinner that night, but Steve remembers cleaning meatloaf off the ceiling and walls. For months we continued to find crusty meatloaf boogers in every crevice. I was in a foul mood for days and he became defensive. He never apologized, never did come around to my point of view.

Did he not know that I was trying to be sexy by posing practically naked for him to photograph? Or was it that he didn't have the kind of filter to screen out the difference between "intimate relations with wife" (Rated "R") from "publicly appropriate content for any audience?" (Rated "G") How could he not know to first share anything and everything with his newlywed bride—before sharing them with his mother?

Today, when I ask Steve about this, he says, "What? What was the problem? You were more covered in that towel than you were in the bathing suit my mom saw you in at the beach. I don't understand what's wrong with that. Women! Stupid!"

All he knew, I suppose, was that in his heart, in his own mind, his intentions were pure. He did not mean to make me feel vulnerable. He did not mean to show anything intimate to his mother. He did not mean to put his mother before me. He loved both of us, his mother as a mother, and me as his wife. As far as he was concerned, I was the one with the problem in my perception.

Now, after the passage of time, we can laugh together about the "meatloaf incident," but back then it sure wasn't funny. I fumed over the honeymoon photos for years. I'm not sure I'm over it, even now.

Daniel's Answers (Age 29)

[I have this in here not just to show Dad's and my differences, but also to admit how I lost my temper, and how out of control I got. Remember that Simpson's cartoon where Marge loses her temper and screams at the top of her lungs to a policeman at a traffic stop—and how we sarcastically made fun of that as being a caricature of me when I screamed at you guys.]

"I remember when you screamed at us. I was scared."

[That is sad. I am so sorry.]

PIECE 14 — SIGNS OF LANGUAGE

One of Daniel's babysitters was also an interpreter for the deaf. She taught him some sign language. He knew a dozen signs before he spoke a dozen different words. At two years old Daniel knew American Sign Language for fish, dog, cat, good, bad, duck, ball, boat, mommy, daddy, yes, no, and stop.

When Daniel was one year and nine months old I included this in a note to his day care: "Talking – Daniel has been slow to talk, but I am not concerned about it. He seems very smart in other ways. The words he knows are: E.T., mommy, daddy, 'boo!' light, water, juice ('doos'), Sally ('saazee'), Mandy ('meemee'), moon, moo, bark-bark, meow, ball, (bird, bear, Grandma Binney are all "bee.") He is very expressive and acts out what he wants. He imitates the sounds of monkeys, birds, elephants, motorcycles, airplanes, etc. When we went to the zoo, he pointed to his neck for giraffe, since giraffes have long necks. He can say 'yes' and 'no.'"

Daniel's bowels went from physically stopped up to intermittently overflowing. In a parallel way, his communication had been delayed and then the words gushed out. Until his second year, he said only a few words. Mostly, he pointed to what he wanted, or gestured.

Steve's closest friend since childhood, Rich, a physician, has known Daniel since birth. Rich used to tease us that Daniel seemed "retarded" because he wasn't talking much around age two, especially compared to his niece the same age… but, he added, "Once Daniel started talking, he was like a genius, like Einstein coming up with the theory of relativity, stating the formula $E=MC^2$."

Nilla's Diary October 8 (Daniel Age 3 ½)
You hound us day and night about what letter starts such and such a word—"Cake starts with a hard C." You want to practice sounds all day long.
Nilla's Diary October 16 (Daniel Age 3 ½)
Learn to pronounce letter "L" correctly but it's so difficult that you exaggerate in search of perfection—said "Puh-l-eeze" in your sleep.
Nilla's Diary October 26 (Daniel Age 3 ½)
At La Petite Ecole you are learning French song "Dites Moi, Pourquoi" and words "J'ai faim, j'ai fois, fatigue, gateau sec."

When Daniel wasn't lecturing, he was asking questions, non-stop, like this series from when he was four years old and I was trying to get him to go to sleep. I told him I couldn't answer all of his questions tonight, but that I would write them down so we could remember to find out the answers together later.

- How long does a panther jump?
- How long does a cheetah jump?
- How long does a tiger jump?
- Which one jumps the longest?
- What is this? (pointing to a tendon in my inner forearm)
- What color are those? (pointing to veins in my arm)

Purple or blue?

- How can God pick up trucks?
- How can He Man pick up trucks?
- How can a man dancer pick up a lady dancer?
- How can a man pick up a lady in a basketball game? (cheerleaders)
- How can wings make bees and things that fly, fly?
- How can God make houses and furniture? How can God make people be so strong?
- How do pigs turn into bacon? Also ham?
- How can God make you strong from tellin' you what to do and helpin' you?
- How can God make everything?
- Why do people want to shoot people?
- How can God make the whole world?
- How can God make you write with a pencil and a marker and a pen?
- How can God make you dance?
- How can God make women's bodies? Boys'? Men's'?
- How can babies grow? Into big boys? That can do everything?
- How can erasers erase drawings off?
- How can some watches be waterproof watches and how can some watches not be waterproof?

I can tell you the rest tomorrow night, okay? And you can write them right here. (pointing to the margin of my paper.)

PIECE 15—TREASURES, TRASHED

Nilla's Diary September 7 (Daniel Age 5)
My heart is hurting. I am too young to have a dead mother. My mother was too young to die. My children miss their 'Mimi.' They don't understand that you are not coming back. I wish you could know how much Daniel loves the 'treasures' he has found at your house. When I asked him if there was anything he wanted at Mimi's house, he said 'the knife on the wall where Mimi's bed is.' It is a beautiful, hand-carved artifact. It is his most prized possession. He has shown everyone every detail of it.

(Daniel Age 20)
One night I came home and noticed things looked different in the den. Some things were rearranged, and others seemed to be missing. I was confused. I stood around for a while, wondering what was wrong.

"Daniel, things look different. Did you move some books off the shelf?"

"You don't need them."

"What? What do you mean I don't need them? Did you put them somewhere?"

"Yep."

"Where did you put them?"

"Outside."

"Outside? Where?"

"In the trash."

"What!?! The trash! What did you throw in the trash? Go get it and bring it back in!"

He didn't say "No." Silently, he walked away, and went back to what he had been doing.

"Daniel! Go out there and get them and bring them back in!" He wouldn't budge.

He didn't apologize. He didn't seem to understand why I was upset.

Steve came home an hour later, and found me clanking around out back. "Look what he did!" I wailed. "He threw my stuff away, and some of David's things, too." My whole body was heaving with deep sobs. Daniel had filled several large black plastic trash bags full of things that belonged to me and Steve and David. Several things were broken.

"He didn't put them aside to ask me about them, he didn't put them in another room. He THREW THEM AWAY! Look! In these STINKY, FILTHY garbage cans! Mixed in with this NASTY, rotting food and your SNOTTY Kleenex!

"And worst of all, look at this! Remember this antique Eskimo knife that Big Dave gave to my mother from his arctic exploration, remember? The one thing that Daniel picked out after Mimi's funeral… the one special thing he wanted to keep… to remind him of her!"

The tears were rolling down my cheeks. "Oh my, gosh, I'm sure he doesn't remember that from so long ago… but he has always said he thought it was 'cool.' How can he throw away something like that—a family heirloom—that means so much to me, without even asking?"

"What if I hadn't noticed these things were missing, and the garbage men had picked them up and if they were in the landfill!?

And look here: these are kitchen utensils that I use all the time! WHAT was he thinking?

"This is my hairdryer!

"Here are some books that David needs for school. I can't believe he did this!

"Look… the glass is broken in these framed photos. And he won't help clean it up."

Steve went inside to find gloves or a towel to use to pick up the glass shards. He asked, "Daniel, why did you do that?"

"They didn't need it."

"You can't just do something like that, just move other people's stuff around and throw things away that belong to somebody else."

Daniel didn't respond.

Steve shook his head and came back outside and helped me carry things back inside.

Daniel never said he was sorry. He never came outside and helped.

Daniel's Answers (Age 29)

[Why did you do that?]

"I just remember seeing stuff that seemed excessive. I never saw anyone using it. I was thinking I would help out by dealing with it myself. I felt like [your response] was an overreaction to it."

STEP TWO
ONTO THE TABLE

Nilla's Method for Completing a Jigsaw Puzzle
1.   First, I turn all the pieces out of the box.
2.   **I plop the pieces onto the table into a big jumbled pile.**

Ninety-seven small cardboard shapes scatter into a chaotic mass on the table. Some land right-side up, some up-side down, ready to serve their purpose. Lifeless, the inanimate pieces wait for human hands to manipulate them into the places where they will belong.

Two pieces fall on the floor. One piece bounces under the curtains. I put on my reading glasses and sweep my hand along the floor. I am careful to look around for any lost pieces. If the dogs find a loose piece before I do, they will gnaw on it until it is unrecognizable. Even if only one piece disappears, the puzzle cannot be completed.

In life, I do worry a lot. I try to think of every possible negative thing that MIGHT happen, as if that worry would help me to prevent bad things from happening. Being anxious is one of my useless attempts to control my world.

Why didn't I recognize my son's differences? Why didn't I notice how homesick he was at college? Why couldn't I have been more patient with him as a toddler? Why couldn't I have made our home more calm, and slowed us down to a pace that quieted my son's anxiety? Why did it take so many years to figure out what was going on?

PIECE 16 — GIFTED

I was so puzzled by Daniel's brilliant mind when he was two and a half years old. I was overwhelmed by how bright he was. I was afraid he needed more challenge for his intellect than I could provide. I didn't want his potential to be dampened by lack of stimulation.

Nilla's Diary (Daniel Age 2 ½)
You love looking through the phone book, especially at names that began with the letter "C."

Nilla's Diary (Daniel Age 3 ½)
After supper I showed you how to write your name for the first time. You learned in about 15 minutes. You amaze me! First time you ever tried to write D, N, and L. You like C's, like in our last name.

Out of all the young children I had known—my sisters, my sisters friends, my cousins, or any children I babysat—I had never known a child so sensitive and tender and observant. I knew this child of mine was someone very special. I felt blessed. I felt honored to be his mother.

Nilla's Diary February 20 (Daniel Age 3)
Director of playcare says they love having you—you are so polite and nice and eager to do activities—would love to have you here more days a week.

Nilla's Diary April 20 (Daniel Age 3)
Out of the blue you say such kind, thoughtful things: "Isn't this a nice day, Mommy?" "Look at those pretty flowers." "This sure has been a fun day!" "I love you, Mommy."

Daniel asked questions incessantly. I felt it was my responsibility to answer his questions, and I felt anxious when I could not. He read at an early age, and continued to read constantly. He wanted to learn everything he could about a subject, whether it was dinosaurs or bears.

Nilla's Diary (Daniel Age 3)
You saw electric cable spool & kept asking me questions I couldn't answer about it so I took you to the library. I read all 53 pages of 3rd grade level book to you.
Nilla's Diary (Daniel Age 3 ½)
You want to know about engines—cars, etc. Go to library for resources. Listen intently to 53 page book *What Makes a Car Go.* Librarian astounded. Thought I was joking at first.

Daniel had an incredible memory for detail, such as in my diary entries below, asking me about something that had happened a year ago—a time period equal to one-third of his lifetime.

Nilla's Diary October 17 (Daniel Age 3 ½)
"I membr when Dand-faw [Grandfather] and I cut dat pumpkin last year and he couldn't throw away the seeds at first 'cause he didn't have a trash can."
Nilla's Diary October 20 (Daniel Age 3 ½)
"Daddy, do you 'member when we saw dat rainbow at Steve's Ice Cream Store at Yana?" (In Atlanta, a year earlier.)
Nilla's Diary October 21 (Daniel Age 3 ½)
"Mommy, show me where you squooshed that spider here last time." It was at grandfather's church, and we hadn't been there in I don't know how long. Incredible memory for details.

I took Daniel to a psychologist for an IQ test. His score was very high, in the "superior" range. We enrolled him in a preschool for "gifted" children.

PIECE 17 — OFF THE HOOK

From our first meeting, I knew Steve was odd in a number of ways. I had never met anyone else like him. I giggled to my girlfriends that he was very handsome, and I loved his big goofy grin, but I couldn't help but observe his unusual physical features: featherweight body topped by an oversized noggin. Small, shapely ears, efficiently cupped for gathering sounds. Standing, his shoes pointed outward like a dancer in second position. Walking, his arms hung like an ape's, palms turned flatly backward. He had a birthmark on his back that looked like a fried egg.

Steve seemed ignorant, like he didn't have a grasp of basic cultural knowledge. Soon after we met, I had to explain to him how to make a long-distance phone call: first dial a "1," then the area code, then the number.

He didn't know how to blow his nose until he was 15 years old. (Our sister-in-law Sharon remembers teaching him how.) He drove using both feet simultaneously: right for gas, left for brakes, instead of one foot alternating between the two.

Among friends, Steve loudly bragged that he and all his friends were members of the B.O.A. (Bachelors of America) Club.

Steve boasted that although he didn't read much, it was because "All books are the same; the words are just re-arranged." He said he was going to publish a book titled *Words Rearranged* to contain all his brilliant thoughts.

His child-like playfulness was so much fun. We had the same goofy friends, we shared the same deep faith, he was a speedy runner, a potter, (how earthy!) and he played the guitar (a man of many talents!). He didn't drink or smoke cigarettes. His quirks were intriguing to me, and in spite of my instincts, or maybe because my instincts overpowered common sense, I was in love with him.

(Nilla Age 20, Steve Age 22)

The first time I traveled back to my parents' home for a long weekend after we were married, Steve couldn't get time off work. My first night away, I called him. The line was busy. This was back in the 1970s—before cell phones. Long distance rates were high, so I waited until after 11 p.m. to call, when the long-distance rates were lower.

The next night, the number was still busy. How could that be? Steve never talked on the phone. Maybe he accidentally knocked the phone off the hook. I called the phone company to have them check the line to see if there was any malfunction. They said it was operating properly; the phone was probably off the hook. I would wait until the next day. I missed him and I wanted to know how things were going. Surely he would wonder how I was doing and call me. Nope.

The third night I tried dialing the number again. Busy. By now I was worked up into an anxious state. I imagined his route home from work, late at night, along winding roads, across bridges, speeding along highways. What if he had been in a wreck? My imagined nightmares escalated; what if someone had broken into our apartment and disconnected the phone so he couldn't call 911 and viciously bludgeoned him to death? After obsessing over the worst possible scenarios for hours, I knocked on my parents' door, tearful, pitiful, asking for advice.

My dad said "I'm sure everything is fine. The phone is probably off the hook."

I overheard my mom sigh and mumble something under her breath to my dad, in a huff, like, "One of these days, he has got to learn to be responsible!"

I resumed my worried sobs.

My dad asked if I knew any of our neighbors. Catching my

breath between wiping my red eyes, I said, "Yes, there is a married couple that lives next door. They are law students. They stay up late studying, so maybe it's not too late to call them, but I don't have their number."

My dad called for directory assistance, and requested their number.

I called our neighbors and asked the man to please go knock on Steve's door to ask him to put the phone back on the hook and call his wife. Steve called a few minutes later, wondering if something was wrong. When I said I was okay, just worried about him, he was angry that I had woken him.

I went back to tell my parents he was fine and apologized for waking them up. I went to my old room and quietly cried myself to sleep.

Daniel's Answers (Age 29)
[About my imagination of what might have happened to Dad:]
"That's an example typical of your overblown worry."

PIECE 18 — TENDER

Daniel's skin was so sensitive. From the time he was a young child, his whole arm would swell up when he was bitten by a mosquito. Even if no one around him felt a single mosquito bite, it seemed all the bugs zoomed in to feast on Daniel's tender skin. All summer long, his arms and legs were spotted with red, irritated, bug bites. His frequent diaper rash was severe and almost impossible to heal.

Daniel was particular about what kinds of fabrics he would wear. The tags in the backs of collars made him itchy. We gave in to avoid the struggle. We let him wear anything he wanted—usually comfy, floppy, loose sweatpants and soft, well worn t-shirts. He liked to wear a few favorite clothes over and over again.

Nilla's Diary April 23 (Daniel Age 3)

Put on own sweater, button, unbutton all by yourself. Say, "I love you, Mommy. Let's not fight and let's not scream and let's not spank… Let's be buddies. Let's do!"

Nilla's Diary April 24 (Daniel Age 3)

3 yr. old check up with Dr. B. You cooperate so well he said, "I wouldn't be tired at night if they were all like you." You have bronchitis. You tell him, "Hey, Dr. B! Purple [medicine] is my FRA-vrit!" You don't cry when nurse sticks finger.

Nilla's Diary November 24 (Daniel Age 3 ½)

Sweet little voice 2 a.m.: "Mommy! Can you come see what I did?" He had thrown up all over himself and his bed. "Daddy, I'm not so proud that I threw up like you. But I'm through throwin' up so I'm glad. I hope I don't throw up again! Let's get another shirt for me."

Soccer Tears (Daniel Age 5)

Daniel wanted to play soccer like other kids his age. I signed him up for a team. He proudly dressed in his white shorts and green team-color t-shirt with his name in bright yellow letters on the back for the first day of practice. I fastened his shin guards and helped him pull up the long socks with the matching green and yellow stripes. I tightened the laces on his cleats just the way he liked them.

We drove to the soccer field behind the nearest elementary school and walked up to the color-coded cluster of kids. I introduced him to the coaches. They directed him to begin dribbling the ball toward the goal. Instead of charging out on the field, Daniel started crying, grabbed my hand, and buried his face in my skirt. The coach looked away, confused, and kind of embarrassed. He wasn't a psychologist or a trained teacher. He was another parent who had volunteered to coach a kids' sport. I'm sure he didn't know what to do when a kid cried about going to play.

I pulled Daniel aside, talked to him, pulled up his socks, and retied his laces. After a while, I convinced him to go out, kick the ball, and run around. I don't remember why we kept going to practices and games, because Daniel continued to whine and cry and hang back. We probably kept going because when we got home he insisted he did want to play on his team and promised that he wouldn't cry next time.

Nilla's Diary November 4 (Daniel Age 5 ½)

Daniel is so sweet. I am enjoying him more and more. He is so sensitive. I am relieved when I see him cry because last year he bottled his feelings in and became frustrated, angry, and sometimes behaved violently. It was frightening. He is more pleasant to be around. I feel less stress, less of a power struggle. His teacher says he is a perfectionist. He won't try something unless he knows he can do it right. This interferes with his artwork because his hands can't produce the clear image in his mind, so either he doesn't try to draw it or he tears it up in frustration. It's wonderful to watch Daniel when he treats David well—he shepherds him along and David grins and loves keeping up with his big brother.

Sunburn (Daniel Age 21)

Our family went to the beach on the South Carolina coast. In the morning, I slathered myself in sunscreen, then handed the tube to Daniel and told him to put it on. He ignored me. At lunchtime his skin was already looking pink. I knew the sun was getting strong. I explained to him, "This time of day, between 11 a.m. and 3 p.m., when the sun is directly overhead, the sunlight is the most intense, and you will get sunburned." I picked up the blue tube of Coppertone and offered to rub it on his arms and back for him, or at least on his reddened nose and his already blistering ears. When he refused, I asked him to at least wear a t-shirt and a hat.

He was out in the sun all day long with no sunscreen or hat or shirt. He was so severely burned the next morning that he moaned in pain and rolled around on the floor, curled into a fetal position. I wet beach towels in cold water and draped them over him and suggested a cool bath. I sent Steve to the drugstore to buy something to spray on his raw skin and gave him Tylenol to soothe the pain. He doesn't much like going to the beach anymore.

Daniel's Answers (Age 29)
[Do you remember crying at soccer?]

"No, but I remember one time I got a bee sting. Grandfather used cigarette tobacco to put on it."

PIECE 19 — RANDOM DRIVES

After Daniel's "Gap Year" between high school and college, when he didn't find a job or internship, we insisted that he enroll again at UNCA where, the previous year, he had withdrawn a week before classes were to begin.

This time we would not allow him to back out. We packed up the same sheets and towels and I drove him up to the mountains and moved him into his dorm. Everyone greeting us was exuberantly friendly. We unloaded the cars, unpacked clothes, and locked up his bicycle. I made his bed, hung up his towels, and stacked his snacks. I introduced us to his roommate and his roommate's mother. I helped him open a bank account, sign up for orientation, and purchase his textbooks.

When we were driving around town shopping for a microwave, a desk chair and a few other last-minute items, I choked up when he said, "I'm really going to miss you, dangit." If only he could have communicated more than that. If only I could have understood sooner the depth of his homesickness.

Email, Daniel to Nilla and Steve August 12 (Daniel Age 19)
Hey peeps, How should we get in contact for the next couple of days? If I can figure out how to call long distance, I will call you as

soon as possible, but it may take a few days. I'm already getting overwhelmed with planning my schedule and stuff to handle; going from relatively slow days to this—and this is just the first day. And I'm already homesick—I guess it will take some time. I'm going to try to get involved and make some new friends here but it will be hard (never been very good at it.) Love, Daniel

Daniel had the best of intentions. He was determined to make it. For the first few days, he kept a strict schedule, until his roommate began keeping late nights and Daniel began sleeping all day.

He was suspended that year for failing grades. After those first few days, he never went to classes again. With gentle questions and a great deal of patience from us, he finally admitted he was paranoid that people were staring at him. The reality was they probably were staring because his gait was so stiff and his walk so stilted. He was absolutely terrified of walking across campus.

He spent most days on "Random Drives" through the mountains. Sometimes he stopped and hiked the Blue Ridge Parkway by himself, which sounded like a wholesome activity until I realized he hadn't considered any common sense safety measures, such as:

1) Tell someone where you are going and when to expect you to return;
2) Take a bottle of water and a snack bar in case you get lost;
3) Bring a flashlight if you hike near dusk in case you are caught in the woods after dark.

No one knew where he was. If he had gotten lost or injured, no one would have known to look for him.

One night he was pulled over by the police for speeding. The officer said he clocked him driving 90 miles per hour in a 55 m.p.h. zone, but mercifully only ticketed him at 70 m.p.h. Steve's and my automobile insurance rates doubled for the next three years. Daniel told his dad about this, but neither of them told me. Later that summer Daniel confessed to his dad that one night he had pushed the accelerator all the way to the max, to 120 m.p.h.

He refused to eat in the cafeteria although we had paid in full for the complete meal plan, breakfast, lunch, and dinner, for both semesters. During the Christmas holidays we chided Daniel for not attending classes and not eating in the cafeteria. He convinced us he would change his ways for the second semester and we believed him. During the spring semester, he never asked for help and never led us to believe he was skipping classes and meals.

Email, Steve to Daniel April 2 (Daniel Age 20)

Daniel,

Your mom and I were talking yesterday about how awesome your story was that you emailed us about all those deer and that drive you took. We are so glad you had this year up in the mountains to be able to experience stuff like that. Unfortunately that came to an end as will your first year in college.

Mom and I were kind of sad that you won't be staying in the Asheville area since it seems you enjoy it there so much. It's obvious that you have taken advantage of the outdoors and we are both amazed at how you have overcome several of your social fears. I wish you were returning but it's too late to talk about that.

So, where do we go from here? Both your mom and I would love to help you talk through what plans you have for mid-May and beyond since that is when you will be out. You are getting ready to turn 20. Man, I can't believe that. You are going to be 20. You are getting older. You will need to be making decisions and we would like to help but it really is going to have to be something you want to do.

What do you love to do? I want you to take some time over the next 10 days and write down on paper what it is you want to be doing. You may want to get in your car, drive to the Blue Ridge Parkway with a pad and pen and just sit, think, and start writing whatever comes to mind. Basically I'm asking for some kind of plan. You really don't need to figure on coming back here with nothing to do. The phrase "I don't know" is illegal so don't even think about using it. We love you and want you to be happy whatever it is you do.

Love from Mom and Dad

PIECE 20 — REST HOUR

year after we were married, Steve and I spent the summer as counselors at Camp Yonahlossee, a private summer camp for girls, the same camp I had gone to from age 10 through age 16. Steve was one of the few male staff members. He and I lived in a rustic room upstairs in a rock building called the "Castle." We led the idyllic life for 10 weeks that summer, with all our meals and lodging provided, though not much pay!

Steve started out as the art counselor, but after a few weeks he tired of sitting in the dank, dreary "art shack" tucked away underneath the assembly hall. He switched to being the "Pioneering" counselor, so he could be outside in the mountains all day long, leading hikes and camping trips.

As tennis counselor, I spent sunny days across the lake, tossing fuzzy yellow balls over the net to clusters of girls of all ages.

Mornings after breakfast we sang camp songs between announcements. After big lunches we enjoyed "Rest Hour" before afternoon activities. Evenings we shared performing silly skits in the assembly hall. Sundays at dusk we sat on stone seats in the woods for Vespers.

Steve and I comforted homesick campers and spun the merry-go-round and played tetherball before meals. We helped the camp director with anything and everything she needed. We drove into town to wash children's sheets; we sat with sick campers at the hospital; we set up for Carnival; we cleaned up the facility between sessions.

We were very happy there, and in great health because of all the fresh air, exercise, and good food. We agreed to return the next summer, and that is where Daniel first came into being.

PIECE 21 — TANTRUMS

Each day began with power struggles with Daniel over getting dressed, and each day continued in this way, with debates and negotiations at every transition. Throughout the day, if things didn't go as planned, temper tantrums resulted. Daniel cried when it was time to get into the pool for his swimming lessons (even though, as I knew, he loved his swimming lessons), and then he cried again when it was time to get out of the pool.

Daniel cried when I left him most days of Pre-K. Patiently, his kind teacher peeled him out of my arms and skillfully turned him to something he was interested in playing with or in learning.

Weekly, when we went to church, Daniel refused to go to his Sunday school class, screaming and crying and pulling on my hand. "No! I want to stay with you! Why can't I go to your class?" I remember taking him outside regularly to spank him for his rude, controlling, disobedient behavior. Every Sunday was stressful, trying to get him to cooperate.

At four years old Daniel tried to control me by pulling on my hand, by wanting me to carry him, by begging me constantly to hold him. He was clingy, demanding, and stubborn. He tried to control me by whining, "Don't walk so fast." No matter how slowly I was walking, he wanted to control the pace. He tried to control by rolling on the ground, climbing, running, jumping, and screaming, and he expressed his frustration by punching his brother or knocking him over.

Nilla's Diary March 3 (Daniel Age 4)
Daniel broke the window pane in the playhouse with a curtain rod—repeatedly and on purpose. Also, he had been told many times not to

lock any doors. For the 2nd time in two weeks, he locked both bathroom doors so no one could get in from either side.

Whenever I disciplined Daniel, whether it was scolding or spanking, afterward I gave him a hug and assured him I loved him. He insisted that I continue to hug him and kiss him a certain number of times, repeated to his satisfaction. He tried negotiating rewards and consequences for certain behaviors. He begged, "I'm hungry," at bedtime, although I knew he had eaten enough dinner to be full.

He alternated between independence and helplessness in dressing, making his bed, picking up toys, and wiping his bottom after a bowel movement. When he was learning how to tie his shoes, even when it was still too difficult for him, he insisted on doing it himself. Each time it took him a painfully long time to do and re-do, over and over to perfection.

Nilla's Diary March 4 (Daniel Age 4)
Daniel was very upset today, and covered his eyes when I told him I gave blood today to help people who are sick. He wouldn't explain why he was so upset. He said, "Why did they do that to you?" [With hindsight, now decades later, I realize maybe he thought I was giving away my life?]

In pre-school Daniel blinked his eyes repeatedly, a clear sign of anxiety, an additional ingredient tossed in with his defiance and controlling tantrums. Our pediatrician referred us to a counselor, who explained that structure, and knowing what to expect, would help Daniel to feel more secure. She helped us set up rules and privileges to establish consistency:

Rules

1) Act respectfully toward adults.
2) Do not scream indoors.
3) Be quiet when someone is on the phone.
4) Obey parents the first time.
5) No whining.
6) No ugly words or name calling.
7) Don't tease David.
8) Rest one hour in bed in afternoon.
9) Calm, in control of self in stores and restaurants.
10) Food only at meals (breakfast, lunch, dinner) except:
    a. Morning: at preschool.
    b. Afternoon: 3 or 4 pm – fruit.
    c. Bedtime: 2 saltines or ½ graham cracker & juice.
11) Do not lock doors.
12) Do not hit.
13) Do not destroy or throw things.

Privileges

1) Have a friend over.
2) Play a game; play cards.
3) Extra books read.
4) Take a walk.
5) Watch "Thundercats" cartoon weekdays 5-5:30
6) Library.
7) Nature Center.
8) Playground.
9) Skating Rink.
10) Play Tennis.
11) Miniature Golf.

PIECE 22 — SUSPENDED

Following Daniel's freshman year of not-going-to-classes, UNC-Asheville suspended him for failing grades. Steve and I asked Daniel to make a list of ideas for what he could do next with his life.

IDEAS (Daniel Age 20)
1) Get enough mowing and computer jobs to stay busy.
2) Get part time job and stay at the church housing.
3) Get full time job out west or anywhere else in country, along with apartment.
4) Travel cross-country on bike doing odd jobs and staying in KOA campgrounds.
5) Do the AT trail.

Daniel decided he would try Idea #2. For a while he did janitorial work assisting the custodian at our church, Redeemer Presbyterian. He lived in a room in a house the church owned, along with several other young guys who worked in church ministries.

One day I went to see Daniel and as soon as I walked in the door I smelled an awful odor. I traced the stench to its origin. The kitchen sink was filled to overflowing with moldy dishes covered in varying stages of decaying food. Daniel explained he never used the kitchen, and he refused to wash the dishes the other guys had dirtied. I wasn't willing to dip my hands in that toxic stew, but I lectured Daniel on the fact that everyone who lived there needed to pitch in and clean up. I explained that the filth could attract not only roaches, but also vermin. Nothing was done. That situation lasted about six months, until the church made other plans for the housing, and so Daniel moved back home.

Soon after that our next door neighbor hired Daniel temporarily that summer to screen-print t-shirts part-time. Steve and I were glad he had a job, even if it was dreary manual labor, but it still wasn't working for us to have Daniel living in our home. We told Daniel he had to move out of the house and gave him a deadline of one week.

Daniel told his dad and me that he was going to try Idea #5, through-hike the Appalachian Trail, starting the following week. His dad agreed through-hiking was a great idea, but cautioned that it required preparation. "You can't just head out one day to hike the Appalachian Trail. You have to train your muscles and break in your boots to get ready for such steady hiking. You have to have the right boots and backpack. You have to plan your supplies and ship food ahead to drop points."

Daniel shifted to Idea #4, and changed his proposed direction from the western U.S. to New England. Daniel decided he would drive north to Maine, sleeping at campgrounds in a tent, until he could find a job and an apartment. He began his adventure in the middle of August. He drove north through Virginia, Washington, D.C., and got lost in New York City trying to find the U.S. Open Tennis Tournament. He pulled off the highway somewhere in New Jersey at a gas station and called me from a pay phone to help him find his way. I answered him on my cell phone while I was in a bookstore in Florida. There wasn't much I could do to help him, other than to suggest that he buy a map and to ask for directions from the attendant.

Daniel's Travel Diary (Daniel Age 20)

Thurs Sept 6 MADE it to my "destination" of Bar Harbor, Maine. Got campsite. Set up tent and did the Loop Road around Acadia. Very neat coastal rocks/cliffs. Tried Cadillac Mtn. for sunset time. I got what I wanted! So did the rest of the crowd sitting on the rocks around me, taking in this beautiful sunset. When it ended everybody clapped.

Fri Sept 7 WOKE up at 4:30 AM. Got some sunrise pictures. Hiked up Gorham Mtn. in Acadia. Great view + weather. Small boats crawling along the coast. Are they dragging nets behind? Checked out photo shop in Bar Harbor to see about developing. Fairly expensive, so I didn't get developing. But, I did fill out an application for work there, since they had a "Help Wanted" sign on their door. Told to come back tomorrow to talk to manager.

Sat Sept 8 WENT to photo store in Bar Harbor again, this time to talk to the manager. She asked me if I could start work that day!

Mon Sept 10 LEARNED some of the photo lab at work. Worked from 10-4. Took nearly a whole roll of film at Thunder Hole in Acadia. Waves come up through a hole on the coast, and the best ones were probably 50-75 feet in the air. Back at campsite at 8—it's dark and nothing to do. Keep meaning to ask out Sara at work but never do. Too nervous, "she wouldn't go out with someone like me" syndrome, + "she has to already have a boyfriend" syndrome. Both probably true, but it will only help to ask. Besides being beautiful she doesn't talk too much like some of the other girls at work, which can get on the nerves very quickly (along with laughing way too much).

Tue Sept 11 GO to work to learn about the worst terrorist act in history has just occurred. Of course I'm talking about the jets being crashed into both World Trade Towers in NYC and into the Pentagon and one that crashed in a field in Pennsylvania. Estimates are 30,000 dead. It's just hard to believe. I had just driven directly by the Pentagon a week earlier, and been in NYC and Manhattan also. I imagine is much like the JFK assassination, where everyone remembers when it happened and where they were. Everybody has a TV or radio on to listen to the news. At campground people are crammed into the TV room to watch the news.

Fri Sept 14 NOT a very good day at work today. Went in from 8-3:30. It's annoying how all people ever do is complain. I would think an event like the terrorist act would make people realize how fortunate they are, but people just whine constantly. It's so annoying and depressing.

Sat Sept 15 WENT to work at 8 AM and stayed until 7 PM. I had a better day today, mainly because Bill wasn't constantly criticizing my work. Sometimes he can act like he might run the place. When he made a mistake he quieted down even more. It is much more enjoyable when there is no criticism and complaining. (I need a new pen!) I just started the Dale Carnegie "How to Make Friends and Influence People" 8-CD set today while driving to work. It has wonderful suggestions—things that it seems anyone would know but so few actually practice. Key points revolve around "Golden Rule", things like "compliment people", "remember and use a person's name", "do not criticize", and "avoid arguing". I plan on writing them on a sheet of paper and looking at it each day. I should probably listen to it more than just once.

Tue Sept 18 WENT in to work today only to find out "they don't need me anymore." My manager told me she already layed off three people. Apparently season has slowed (stopped) faster than usual. Maybe terrorist attack (planes being stopped) is what caused tourist slow down. Before today I thought my job might last another month.

Wed Sept 19 GOT paycheck today - $300! Much more than I expected. I don't think taxes were taken out. This money will get me back home. I was down to no money, having spent it all getting here and staying in $20 campgrounds. That equals $600/month, a good apartment cost. Dad also told me on the phone that Mom will deposit $80 in my account today to help out. $0 - $400 in one day – I feel much more relieved. Today I will start my trip home.

We were all grieving after 9/11, but Steve and I still insisted that Daniel find an apartment. I gave him the newspaper and suggested he look in the want ads. He didn't know where in the paper to look. I showed him the page, the section, and circled a few possibilities. I explained to him how to choose an area, how to read an ad, how to look for how much rent they are asking, how many bedrooms, how to compare options, and so on.

Daniel looked at one apartment. He signed up for the first and only apartment he saw. It was a dark, grimy, studio apartment next to the highway. It was a tiny space, eked out of a one-car garage. Literally, he had to turn sideways to enter the bathroom. Daniel's landlady, an older woman, lived in the house, and her boyfriend lived in the garage apartment above Daniel. She was brusque and business-like, but once she got to know him, sometimes she brought him a slice of pound cake. He loved that.

Daniel's Answers (Age 29)
[Why didn't you look at more than one apartment?]
    "I didn't have any problem with the first one."
    [Remember, though, it was so small you had to squeeze into the bathroom?]
    [Shoulder shrug.]

PIECE 23 — GREAT EXPECTATIONS

Our real estate agent was proud to sell us our first home: a cute little two-bedroom, one-bath brick ranch. We could afford it because it was located in a flood plain on the "wrong side of the tracks" in southern Atlanta. Steve refinished the hardwood floors, sanding and staining them a dark brown. My uncle gave us some furniture and lamps he no longer needed. We hung bamboo-patterned wallpaper in the hall. Steve and I made our first big purchase together: an avocado-colored refrigerator.

Heavy rains swelled the dry creek in our back yard into a swirling lake to within an inch of our newly varnished floors. I screamed to Steve when I spotted a large rat dog-paddling across our property. When it wasn't flooding, Steve and I laid in bed hot summer nights listening to "gangs" of teenagers hanging around underneath our bedroom window, laughing, smoking, drinking, shouting, and running around the neighborhood. We weren't sure of our investment until we sold our "Misty Valley" home for more than a 50% profit. We had paid $17,000, fixed it up a bit, and sold it only a year later for $26,000.

By December, Steve and I had both completed our undergraduate degrees, and I had finished my three-month paralegal training program. I was five months pregnant and wanted to move "back home" to Winston-Salem where my parents and sisters lived, before the baby arrived.

On a snowy January day we drove our U-Haul truck to the new home we had found in the "country." The rustic outbuilding that Steve could use as his artist's "studio" made the house perfect. He set up his pottery wheel and kiln in the back room and set his painting easels in the large, windowed front room. I set up my weaving loom on the sun porch of the main home. We settled into our two-story yellow clapboard home on a corner lot. We loved to swing on the front porch, although it overlooked a busy rural highway, separating us from the county cemetery. Our gravel driveway entered off a quiet road lined with a row of white pine trees that reminded Steve of a painting by artist Andrew Wyeth, his hero.

Only three months until the baby was due. I found my old crib in my parents' attic and set it up in the baby's nursery. I sewed blue gingham cotton fabric into simple curtains and matching crib pads. We bought a changing table. Through a friend of a friend, my mother found a job for Steve. He was hired as groundskeeper and janitor for a mental health facility. It was manual labor, but ideal for him at the time because he worked early hours, from 6 a.m. to 3 p.m., which left him time to paint in the evenings.

Only three days until the baby was due: April 1st. I had everything "just so," ready for the huge life change, ready to welcome our baby into our perfectly prepared home. I came home from the grocery store to find that Steve had stripped the surface from the kitchen counters. He was fascinated by the grain of the plywood and had decided impulsively he would sand them down and seal them. I guess he never thought about how I, as an anxiously nesting mother-to-be, would react on the verge of labor. I was furious. I went into a melt-down, screaming, "You CAN'T have PLYWOOD kitchen counters!" Even though we couldn't afford it, I insisted that he hire someone IMMEDIATELY to install kitchen countertops. I guess that was the "April Fools" joke Steve played on me that year.

PIECE 24 — "YUMPS"

illa's Diary March 11 (Daniel Age 3)
Daddy waited about an hour for you this AM while you tried to dress yourself—snapping each snap on your cowboy shirt! We don't have enough patience—a constant struggle.

"Mommy, I got yumps in my socks!" Every morning before preschool, the getting-Daniel-dressed-routine felt like torture for both of us. Underwear was not a problem. Maybe there was no power struggle because he liked the He-Man cartoon characters printed on the cotton briefs. Or maybe it was because, since he had slept in them, they were already on so no affirmative or negative decision existed to be considered.

Next, I would suggest pants and a shirt. No matter what I offered, he always insisted on different choices. We negotiated whether it would be the blue pants or the red pants. He wanted to see every option in the drawer. Then, would it be the striped shirt or the alligator shirt? He fingered every shirt in the dresser, evaluating each option.

Early on, I tried to steer him toward reasonably fashionable matches, but after weeks of daily power struggles I weakened and gave in to anything, whether it matched or not. After months of daily power struggles, I gave in to his insistence on wearing only sweatpants and t-shirts.

Briefs, pants, shirt; we were almost there.

We both sat on the primary yellow carpet next to his bunk bed. I, the mere adult, cowered next to the scrawny little toddler, who acted like he was He-Man the almighty himself, and gingerly pulled the small, plain white cotton crew sock onto his left foot, wriggling the seams to adjust it.

Inside, I was begging, pleading, holding my breath, "Please, oh please, let this be acceptable to his highness."

Then I reached for the second of the pair, put my fingers inside, stretched it, and slipped it delicately over his right foot and five tiny toes—again, under-the-breath prayers to the sock-gods.

I had looked through every store in town, searching for the perfect sock, the sock with no seams, the sock with the perfect fit, but it seemed the perfect sock did not exist.

Okay—briefs, pants, shirt, two socks on—so far, so good.

Only two little shoes to go: cool-looking, red canvas Stride-Rite sneakers with blue laces. One at a time, I opened up the tongue, spread the laces wide, and evenly slid the left shoe over the sock, holding the cotton fabric in place to keep it taut. I replaced the tongue and pulled the laces snugly, evening out the pressure on each side of the lace.

Same story with the right shoe: squeeze it tenderly onto his wiggly foot, tie each lace not-too-tight, not-too-loose, and the lace ends must be even.

All dressed! Ready to go?

Nope.

"Mommy," he whined, accusingly, as if I intended him great harm, "Yumps!" he shouted, "I got yumps in my socks!"

If his shoes and socks didn't feel right to him he would pull them off and insist that they be put back on again, straighter this time.

"NO! There's a yump, right there!"

I pulled Daniel's socks on, put his shoes on and tied the laces evenly, then took them off again. I would repeat this pattern dozens of times until he was satisfied there were no more lumps or wrinkles, especially around his toes.

Whining, "More YUMPS!"

This same miserable getting-dressed process repeated… every single morning… and all this before Daniel ever left the house.

Daniel's Answers (Age 29)
[Do you remember anything about this, about having lumps in your socks? You were so young. You probably can't remember that far back.]

"You were probably hurrying me, like you do now, like, related to the dogs, when you hurry to get their leashes and get them out the door before they calm down, or when you plop their food down in their bowls without waiting for them to calm down first."

PIECE 25 — APART-MENT

D aniel continued to have panic attacks, even when he was alone. One day he called me from his job at the screen printing shop and said he was having a panic attack, and that he didn't know what to do. I drove out to his work place, brought him some lunch, and sat with him for an hour until he decided if he could stay at work or if he needed to go home for the day.

Nilla's Diary, September 10 (Daniel Age 21)
Steve and I came home today and found a pile of notes on our bed, Daniel's way of asking for help. They were heart breaking and touching notes. He said he felt so lonely in his apartment and had so

much anxiety that he didn't know what to do about it. One of the notes said "Thank you for being great parents." That note shocked us because we thought Daniel "hated" us, like many typical teenagers say when they go through a phase where they can't stand their parents.

I made an appointment for Daniel the next day with our family doctor to have him evaluated for depression. They did blood work to test his thyroid and prescribed anti-depressants. He told the doctor that when he became anxious, he worried about losing someone in his immediate family such as a parent or his brother. Initially he believed a lot of his anxiety stemmed from moving a lot when he was a pre-teen. He reported getting nervous with public speaking and said he had poor social skills.

Daniel read a lot on his own about changing his thinking patterns. He discovered a therapeutic method called Cognitive Behavioral Therapy and I helped him find a psychologist who practiced CBT.

A month later, at his re-check appointment, he told our family doctor he was beginning to feel "normal," the only way he could describe it. He said he was working hard to get better, on his own and with therapy.

Contract between Daniel and Mom and Dad
September 24 (Daniel Age 21)
Daniel will rent the back room of our home as his self-contained apartment beginning October 1 until no later than September 30 next year. Mom cannot change her mind after a short period of time for stupid or temporary reasons. Daniel can move out at any time. The intention here is that Daniel is living independently.

The purpose of this arrangement is to encourage Daniel's continuing improvement in addressing his social anxiety and panic disorder. Daniel will use this opportunity to challenge himself to reach out to meet people and form new relationships. During the year, Daniel can look for roommates and other more permanent living arrangements.

Daniel will pay parents $100/week. Parents will in turn pay $110 for weekly appointment with psychologist Dr. Campbell.

Daniel will continue medication as recommended by Dr. Lyons, primary care physician. Daniel will attend an anxiety support group twice a month, as well as the weekly psychology appointments.

Entrance and exit will be through separate door.

We will all help each other out with household chores. Daniel may use the kitchen and the laundry room. He will have a shelf in the pantry to store his foods. Daniel will not hang out in the rest of the house without invitation. We will not enter Daniel's apartment without invitation, even to watch TV/DVD. We can eat meals together and visit and have normal family relationships.

We can make additions and subtractions to this contract as long as we all agree and initial this contract. Contract will be reviewed in six months.

Signed,

Daniel Childs   Mom Childs   Dad Childs

PIECE 26 — ENCOPRESIS

Encopresis is the inability to control defecation. It basically means pooping in the pants. It is an unpleasant subject to talk about or read about, but even more unpleasant to deal with several times a day, every day, for many years.

Daniel's first grade teacher had to call me almost every day to come to school to clean him up. I would leave my full time job as an insurance office manager, drive across town, walk into his classroom and smell the horrid, rotten stench. I was embarrassed that the children and this dedicated teacher had to endure this every day. I felt sorry for Daniel, having to sit in dirty underwear, but I have to admit

I think I usually felt angry at him. I couldn't understand why he couldn't control it.

It seems like we tried everything to prevent it. I begged him every morning before he left for school to go into the bathroom, take his time, and do what he needed to do. The psychologist recommended that the family take a walk every morning to get his bowels going. Our "morning walk" tradition is now a good memory to look back on, and it may have helped him somewhat, but not completely. He didn't have one bowel movement a day; he had three or four.

We didn't know if Daniel's physical condition was a result of his surgery for Hirshsprung's Disease when he was an infant, so at first, we dealt with it kindly and with patience. We took him to the pediatrician, and then back to the surgeon who had operated on him, to see if they could find any lingering abnormalities. They weren't sure because Hirshsprung's Disease is rare, and they didn't see cases of it regularly. But the physicians and the psychologist all agreed they thought the cause was likely not physical, but more likely psychological, and probably related to anxiety.

When Daniel had an afternoon activity like sports or music, he would have to come home first and get cleaned up. When Daniel was invited to play at a friend's house he had to take a change of clothes. He usually couldn't clean himself up so I would be called over to help him. This went on for at least four years. I remember going to his first grade class to clean him up and I'll never forget smelling that foul scent when I picked him up from clarinet lessons after school in fourth grade, where I usually found him hiding under a table, giggling, with the teacher either ignoring him or asking him to be quiet and pay attention.

Mothers Day Antelope Island (Daniel Age 12)

David, Daniel and I joined a group camping on an island in the middle of the Great Salt Lake. We had a magical time, climbing to the top of a mountain to count the many wild buffalo watching hawks soar, and spotting other wildlife. We cooked out on a campfire and both boys gave me hand-made cards for Mother's Day. It would have been a perfect weekend, except that Daniel soiled his pants. There was no easy way for him to clean himself up without showers, so he stunk up our tent.

PIECE 27 — OASIS TO OASIS

In the late '80s, Steve had a two-year backlog of painting commissions. We had plenty of money to pay our bills, and then some. We joined a country club. On hot summer days we enjoyed splashing in the cool swimming pool and I loved chit-chatting in the company of other mothers of young children. The four of us played tennis on the clay courts, the boys took golf clinics, and Steve and I invited our friends to dinner out at the club.

Daniel and David attended The Summit School, a wonderful private school, for their kindergarten and early elementary grades. They had plenty of friends, play dates and sleepovers. They played soccer and baseball. They went to summer camps. We bought a home on a golf course so we could walk out our back door summer evenings and drive a little white ball down to the lush, trim, grassy green. Our home was located within the campus of Wake Forest University, so our family frequented college sporting events and walked around the quad.

We renovated the brick ranch home, knocking out walls to transform the two small bedrooms and two baths into a huge master suite with spacious tile shower, whirlpool tub, and pedestal sinks. We turned the 1950s dark paneled kitchen into a modern show place with all white cabinets, new appliances, and a curvy, custom-designed granite counter-topped island: my dream kitchen.

Within a year, Steve's commissions had dried up. I hadn't worked full time in several years. The economy was in recession. We had no income and nothing on the horizon. We canceled our country club membership, withdrew the boys from private school and toured public schools for the fall. We canceled our newspaper and magazine subscriptions and everything else we could, even our membership in the YMCA, to save money. In order to pay our mortgage, we realized, we needed to rent out our newly remodeled house, now in perfect condition with fresh paint and newly refinished wood floors.

With our lives now upside down, Steve and I began to dream about a kind of "sabbatical" year in a different location. I wanted to move the family to France, where our sons could become fluent in a foreign language, but Steve didn't speak a word of French and that sounded like torture to him. He wanted to move out west, where we could experience all that the "Great Outdoors" had to offer.

We set off on our year of adventure. We traded our two small Hondas for a used GMC Suburban with four-wheel drive to tow a U-Haul trailer filled with only the bare essentials. We created a simple life in Logan, Utah, a small university town in a mountain valley between Salt Lake City and Yellowstone National Park, where the cost of living was much lower.

We were able to rent a two-bedroom, one-bath house across the street from the boys' elementary school, with an incredibly scenic view of the mountains. We furnished the little home with folding chairs and a card table for the dining room, a futon and TV tables for the living room, and bunk beds from the second-hand store.

Though the indoor space was small, the outdoor space was unlimited. Endless hikes waited for us right outside our front door. The crisp, dry air tempted us daily out into the sunshine to picnic at the park, to shoot basketball, to bike around town, to play tennis on the public courts. I won first place in the city tennis tournament and Steve and Daniel placed second in the father-son tournament. Our backyard vegetable garden flourished in the perfect weather conditions.

We knew one local family who introduced us to their friends. We spent weekend evenings playing lively board games, joined in Wednesday night church activities, and were quickly surrounded by a warm, happy community.

Steve and I both applied for, and were accepted to, graduate school at Utah UNCA. Tuition was low, and we were able to buy health insurance and obtain other benefits through the university. I bicycled down the hill to my part-time job at Zollinger apple farm in the valley. We enjoyed gallons of fresh apple cider that fall.

We were able to travel inexpensively throughout the west, to the Grand Tetons, Yellowstone, Glacier, Zion, Bryce, Arches, and Grand Canyon National Parks. We mined gems in Montana, climbed black lava fields in Idaho, and camped in the scorching Nevada desert. Summers we went tubing in irrigation canals and hiked up the Wasatch mountains, the steepest range in the U.S. When frigid weather arrived, we took advantage of the powdery white stuff by downhill skiing at the resort near our home. We cross country skied to cut down our Christmas tree in an Idaho forest.

It had been the best year of our life as a family, so we decided to stay another year in paradise.

PIECE 28 — EXPERIMENT

Each morning of his fifth grade year, Daniel waited as long as he could before leaving for Hillcrest Elementary School, located across the street from our house. Daniel had it timed down to nine seconds. He set his watch alarm and left home… nine… eight… seven… six… five… four… three… two… one… RRRIIINNNNNG! By the time the school bell rang, he would be seated at his desk. Every single night he had to use colored pencils to carefully "color in the lines" some map or diagram—his homeroom teacher's favorite homework to assign.

When he moved up to the sixth grade Daniel was anxious about going to Mount Logan Middle School, a huge building with 1500 other students. The halls were crowded during the frequent class changes and Daniel could hardly keep up with where he was supposed to go each class period. Every night he talked about rules, tickets, points, wasted time, and large classes. He said it was set up to "learn more about rules than learning." He was so stressed, that I feared his curiosity and joy in learning would be suffocated. I began to consider home schooling him. We knew several other families who were teaching their children at home and I asked them for advice.

I knew with individual attention Daniel could pick up information quickly. Learning would be more efficient. I could work with him one-on-one and get into a subject in greater depth. I could tailor subjects to his interests. There were so many opportunities in our mountain valley out west. Instead of P.E. class, he could go cross country skiing or downhill skiing with his dad up the canyon. For art class his dad could teach him drawing, outside in a park. He could take workshops at the art museum where I worked. His brother David was so jealous that Daniel didn't have to go to school.

For social opportunities there were sports and church activities. He played flag football, baseball, and tennis. He was part of a puppet troupe at church, as well as weekly Awanas activities. He was a member of the Junior Naturalists. He was in an accelerated math club, a history club, and an earth action club. Another home-schooling mom agreed to tutor Daniel in math and science in exchange for Steve tutoring her two sons in drawing.

I filed my "letter of intent" with the local school board. They had started a new program where they supplied a tutor twice a week to any family who was interested. Mrs. Bowman taught Daniel geography throughout the year.

I set up Daniel's reading list and curriculum for the year: math, reading, writing, spelling, history, and Latin. I ordered text books. I named our school N.O.I.S.E. which stood for Natural Occidental Interdisciplinary Serendipitous Experiment. Teaching Daniel went hand-in-hand with my study in my master's program. I was studying folk lore and how people learn in non-traditional ways, such as in museums.

We took advantage of everything on the university campus. Daniel attended performances, toured science labs, and stargazed through telescopes. When we studied the government, we toured the state capitol and other civic buildings and sat in on courtroom proceedings. We became familiar with the public library. I checked out from the hospital library complete, life-size anatomical models. I used cooking to demonstrate measurements (math) and chemical processes (science.) We visited sheep ranches, deer ranches, and elk ranches. We toured "living history" pioneer villages and observed Native American "rendezvous." We took our binoculars outside and went bird watching. We identified trees, flowers, wildlife, rocks, animal scat, and clouds.

Daniel and his two home-schooling buddies entered the National History Day competition. They came up with a plan to reenact the journey of early explorers, whose photography, sketches, journals, and scientific data led to the designation of Yellowstone as a national park. Each of the three boys would play a role as one of the three main characters in the expedition. We took a real trip to Yellowstone National Park to reenact the historic journey. The boys wrote up their research, made their presentation, and won first place in the local area! They went on to win second place in the state competition, which meant they were eligible to go to Washington, D.C. to compete nationally.

We two moms took the boys to the nation's capital where they presented their project. Kids from all 50 states exchanged buttons as mementos. We toured the U.S. Capitol where our state's senator put his hands on Daniel's shoulders in the group photo. Daniel was the only student wearing a three piece suit. We visited monuments and museums before returning west.

A year later Daniel wrote a school report on his experience, "In sixth grade I went to middle school for nine days. I did not like it so my mom decided she would home school me. I was very happy. My mom and I thought that would be a good experience for both of us and we were right. We did mountain hikes and I wrote poems about nature. I joined nature groups and writing groups. I studied Latin from cassette tapes and many other things, but the only subject that we took right out of the book was math."

Daniel's Answers (Age 29)
[What do you remember about home school?]
"I remember it being fun."
[What if you had stayed in public middle school for sixth grade?]
"Probably would have had more social opportunities."
[So, in hindsight, would it have been better to stay in public school?]
"Yeah."

PIECE 29 — FRIENDSHIP CLUB

We moved from a small town in the western U.S. to a big city in the Southeast: Atlanta. We rented a two-story brick home in Marietta, a suburb known for its good schools. The highlight was living near enough to Steve's family to be able to go hiking with them almost every weekend.

There was no possibility of home-schooling Daniel that year. Each weekday morning, I commuted 30 miles down I-75 in rush-hour traffic to my full-time job downtown at the High Museum of Art. Steve would be the stay-at-home dad and paint in his studio above the garage. David attended the elementary school a mile away. Daniel entered seventh grade in a huge, newly constructed middle school. On parents' night I bee-lined it to the table labeled "Friendship Club" and begged the volunteers to get my quiet, shy son involved.

David quickly found a friend in the neighborhood and frequently had friends from school over to play. There was a boy Daniel's age a few houses away. His mother and I played on the same tennis team. I encouraged Daniel to go play tennis with him on our neighborhood courts, but that never happened.

I don't remember any human friends Daniel made that year, but I do remember this was the year he became intimately connected with a computer. We bought our family's first personal computer for Christmas that year. When I imagine Daniel, I see him sitting in front of that monitor. Steve's brother Kirk was a professional computer programmer and Daniel lived for the Saturdays that Uncle Kirk came over to solve some computer glitch for us. That was when Daniel was most animated, as he and Uncle Kirk sat together staring at the screen for hours, discussing features or solutions.

Steve and I searched for a church we could attend. I found a church that was known for its friendly youth group for teens. I called the youth leader and found out about their programs. One Sunday afternoon I pleaded with Daniel to try the youth group. I assured him the leader was great, the group was small, and the activity would be low-key. "Just give it a try. It can't hurt." I tried to persuade him this was a good way to get to know some other kids. The more insistent I became, the more he resisted.

I'll never forget the hopeless feeling I had that day as I went from verbal order… to waiting in the car with the engine running… to gentle honking… to going inside… to physically trying to pull him out to the car. I patted his back, "Come on, hon." Blank stare, solid stance. Desperate, I tugged on his shoulders trying to force him to obey. His feet became concrete blocks, cemented to the foyer floor. The more I tugged, the more his body transformed into stone. Before my eyes my son was converted into a marble statue: impossibly heavy and permanently immovable.

Daniel was successful academically, making straight A's in his classes, though he usually expressed boredom with school. I investigated getting him registered for the gifted and talented program. His previous testing would qualify him, but the school district required more recent results. I made an appointment for him to be re-tested. Several weeks later I got a letter in the mail reporting that Daniel did not meet the criteria. The results showed his IQ at

70%, significantly below his several previous scores around 96%. This didn't make sense, because IQ results are typically stable across a lifetime. I asked Daniel about the testing. After some digging on my part, he remembered getting lost trying to find the testing room that day. He had arrived late and was, by then, stressed and behind. Also, he confessed, he "didn't really try that hard." I asked him why. He hemmed and hawed. Finally, I pulled out of him that he had thought the gifted and talented program would be more academic work in *addition* to his regular school load. He didn't understand that it would be *instead* of his regular classes.

I appealed to the school district. I assembled a notebook full of his previous IQ test results, along with a full history of his academic testing results: First grade: 99%. Second grade: 99%. Third grade: 98%. Fourth grade: 98%. Fifth grade: 95%. The school district stuck with their own testing results and denied Daniel access to gifted classes.

After only one year in Atlanta, our family moved again, this time to the Midwest: Kansas City. I found a much better job with a huge jump in salary and fantastic benefits. We couldn't afford not to take this great opportunity. Unfortunately, it meant that Daniel and David had to switch schools, but fortunately, we were moving to Blue Valley, an area reported to have the finest public schools in the nation. I didn't mind my thirty minute commute to work each way. The drive was worth it to provide the best setting for my two smart and wonderful sons.

We moved in the middle of the school year, over their spring break. On the boys' first day of school, I hadn't yet started work, so I was at home in the afternoon. The doorbell rang. I opened the door to see an exuberant boy on roller blades, with a big smile on his happy face. "Hi! I'm Bryan. Is Daniel here?" I couldn't believe my ears. I opened the door wide. "Yes! Come on in. I am Mrs. Childs. Glad to meet you." I shouted upstairs, "Daniel? Bryan is here to see you!" The guys went outside. I ran to Steve's studio to tell him what happened. "Steve, you won't believe it! Isn't that the nicest thing? How thoughtful! To welcome a new kid to town, by coming over to visit the first day! Wow!"

During the next few months, Bryan was a frequent visitor in our home and he started bringing other friends over with him. Daniel's birthday was within a week or two of our moving to town. I was afraid it would be a lonely, boring, just-family occasion, but no! Bryan brought over a group of six or eight friends for the party. I fixed barbecue chicken, corn on the cob, and birthday cake. Daniel's present from me that year was a Polaroid camera. The kids posed in groups with goofy grins and giggled at the instant photos. Soon, there was a "gang" of guys and gals hanging out at our house, playing board games, laughing, running around, playing ping pong in the basement, and watching movies. Steve and I had never been so happy to have friends of Daniel's, teens hanging around the house, who even seemed comfortable being around us adults. The "gang" rented a limousine to go together to the eighth grade dance. They went out for dinner downtown before the dance. Daniel got all dressed up. Steve tied his tie for him. That heavenly phase ended too soon.

Daniel's Answers (Age 29)

[What happened to your friendship with Bryan and that "gang" of friends?]

"Moved."

[No, we lived there for five years.]

"Moved."

[Oh, I guess you did change schools, from middle school to high school.]

"Yeah."

PIECE 30—HIGH SCHOOL LOWS

D aniel attended Blue Valley North, one of the best public high schools in the country, ranked according to their overall academic results and college preparation. He earned all A's and B's in 9th and 10th grades. His national standardized testing resulted in a 98% composite score. Daniel was a strong player on their tennis team. He participated in debate club competitions.

Our family found a church we were all comfortable attending. Daniel joined the youth group and went on a week-long summer mission trip with them. He developed several solid friendships there with two guys, whose parents were also becoming friends with Steve and me. The youth director met individually with Daniel weekly to study a discipleship program together. The church community became like our extended family. David felt at home there too, and made lots of friends in the neighborhood and at school and church.

In 11th grade, maybe from the physical and emotional stress resulting from a severe dental infection, Daniel started having panic attacks. He began meeting with a school counselor, who suggested that he withdraw from Spanish class to lighten his load. He barely passed chemistry class that year.

The next year, David would be going to boarding school, and we offered Daniel the opportunity to go to McCallie as well. Steve and I told Daniel it was his decision to make: stay at home with us and continue to go to the same high school, or go to McCallie out of state with his brother David. I tried to help him evaluate his choices.

"Daniel, what are you thinking, about next school year?"

"School is boring."

"Do you want to be bored?"

"No."

"Aren't you lonely here on your computer by yourself all the time?"

"Yes."

"Do you want to be lonely?"

"No."

"Do you have any friends?"

"No."

"Do you want to be by yourself?"

"No."

"A good high school can lead to a good college which can lead to a good career."

[Silence]

"What do you think your major would be?

[Silence]

"What kind of work do you want to do when you finish school?"

"Computer. But computers are stupid. I've wasted my whole life. School is boring."

"When we looked at McCallie last week, the guys seemed to be working together in labs, helping each other, and interested in what they were doing. They didn't seem bored to me."

"Boarding school is not worth it. School is school. We can't afford it. I will probably go to a cheap college, too, in-state."

Daniel wavered up until the deadline we gave him to make his decision. He told us he decided to go to the boarding school.

As a parent, I felt more connected to the boarding school 1,000 miles away than I ever had to the local public school three miles away. Their faculty and administrators were much more accessible to me; communication was as simple as a phone call or e-mail.

Teachers evaluated students with written comments rather than just a letter grade. "Daniel seems far away, uninvolved, unconcerned, tuning out. His effort is sporadic. It seems he does not care. He is not engaged. He rarely participates. Daniel keeps to himself, preferring to sit silently in the rear of the class. Daniel is a talented student, but he does not apply himself. He makes little effort. He does not complete his work. He doesn't seem to try." His Ethics teacher commented that Daniel seemed "morally rigid." From the computer professor: "Daniel could do the work with ease; but he often comes to class totally unprepared." Another said, "Daniel is gradually thawing. He is becoming well-liked by his classmates, who also think he is a fine guy."

Daniel made mostly A's and B's, with one C. He withdrew after failing physics, although reluctantly, because he wanted to remain in the class because he wanted to learn the subject.

I asked the school counselor to have Daniel evaluated for depression. The counselor assured me not to worry, saying Daniel seemed "fine."

STEP THREE
TURNING OVER

Nilla's Method for Completing a Jigsaw Puzzle
  1.   First, I turn all the pieces out of the box.
  2.   I plop the pieces onto the table into a big jumbled pile.
3.   Turning over each upside-down piece right-side up, I begin to see what I have.

Progress on a jigsaw puzzle happens one piece at a time. This phase of turning over up-side-down pieces is tedious, but it must be done. It requires patience and time. As you turn over right-side up each blank grey cardboard piece that landed up-side down, you discover the other side of each puzzle piece is colorful. Each piece's unique design contains clues as to where it belongs.

Daniel may have felt bland socially, that he didn't have anything to offer, that he didn't know what to say in conversations. His facial expression was often blank. He may have felt like he didn't fit in anywhere. With patience and persistence, with time and careful, intentional training and support, Daniel's world began to be turned right-side up. He began to understand himself better. He began to feel like he belonged.

PIECE 31 — CALM BEFORE THE DORM

In June, before his return to college, Daniel and I, and our eight-year-old, energetic Standard Poodle "Indi," went hiking in Shenandoah National Park in Virginia for two weeks. Steve had been studying lightweight backpacking methods. He became obsessed with every ounce, so he could get his pack weight down from an obscenely heavy 60-pound pack to a manageable 13-pound pack. Steve let us borrow his camping equipment. He showed us how to set up a makeshift "tent" using our hiking poles as support structure for a flimsy green tarp which was folded into a triangle and hung over a cord. The "floor" of our tent was a scrap of Tyvek waterproof sheeting purchased second-hand from a home construction site. Our cooking stove was crafted from an aluminum soda can, cut in half, with a small solid cube of specialized camping fuel.

Daniel and I hiked and camped out in all kinds of weather— beautiful, hot, sunny days; foggy, humid, overcast days; and freezing cold, pouring rain that soaked us through to the skin. Indi slept in the tent curled up between us. We tried to keep our stuff dry under waterproof pack covers, but it was difficult setting up and breaking down our tent in the pouring rain. We warmed up when we could with hot showers in the campgrounds we passed through. Some nights we spent in a rustic cabin just big enough for a wood stove and four bunk beds, where I screamed and jumped out of the top bunk when I felt ticks crawling on my scalp.

We alternated "roughing it" with a night in a motel in town, where we washed our wet clothes at a Laundromat and went to an animated movie. On my 45th birthday, we splurged and stayed in the Big Meadows Lodge with a roaring fire in the huge stone fireplace in the lobby. Steve joined us for the last few nights, as it was our 25th wedding anniversary. We hiked the Appalachian Trail during the day. At night, he and Daniel created a makeshift chess set by drawing a board on a piece of paper and forming chessmen out of pennies, rocks, and other found items.

We toured Luray Caverns. We attended ranger talks in the park amphitheater about bears and birds of prey as well as a ranger-led twilight walk through Big Meadows. We hiked to view peregrine falcons nesting. Daniel thrilled me by agreeing (for my birthday) to take with me a white oak basket-making workshop led by a mountain man on the front porch of the Lodge. We attended the "Drama of Creation" lighted evening choral performance at Natural Bridge, one of the Seven Natural Wonders of the World.

Daniel's Answers (Age 29)
[Do you remember when we went hiking?]
"Yeah. Didn't we both wear Waldies?" [Now called 'Crocs']

PIECE 32 — MAKESHIFT

Two years after Daniel had been suspended from college, he realized that he needed more credentials than a high school diploma to get a decent job. In August he returned to UNCA at age 22, but this time he was provided disability services via his diagnosis of severe social anxiety. With a doctor's note, he was provided a single dorm room. A student "tutor" was assigned to take notes for him in his most difficult class, Humanities, and a student "mentor" was assigned to walk with him to and from each class because he was terrified walking in crowds and across the quad. Another student was lined up to walk to the cafeteria and sit and eat with him. Daniel was exempt from making class presentations and the writing lab was available to help with composing papers and reports.

Daniel's advisor, Dr. Kaplan, was also the disabilities advisor. She had some physical disability that required a wheelchair and made handwriting difficult for her. I think her differences made Daniel feel more comfortable. Dr. Kaplan was very kind and patient with Daniel; she had a calming presence. She listened to me describing Daniel's needs and answered in a matter-of-fact way what could be done to support him.

Dr. Kaplan moderated a weekly lunchtime "disabilities" discussion group, which included an assortment of students of all ages with many different forms of disability. One student was paraplegic. One was a 40-something-year-old man I'll call "Spaugh" who had recently returned to college after being diagnosed on the autism spectrum. Another student in the disabilities group was a young woman I'll call "Charity" who had had a stroke and lived at home with her parents.

I called Reformed University Fellowship, found out the name of the area's campus pastor and set up an appointment for him to meet Daniel. The two of them continued to meet together weekly throughout the year, sometimes joined by other students.

Nilla's Diary August 12 (Daniel Age 23)

Daniel called six times last night. We talked for two hours. For 15 minutes of that time I listened to him crying in silence. He told me he had taken a kayaking class in the indoor swimming pool, and had walked two hours on the track, trying to while away the time to distract himself from the loneliness. He was trying to adjust, but this was so very difficult for him.

Intentionally, Daniel did not bring his car with him so he would not be tempted to take "Random Drives," which had been a major distraction to him his previous time at college. He decided not to have a TV in his room and he gave up drinking caffeinated sodas "cold turkey."

Almost every weekend that fall and spring I drove up to the mountains to visit Daniel so he wouldn't be lonely. When he called during the week, discouraged, I would cheer him up by saying, "It's just a few more days until the weekend. I'll bring Indi up with me and we'll go hiking on Saturday. You pick out a trail for us, okay?" Sometimes David came with us, and brought his dog Zuka as well. We stayed in a motel that allowed dogs and also had a miniature golf course and plenty of land for exercising the dogs. The guys spent the evenings playing chess in the room while I washed, dried, and folded Daniel's laundry for him to wear the next week.

Home again during Thanksgiving break, Daniel handed me a copy of a national magazine. He pointed to a picture of a man inside and said "He's in my lunch group."

I tried to engage him more in conversation, like, "Tell me about him," or "Why did they write about him?"

The only answer I got was a pointing finger, meaning for me to read the article. "Oh, yes, I'll read it." I flipped through the pages, glancing at the photos. "Hmmm... how interesting... how about that. I will save this copy for you as a keepsake here in your box of memorabilia in the closet."

Daniel nodded and walked out of the room.

I looked at the magazine and read the article. The photo was associated with the cover story on autism. This man, "Spaugh," Daniel's friend, had finally been diagnosed on the autism spectrum in middle age, only as the result of his 13-year-old son first being diagnosed.

Daniel was home with us for a nice long time during Christmas holidays. In early January, I asked Daniel, "What classes are you registered for, this semester?" When he replied, "What's registration?" I realized he had "missed" the deadline to register for spring semester. I couldn't believe it. I was furious! In hindsight, I wondered if this was his passive-aggressive way to resist having to return to school.

I called the registrar's office and begged them for an extension, but they insisted the form had to be delivered in person. I told Daniel to get in the car, because we were going to drive the two hours each way to turn in the flimsy piece of paper he had neglected to mail.

Spring semester followed the same pattern as fall semester. Every weekend I drove up to the mountains to visit Daniel, to give him something to look forward to each week, to get him through.

Daniel was on a low dose of Paxil to help with his anxiety. He met with Dr. Maggie in the student counseling office, but Daniel said it didn't do any good to meet with her because "She won't tell me what to do." For example: before coming home for Thanksgiving break Daniel expressed his worry that after a long weekend at home, he would get out of his good habits he had carefully established at school. I suggested that he talk about this issue with his counselor. He says when he did ask her, she turned the question back to him, "What do you think?" To which he replied his usual, "I don't know." And that same helpless cycle repeated over and again, with no progress achieved.

Daniel had made it through the school year relatively well, thanks to all the supports provided him. He passed all his classes except for the two semesters of Humanities, which met in a huge auditorium with hundreds of students, all of which he found totally overwhelming. He had accumulated less than a year's worth of credits in the same period of time his peers had graduated four years of college.

Daniel's Answers (Age 29)

"I remember I was the one who called the RUF pastor. I remember being frustrated with Dr. Maggie. All she would do is ask questions. It was like that was their solution, to shut their brains off and to get through the day."

PIECE 33 — BEJEWELED

The year Daniel went back to UNCA, this time supported by disability services, I called a local church and asked if there was anyone there who could meet with Daniel to help him become acclimated to their church. We met the most wonderful woman, whom I will call "Jewel." Before we met, I had explained on the phone to Jewel that Daniel had severe social anxiety. The three of us met at a coffee shop in the charming, artsy downtown. Later that weekend, she invited us to her home for a simple supper where we met her lovably ugly pug.

Jewel continued to meet regularly with Daniel. She picked him up Sunday mornings to take him to church and took him to young adult fellowship group meetings. They had regular, long walks and talks about spiritual subjects. She was very patient with him and "took him under her wing."

Later that fall I invited Jewel to join David and Daniel and myself for dinner and a show, *The Importance of Being Earnest* at a nearby resort. Over the next few months Jewel became for Daniel "...the best friend I've ever had."

Voicemail, Nilla to Jewel March 15 (Daniel Age 22)
"Jewel, I'm not calling on Daniel's behalf. Daniel is home for spring break and I asked him how you were doing and he said you asked him to never call you again.

"He explained that back before Christmas break he gave you a notebook full of notes he had written down after every meeting with you, and that it contained practically word for word what the two of you had discussed. He told me he wrote them down because he wanted to be sure he was listening to you. He said he also gave you a list of questions and wrote that he wanted to talk about them with you when he came back from Christmas break.

"He said that you had no contact for two and a half months, and then you met with him and told him that the notebook made you feel like you were being watched. You said his response was that he shrugged his shoulders and did not apologize. You told him you felt he was not taking it seriously and asked him to never contact you again.

"I am sad you were hurt. I know he did not mean to hurt you. He is socially *dis-abled* and was totally inappropriate. I wish he could learn from what happened with you instead of being cut off, but I understand your need to protect yourself.

"Anyway, I just wanted to call you to thank you for all you have done for Daniel. I credit you with his staying in school and his turnaround this year. You are an amazing person. Even though I am saddened by this ending, I'm still so grateful to have known you and I wish you all the best."

What Daniel did, by keeping a notebook of what he heard, was nothing harmful in itself. What he did illustrated his skills as an observer, essential for any writer. In fact, it is identical to what I am doing here, by writing this book. Over my lifetime, I have observed myself and others. I am telling that story now.

Daniel's only flaw was in his innocence, his naïveté, his social mis-understanding. He is such a forthright person; he would never have thought to conceal his writings from Jewel. He knew that his intentions were pure. But he could not imagine what her reaction would be. He could not anticipate that she would be offended, that she would feel "watched," if not "stalked" or emotionally "violated." Daniel knew he had not intended any harm, but he did not know how his actions might affect another person.

Charity

Through the weekly disabilities lunch, a girl I'll call "Charity" had befriended Daniel. Occasionally, her parents drove the two of them to the movie theater. Their family gave Daniel a small television set they had won in some contest, which they said they didn't need, so he could watch a few shows in his tiny dorm room.

It seemed to me that Charity had a crush on Daniel, but that he didn't feel the same way about her. Later in the year, he complained to me that she wouldn't stop calling him, even though he asked her not to. She particularly called early in the morning when she knew he wanted to sleep in.

I suggested to Daniel that he have the phone company block her number, but I doubt he ever followed through with that. I was afraid of what else this woman might do. I had never met her, and I couldn't discern the level of danger she posed.

Daniel's Answers (Age 29)

[What do you remember from this?]

"I just didn't understand her [Jewel's] response. It was totally from left field."

[Did she explain it to you?]

"She explained the way she interpreted it. It wasn't enough for me to understand it. It was a waste. If I could have at least learned from it. [Instead,] it was [like] chopping it off and dying."

[I remember how significant she was to you, in your spiritual life.]

"Yeah, that's what made it especially hard. It's difficult when someone you trust like that, to just cut you off."

[Did you have anyone else you could talk to about it?]

"Yeah, I talked to my RUF pastor about it."

[Oh, I am so glad you had someone to listen to you then. I think you found out about this in January, but you didn't tell me about it until March or April of that year.]

[What do you remember about the situation with Charity?]

"It really was a parallel situation. That's what made it so weird."

[About danger:]

"I thought it was strange that you were worried about the danger. I never felt in danger from her. Just annoyed."

PIECE 34 — SURVIVE THIS

Email, Nilla to Daniel July 8 (Daniel, Age 23)

Hey, Daniel. You CAN do it. You CAN make it through three measly little weeks. You CAN survive this. First of all, get some sleep. You can't function without sleep. Then, go to your teacher from the first summer term, and ask about your grade. I'm sure he knows what it is by now. See if you passed, or if you have the grade you need to continue at UNCA. You want to quit, but that brings on so many other problems: housing, work, etc. The easiest route is for you to stay in school for the next few weeks.

Three weeks will go by very quickly. See if you can make an A+. Then you will have another class "under your belt." It is easier to concentrate on one class at a time, like how it is scheduled during the summer session, than during the rest of the year, when you have three or four classes at a time. Study, read, and go to the teacher's office to fulfill your "class participation" requirement.

Whether you decide to stay in this term or to leave, I insist that you get another psychological evaluation. You need to be on the appropriate dose of an effective anti-depressant/anti-anxiety medication. You really can't say no to medicine when your life is not functioning at a minimal level. You need to meet with a counselor once a week, on a consistent basis. Those are not optional. They are essential for you, while you are learning and improving through cognitive/behavioral means you are working on.

We LOVE YOU!!! You are a fine and wonderful person. You have so many gifts to offer to the world. You need some consistent support and proper tools. You will be OK, hon. Talk to you tomorrow. Love, Mom

If Daniel couldn't make it on his own through two short sessions of summer school, I knew he needed more help. What on earth could explain how a smart boy like Daniel could be struggling so much? He wasn't even attending an academically challenging university. He had all the supports anyone could ask for. And he was still just barely keeping his nose above water.

Something crept into my mind about that magazine Daniel had given me last fall. I slid the closet door open, rustled through several stacks of boxes, fished it out of Daniel's keepsakes, and re-read the article. I began to wonder if Daniel might have some of the same characteristics as Spaugh. I started looking for other materials to find more information about the autism spectrum. I knew I couldn't rely on the accuracy of information found on the still relatively new World Wide Web, so I followed up my research with phone calls. I discovered a new program for college students with Asperger syndrome. It was in Florida, just 30 minutes from where my aunt and uncle lived, and I begged Daniel to go with me to look at it and consider it.

PIECE 35 — COMMITTEE

On the 14-hour drive south, I asked Daniel to read about Asperger syndrome and what I had printed off the internet about The Program. While he was reading, or, at least, staring at the pages, I burned up my cell phone minutes trying to get The Program to hold their last open slot for Daniel. In the car Daniel and I were able to talk better than at home.

"If you refuse to go to The Program we may need to commit you for mental treatment, for depression."

"You can't do that."

"Yes, I can."

"How many people do you need to get someone committed? Because I'll get you committed first."

Full of pity, I rolled my eyes. "Go ahead."

We drove late into the night so we could arrive in time for the only remaining interview. We stopped at some random motel within stinking distance of the odorous paper factories in Savannah.

Early the next morning, we buckled back into the leather seats of our Ford Explorer for hundreds of more highway miles in silence. Finally, in the glaring high noon of Florida sunshine we found The Program, in a small office complex behind a strip mall, with a cluster of six apartments across the parking lot.

We met Dr. Kathy, a middle-aged blonde professional, whose teenage daughter served as our receptionist. Daniel looked petrified. Dr. Kathy introduced Daniel to Mack, former Navy cook in charge of the culinary training. She sent them to tour the apartments while she and I talked. Then we reversed—Dr. Kathy met with Daniel and I got the tour. I knew we were in the right place when Dr. Kathy asked Daniel a question to which he answered, "I don't know," and she snapped back sharply: "It's a yes or no question. Which is it, yes or no?" She got him to answer her.

Already discouraged about finances, I found out their exorbitant fee didn't include housing expenses. I didn't know how we could possibly afford The Program. The only way would be to use Daniel's college savings, which would be wiped out in a year.

That night Steve talked to Dr. Kathy by phone for over two hours. Steve called me later and told me about their conversation. She told him she had never called a father before, but in this situation she was so concerned about Daniel. She told him we were lucky Daniel didn't kill himself the night we kicked him out. Steve was devastated. He hadn't realized how serious it was.

Steve tried to explain Daniel's defiant attitude and gave this example: "He won't even make himself a sandwich! He insists that I make a sandwich for him." Exasperated, Dr. Kathy sparked back: "That's the very kind of thing that these kids *cannot* do. To you, making a sandwich seems very simple and straightforward. But believe it or not, it is actually a complex operation that requires multiple steps and sequencing... is it bread first and then mustard, or turkey first and then lettuce? Not to mention remembering what ingredients are needed, and where to find them: bread from the drawer, meat from the refrigerator, mustard from the refrigerator door. Get a plate out, get a knife for spreading the mustard."

"I never thought of it like that. Wow."

The next morning, I woke up worrying. The clock glowed 3:30 a.m. I couldn't sleep. Even if we decided to enroll Daniel in The Program, what would we do with him for the next week before it started? If we drove back home the next day, I knew I would never be able to get him back down there.

3:45 a.m. I went upstairs to my uncle's office to search the internet for mental health treatment facilities.

5:00 a.m. Uncle Jack woke and was surprised to see me in his office. I told him I couldn't sleep, worried about Daniel. I started crying and he didn't know what to do with me. He went back downstairs to get his coffee.

5:30 a.m. Aunt Sally came in. "Uncle Jack said you were up here." I told her about my call with Steve last night, about his talk with Dr. Kathy. She helped me think. Uncle Jack came back upstairs to see how he could help. He took a quote out of his wallet and made a copy of it for me. "Good morning. This is God. I will be taking care of your problems today. I will not need your help. Good day." I smiled and felt comforted temporarily, as he reminded me that this dark moment would not last forever.

7:30 a.m. I woke up Daniel thirty minutes before we had to leave. I went to finish eating breakfast.

7:35 a.m. When I came back in his room again, he hadn't budged. He was still under the covers, a lump of sleeping mass. "Get up!" I tried to pull him up. As I pulled and tugged, he slowly rolled off the bed, dead weight, and thuh-whumped on the floor. I left him there.

7:45 a.m. When I came back in, I truly wondered if he was dead. I saw no movement, no response. "Daniel!"

[Silence.]

Daniel was lying there on the floor with his eyes closed. I put two fingers on his neck to make sure he was alive. I felt a pulse. The only movement in his entire body was a bit of blood pumping through his jugular vein. Then he started laughing, as though he couldn't hold the stone face any longer. He was smiling. It felt like he was mocking me while I was feeling tormented and desperate. I put a cold wet washcloth on his forehead to try to wake him up.

7:55 a.m. There was no time for a shower or breakfast. I told him if he wasn't in the car in five minutes I was calling the police.

[No response.]

Resigned, I walked into the kitchen and asked Auntie for a phone book. "He's lying on the floor. He won't get up. I'm calling the police and having him committed." I burst into tears. Auntie hugged me.

Uncle Jack stood up from his Wall Street Journal, "No, honey, you can't do that. Let US go talk to him." They both walked back toward the guest room as I thumbed through the yellow pages, now blurry through my wet lashes.

What do you know—there came Daniel, walking down the hall, coming out to get in the car. They were shocked. I was shocked.

Auntie had cooked bacon for us, but now there was no time for scrambling eggs. She threw the bacon on a paper plate, handed it to Daniel, and shoved two water bottles into my arms.

My tears steered the car; the weight of my heaving sobs pressed down on the accelerator. I called Steve and told him what was happening. "Will you please call Rose and ask for prayer for us?"

"Who is Rose?"

"She's our church's prayer 'chain' coordinator."

"I don't know how to find her number."

"Look up her name in the church directory."

"Where is that?"

"It's in my home office, on the white shelf, at waist level, center, on the black wire organizer."

"I don't know what to say."

"Just tell her what's going on and ask for prayer."

9:00 a.m. We arrived for our meeting. I didn't want Daniel to have the car keys because I was afraid he would drive away. I went to the car to get a dry shirt he could change into. He was still wet from the washcloth and he was shivering (probably also from nerves.)

He was shut down, not speaking. I called Dr. Michael's cell phone to see if we were in the right meeting place. The ringing located him: over by the fireplace, looking for us as I was looking for him. I had imagined someone much older. He looked too young to be a grandfather, as he had told me earlier. Then I noticed someone else with him.

Dr. Michael introduced "Levi," a tall guy with reddish blonde hair, about Daniel's age, with a heavy mid-western accent. He shook my hand with strong confidence and a warm smile.

I warned them that Daniel and I were both very emotional, that we had had a difficult morning. The experienced psychologist Dr. Michael asked of Daniel, "Oh, really? Tell me about it, Daniel."

Daniel didn't respond, so I answered for him: "Daniel didn't want to come. He wouldn't get out of bed, so I pulled him, and he was lying on the floor, motionless, and I thought he was dead. Then he started giggling."

"Oh. Daniel, what was that about?"

[Nothing.]

"Sometimes stress shows itself in inappropriate ways, as giggling, when we don't know what to do."

Almost imperceptive, Daniel nodded his head.

It was too noisy in the busy bagel shop to concentrate on what Dr. Michael and Levi were saying. Daniel's face looked blanker than a sheet of white paper. I asked if we could go over to their office. I had helped Daniel think of some questions to ask so we would cover everything. I put those notes on the table in front of Daniel so he could ask them. Dr. Michael had a quiet, calming nature and I knew I trusted him right away.

Daniel's Answers (Age 29)

"I mainly just remember I felt like that was not very cool for you to do that, about having me committed."

[You mean you think it was cruel?]

"Yeah."

[I'm sorry.]

[What do you remember about seeing The Program for the first time?]

"I had a bad first impression. I thought it was a bad decision. A mistake. I did not have a real good feeling about it."

[You're laughing about the sandwich thing.]

"That's totally silly."

[It seems a good way to me, to describe how something can appear so simple but it can be so difficult for someone else.]

"It's fine as an analogy, but making a sandwich, I know how to do that. I shouldn't even have to tell you that."

[I really did think you were dead when I came back in and found you motionless on the floor.]

[Daniel, laughing,] "That's your over reaction right there, another place for it. I was doing that on purpose! I just didn't want to go to the stupid place and I didn't know how to get out of it so I was trying my best."

[I think you did the same thing the day you had your interview at the private boarding school.]

"Yeah, probably same thing."

[I say here I trusted Dr. Michael. Did you?]

"Yeah, but it didn't really matter, cause he was never there. He came in to sell it at the beginning, but that was about it. At the end he was more involved, maybe because they didn't have enough staff."

[What did you think of Dr. Kathy?]

"I thought she was good. That's why I was shocked when they fired her. They never did explain."

[I have a theory about why she was let go, probably having something to do with 'politically correct' reasons.]

"Probably so. That's why I liked her; because she did what she thought was right. She didn't try to do what other people expected. She wasn't fake." [I noticed from the beginning she was good at getting through to you.] "Yeah."

PIECE 36 — THE PROGRAM

D aniel was not convinced that this was what he should do. After we had all the information we needed, and after I had talked Daniel's ears off, I asked Steve to talk to him. I drove to the beach where we could watch the powerful surf pound the sand, where our nerves could be soothed by the repetitious waves, and where we could sit and think.

First I had to convince Daniel to wear sunglasses so he wouldn't burn his eyes in the bright glaring sunlight. I had an extra pair of really fine sunglasses with me. I begged him to try them. He wasn't interested. I described how much I loved my "Happy Glasses." This specific lens had a tint that made the light more crisp and made any scenery more beautiful. These were my version of rose-colored glasses. "Here—look at the sky. You won't believe how blue it is."

He tried them on. "Whoa!" He agreed to keep them.

I called David and asked him to talk to Daniel, to help him decide what to do. I walked away, down the beach. David told Daniel he had been studying research in his college business class that the most important characteristic to have is networking. Regardless of academic achievement or talent, being able to get along with people is the most important skill to have. David told Daniel that this should be his top priority.

At age 23, Daniel reluctantly entered a year of "treatment" at a training program for ten guys on the autism spectrum. Each guy shared an apartment with a roommate in the program. They received individual counseling and group therapy. They learned about their "pervasive developmental disability."

Teachers guided them through a curriculum of lessons on social skills, sensory integration, cooking, budgeting, recreation, fitness, laundry, and hygiene. "Peer mentors" were assigned to participate with them in recreational activities. Some guys worked; some attended community college; others received tutoring in basic academics, depending on their needs.

In the first weekend Daniel went bowling, to a science museum, and to the grocery store. He also began to develop a friendship with one of the other guys, named Sam.

Talking with Daniel on the phone after two weeks was painful because he sounded just like he used to at his worst. Steve talked to Daniel too and says he sensed the same sadness. Daniel's few responses to us were the same old… long periods of silence, or "stuff" or "I don't know." My guess is he was on the computer all weekend? He had not eaten dinner yet at 9 p.m.

During parent's weekend in October I was grateful to see Daniel laughing and talking with his new "friends" in The Program. When we went to a book store he held the door open for me. He fixed the seat of the car so I could get out of the back. He asked me, "Mom, do you want a pillow for the car so you can sleep?" He pointed to the sheet on the refrigerator door, "This is our menu," obviously proud to show us. He gave us a "tour" of his refrigerator and freezer, pointing out his new discoveries from his grocery shopping trips: soy ice cream, rice milk, soy chocolate pudding, soy milk, soy cheese, and tofutti popsicles.

I was impressed with Mack's manner with the guys and the matter-of-fact way he instructed them in preparing a meal. When Daniel first came home, he was so proud to tell us about the barbeque cups he had learned to make from ground beef and the salmon he had learned to sauté. He prepared those meals for our family. He learned from Mack to add lemon pepper, especially to scrambled eggs, as a healthier alternative to salt.

I liked Daniel's advisor instantly when I met him. I liked his calm and assuring presence, I liked his voice, and the way he interacted with Daniel.

Daniel didn't seem motivated to do anything except play online poker. He took two classes at the community college, then dropped one with no real reason, and did so-so in the other. We paid all that out-of-state tuition and he simply dropped the class. He waited until right after the drop/add period, so no tuition was refundable. His advisor was very frustrated with Daniel. He tried to help Daniel get permission to change classes or something. He went to a great deal of effort to get the professor's permission, and then Daniel didn't show up to get a signature.

Evaluation

I wrote a thorough, in-depth evaluation of The Program, with my compliments and criticism covering five full, typed, single-spaced pages. Daniel's advisor let me know that at first he felt offended by my comments. After The Program Director suggested that he look at them as a roadmap for improvement, he began to view them as constructive.

We had arrived at The Program at a point of maximum stress. We were faced with multiple disadvantages. While other families were already accustomed to their chronic situation, we were in the middle of a crisis situation. We were at the beginning stage of an intense grieving process. Everything was new and foreign. We arrived in a panic only one week before The Program began. The move-in was confusing. It seemed that everything that COULD go wrong DID go wrong.

Daniel had not yet been diagnosed. He needed to see a psychiatrist immediately to get meds for anxiety, but couldn't get in as a new patient for several months. He had never had disability services, not even an IEP (Individualized Educational Plan) in school.

Daniel's needs were so different from the needs of most of the other students. He had no trouble keeping up with his bank account; he had no trouble doing his own laundry. He did not need academic tutoring. His needs were specific: he needed accountability in attending classes. He needed help mending problems communicating with his professors. He needed to be required to shower daily. He saved money so obsessively that he needed help learning how to spend money occasionally. He needed help understanding his own wishes.

In almost every area, Daniel was receiving services he did *not* need and was not receiving services he *did* need. Even in a program for people who were different from typical, Daniel was not fitting in. He needed a very individualized program, modified for his particular needs.

"Daniel's dad Steve won't fill out the evaluation 'cause every question he says 'I don't know.'" When Steve saw me write that, in reaction he came up with this paragraph: "I haven't noticed many changes in Daniel. When he came home Christmas I couldn't tell much has changed. When I talk to him on the phone I can't tell much has changed. The only thing I can tell is when we were down there in the meeting in the conference center, he seemed to be a little bit more assertive, but later when we had a conference call, he just said, "I don't know" and didn't participate. I haven't seen Daniel since Christmas, and he won't talk on the phone, so I wouldn't know if he's changed. I can't say either way, because I haven't seen him."

The most significant skill Daniel learned that year was to keep a cell phone with him at all times (and to keep it powered on!) That way he could ask for help if he needed it, I could check on him periodically to see how he was doing, and it served as an alarm clock and calendar so he (theoretically) missed fewer appointments.

Daniel told me, "I don't know if The Program has been successful, but the *group* has. Being with the group is positive. I'm friends with all ten. I want to go back."

Daniel's Answers (Age 29)

[Do you remember what David told you that convinced you to give The Program a try?]

"I was thinking it was too much money. David said 'after this year you'll be fixed and you'll be making a lot more money, so it won't matter.' In the back of my mind, I was thinking it would not really happen that way, but I just figured I would be optimistic."

[So what do you think now, about going to The Program that year?]

"It's not good to make choices out of fear. You wouldn't make decisions about any other organization, like choosing a bank or a college, like that."

[What was the deal with your roommate? I kept asking The Program to move you out of rooming with Walker, but they kept telling me that you didn't mind, while I knew you did mind.]

"In one way, it was good. We probably helped each other out, being total opposites. But also, it would just get annoying. Like Cesar Millan says, 'You get the dog you need, not the dog you want.' I thought instead of changing roommates, splitting up, and going our separate ways, that wasn't the solution. We were there for a reason, to learn to deal with things. But the trouble was that they never dealt with it. They would just brush it off."

PIECE 37 — UMBILICAL STEEL

The Program Director explained that people with Asperger syndrome are often connected to their mother as if by a steel umbilical cord, as though their connection had never completely been severed at birth.

I had spent a lifetime trying to compensate on Daniel's behalf for any skills he was lacking. Since Daniel had poor communication skills, I stepped in as his "translator." I explained his idiosyncrasies so that other people would accommodate him into their activities. I became his "adapter," like the electrical converter American tourists take to Europe so they can use their own razor or hairdryer from home. Knowing Daniel had trouble with planning and organizing, I looked for ways to prevent anything from "falling through the cracks." I questioned him, tried to prevent missed deadlines and worried about anything that might have been overlooked.

When it was time to leave Daniel at The Program that first day I felt I was leaving a helpless child in an unsafe environment. It was The Program's first year of operation. They were not exactly organized.

As we were leaving, Daniel looked around, confused, with a panicked look in his eyes. He literally did not know where to go next. No one said, "Go to your apartment and we will meet up later this evening," or "We will meet again tomorrow morning," or "Ask your roommate to walk to the store with you or go out to dinner together." There was no assigned activity like "Go to your apartment and finish unpacking," or "Go play cards or a video game with your roommate."

There were no activities planned, no agenda. Just open-ended nothingness—the worst possible situation for someone with Asperger syndrome whose parents were leaving him at a place he did not want to be, where he knew no one, where everything was frightening and unfamiliar.

The Program as an organization seemed to share the same characteristics as an individual with Asperger syndrome: it exhibited poor executive function, almost non-existent communication, and poor social skills. I couldn't believe they expected ten guys with AS to "hang out" indefinitely, with no direction, in their first hours on their own in a strange environment. This was an ominous start, and as Daniel appeared to be on the verge of a panic attack, I could also feel anxiety welling up in my gut.

I found Dr. Kathy and told her I wanted to talk to her immediately. She invited the three of us (Daniel, Steve, and me) into her office. I voiced my/Daniel's concerns. She quickly snapped at me that I was too connected emotionally to Daniel. She described our situation as being like Elliott and E.T. in the movie "E.T. the Extra

Terrestrial."

At that moment I couldn't recall the story, so she explained: The alien E.T. was abandoned on earth and the boy Elliott found him and began taking care of him. Slowly, it became apparent that when E.T. felt hungry, Elliott suddenly felt hungry and looked for food; when E.T. was tired, Elliott became tired and fell asleep; when E.T. was afraid, Elliott shared that fear. Their supernatural connection was E.T.'s way of getting his needs met.

The story was coming back to me, and I figured out where Dr. Kathy was headed. She went on to describe the end of the movie where Elliott was so connected to the alien that when E.T. became very sick and almost died, the same process was occurring with Elliott—he was getting sicker and sicker and near death. Finally, E.T. disconnected himself so he wouldn't continue to harm Elliott. Dr. Kathy's message to me was that I needed to disconnect from Daniel. She didn't say it, but her implication was that my anxiety was contagious and was contaminating my son; that I was killing him with my over-involvement. Dr. Kathy was right about the movie paralleling our situation. It hurt! It felt like dying. Ouuuch!

Steve and I left Daniel, at least knowing that Dr. Kathy was now aware that Daniel didn't know where to go or what to do. In our little meeting, she explained to Daniel what would happen next. She gave him minimal direction, enough to satisfy me, and hopefully enough to keep Daniel from falling into a cave of panic. I gave Daniel another hug and assured him he would be all right.

Once we pulled away in our car, I collapsed emotionally, heaving with sobs. Steve said he couldn't just get on the highway and drive home with me in that condition. He pulled over and let me cry for an hour or so while he rubbed my neck and gently stroked my back.

The next three weeks were a blur to me. I spent them in bed, as if I was sick. I don't know if I have ever had a nervous breakdown, but if I have, this was it. I felt like I couldn't function at all. Normal was nowhere nearby. It was a season of grief and recovery. From the years (more like decades!) of trying to figure out what my son needed, to forcing him to leave our home that night when it felt like my leg had been amputated, to this moment of feeling like I was abandoning my little child in a scary place.

I was physically and mentally exhausted from the 10-day ordeal of getting Daniel to Florida, living away from home in a tense situation, evaluating The Program and whether it was right for my son, persuading my husband that it was the right thing to do, and convincing Daniel that he should stay there for a year.

Even the practical tasks had been tiring: purchasing everything Daniel needed for a year away from home, cleaning the mouse poop out of the kitchen cabinets, setting up his apartment, getting two new cell phones and service contracts, filling out applications, and writing that massive check for the first semester.

PIECE 38 — EVACUATION

The Program was new. It had just opened its doors and didn't yet have an emergency plan in place. This was the year that Florida was walloped by four hurricanes in one devastating season.

As the first of the four hurricanes approached I sat anxiously by the television, four states away, tuned to the weather channel. I watched the ominous system approach like a bulls-eye on a target to the very town where my son was located.

I tried phoning Daniel, but he had not yet learned to leave his cell phone turned on. His advisor was not returning my phone calls or emails. The director of The Program lived in New England and could not be reached. Three days passed with no word of any plans to evacuate to storm shelters or plans to send the guys home. I was a nervous wreck.

On the fourth day, Steve convinced me to leave my worrying

post and to take a leisurely Sunday drive with him to the mountains for the day. While I was out of cell phone service, someone from The Program called and left a voicemail message that we needed to get a flight home for Daniel right away, that they had decided to close The Program and evacuate the residents.

The Program itself seemed to exhibit symptoms of Asperger syndrome, because with no advance planning, it was too late to get a flight out. Everyone was fleeing the state. I had been exasperated by the lack of information and the lack of communication. I was angry that my son's safety and survival was in the hands of nincompoops!

In desperation, I left a voicemail telling them I would leave immediately to drive the 10 hours south to pick up Daniel and bring him home. More confusion erupted, as most of the staff had already evacuated themselves. Only one staff member remained and he drove four of the 10 guys to the home of one of the residents in northern Florida, again a poor choice because it happened to be located in the direction the most dangerous part of the storm was heading. I tried to recommend a different strategy, but the staff member in charge was not a flexible thinker. He would not adapt to urgent new information and stuck to his original plan.

The next morning, cell phone service was sketchy, and the storm was making reception even spottier. We finally managed to connect at some random gas station. It was raining cats and dogs by that time, and winds were howling.

The new plan was for me to drive several guys four hours further north to the Atlanta airport where they could catch their flights to the northeastern and northwestern corners of the United States. Daniel and two other guys got out of The Program's van and hopped into my SUV. The staff member, Mack, did not give me any information about the guys or what they needed. He drove off within a few minutes of our meeting, presumably so he could get to where he needed to go. Cell phone service was unavailable.

PIECE 39 — SPONGEBOB

One of the guys I'll call "SpongeBob" seemed particularly child-like and very needy. He loved animated cartoons and eating candy. No one had thought to provide any kind of instructions for me, his temporary guardian. I didn't know when he needed to take his medication. I tried to get information out of Daniel, like "What does SpongeBob usually eat? What does he need?" but Daniel didn't know. Keep in mind, all these guys were in their 20s.

I asked the other guy, whom I'll call "Pilot Man" if he knew anything about SpongeBob. He didn't, but he was interested in telling me about airplanes. He knew every airport in the U.S., and could tell me the approach directions for every runway. He knew every make and model of airplane and every technical detail about each one. During the rest of our drive, he educated me about fuselage, wingspan, airspeed, and so on. Though it all went over my head I was grateful for the distraction.

The guys were hungry so I polled them on where they would like to eat as we passed each exit and reviewed the fast food signs. The consensus was Subway. I pulled over at the next exit. I reminded them to take advantage of the restrooms while we were here. I helped them figure out what to order, although I didn't know if the guys had any dietary restrictions. I paid for their meals and handed their individual bag to them once they were sitting in the car. We didn't have time to eat inside the restaurant. We had to keep driving, to get them to their flights on time.

We had just turned out of the parking lot when SpongeBob whined loudly, "Why did you cut my sandwich in four halves?"

"So that it would be easier to eat in the car, so it wouldn't be messy and spill loose food all over the seats."

"But I didn't want my sandwich cut into four halves!"

"I'm sorry, that's just the way it is."

"Go back!" he yelled, "I want another sandwich! I don't want this one!"

"We can't go back. You'll have to eat that one or stay hungry."

"Why did you cut my sandwich in four halves?" he repeated.

Finally, after what seemed like an eternity, we arrived at the Atlanta airport. I dropped "Pilot Man" off curbside at the terminal for his airline. He assured me that he was very comfortable finding his way around airports, that he had flown independently before and would be fine.

I knew I would need to wait in the airport for an hour or two until SpongeBob's flight departed. Daniel and I would be staying in Atlanta that night with his Aunt Sharon and Uncle Kirk. I gave Daniel the option to wait around with us, or to ride the MARTA to his Aunt and Uncle's house. He chose the rapid transit route. I gave him cash and instructed him how to purchase the token he would need and I reminded him to leave his cell phone turned on so he could meet up with his relatives at his destination.

Now it was just SpongeBob and me. We waited in the long lines, made longer due to the migration of people fleeing the storm. We finally reached the counter. I paid for SpongeBob's plane ticket and called his father to arrange for him to mail a check to repay me.

SpongeBob whined loudly, "I want to change clothes!"

I told him he couldn't change clothes because I was a girl so I couldn't go into the men's room with him to help. I said he could go in by himself and I would wait right outside the door for him.

"But I can't do it by myself."

"Okay, then you will just have to wait until you get home. You could just change your shirt out here if you want to." He did. I helped him pull it off over his head and slip the other one on. He didn't want to be wearing a t-shirt when he saw his father.

He didn't want to stay with me in the airport. I told him he had to. He was already stressed out from all the changes and uncertainty. I could tell he was headed for a major meltdown. I had him call his parents so they could persuade him to calm down and follow me to get on the plane. They asked me if he had taken his medicine. I told them I didn't know. They asked him. He didn't know. They talked him through it and figured out where, in what pocket of which bag, he did have a supply of meds. They told him to take one blue pill. I found a cup of water for him so he could swallow it.

Now SpongeBob was creating a scene. He was yelling into the phone to his dad. I was embarrassed as we stood there with everyone around staring at us. He complained and begged and negotiated with his parents until they gave him permission to go buy some candy. That was his bribe to get him to follow me to the gate. The airport store didn't have the kind of candy he wanted. He wanted to keep looking for other stores until we found the special brand he wanted. I convinced him this kiosk had the best selection, that there were no other stores that had his favorite, and I steered him toward a similar choice.

I knew I had to walk him to the gate, but signs everywhere said only ticketed passengers were allowed past the screening stations. I went to a customer service counter and then another until I found out how I could get permission to accompany SpongeBob through security and stay long enough to get him settled at the gate. This was post-9/11 so it was difficult to obtain an exception. We had to go through a special line for people with disabilities.

I had heard Daniel and Sam tell about SpongeBob and how he would get hysterical if anyone touched him. I had experienced enough of his meltdowns for one day. I wanted to do anything I could to prevent any further incidents. We waited in line, waited, and waited, all the time SpongeBob asking me, "Why are we waiting here? Why can't we go to my plane? I want to go see my Daddy now!"

I kept repeating my explanation, "We have to wait here until it is our turn. We are going to your gate. You will get on a plane soon to fly home to your parents."

As we reached the front of the line, I leaned over and very quietly warned the security screener standing next to us, "Excuse me, if you do not mind, when you search him, please do not touch him. He is autistic and is sensitive to being touched."

The guard turned and whispered/yelled across the hall to the guard with the scanner wand, "Hey! He's *artistic!*" "What?" "He's ARTISTIC!"

I tried not to laugh, but at least the guard got the point. He was very patient and gentle. After being scanned myself, I had to wait at a distance. Then the two of us were on our way toward the gate again.

I asked the airline personnel at the gate to be sure that SpongeBob got on the next flight. I made sure he was comfortable with his candy and that he had his cell phone handy in case he needed to call his dad again. I called his father and explained where he was, and asked if he thought it was okay to leave him at that point. He said yes. I talked everything over with SpongeBob again and told him if he had any questions he could ask the airline person behind the desk. "Goodbye, SpongeBob, have a good flight."

Dazed, I walked out of the airport terminal, reached my car, and phoned Daniel to be sure he had connected with his aunt and uncle. I drove through rush-hour traffic (exacerbated by thousands fleeing the storm) to my in-laws. Gratefully, I accepted a big hug from my sister-in-law, who could see the stress in my eyes and the tension in my forehead. I took a rare Xanax and a long, long, nap. That night the storm followed us north. It knocked out the power and a huge hardwood tree fell on the house where we slept, but no one was injured.

Daniel's Answers (Age 29)
[What do you remember about "SpongeBob?"] [Instant smile with quiet laugh]

"Funny."

[What was funny?]

"Comments Sam would make. Walker reacting to 'em. Walker and his friends trying to take advantage of him."

[Like how would he take advantage of him?]

"Try to use his music player or get his candy or stuff like that."

[So they would tease him?]

"Yeah."

[I remember you telling me someone stood up for him.]

"That probably would have been Sam."

PIECE 40—FOOL ME TWICE

Remember I said The Program was behaving organizationally like it had Asperger syndrome? One characteristic of Asperger syndrome is the inability to generalize, which means not being able to learn from one situation and apply the learning to a different situation later.

When the next hurricane approached, in spite of evacuation recommendations, The Program decided to stick it out. They huddled the 10 students and a few staff inside the classroom building with emergency food, water, supplies and flashlights.

Once again, I stayed glued to the tube watching the weather reports. Again I was angry that my son was helplessly dependent on the poor judgment of this expensive institution. The group had a scary night or two with no power, with spectacular thunder and lightning storms, high winds, heavy rains and flash flooding.

I had asked Daniel to call me periodically to let me know how he was doing. He never called. At least, by this time, he had learned to leave his cell phone on, so I was able to call him before his cell phone battery died as the power was knocked out and he was unable to re-charge it.

Thankfully there were no injuries and no major property damage and thankfully the next two hurricanes to hit Florida that year were weaker and less of a concern for their specific locale.

Daniel's Answers (Age 29)

[Will you describe what was going on while you were waiting out the storm?]

[No response.]

[Tell me what it was like. Were there heavy winds and rain and lightning?]

"It was a hurricane."

PIECE 41—SCRUBBING BUBBLES

After I had to use Daniel's bathroom in his apartment at The Program, I went out and bought cleaning supplies.

"Let's clean up your bathroom."

"I just cleaned the toilet."

"What? This is one of the filthiest bathrooms I have ever seen!"

"This is the cleanest bathroom at The Program."

"That just shows our different perspectives." I stood there not knowing what to do. I decided to plunge ahead.

"Come over here, look at how the 'scrubbing bubbles' cleanser works. You spray it on and, like the TV commercial, the bubbles get to work, foaming away." He actually came in and watched and participated, as if I were Mack showing him how to do something. I handed him the spray and a sponge. "Will you please spray the shower and tub while I clean the sink?" That accomplished, I asked him to do the same to the toilet.

"When you get back after the holiday you can clean the floor like this, and wash the mat."

"Why does the floor need cleaning?"

"See the spider webs in the corners?"

"Spiders are good. They eat mosquitoes. And why does the mat need washing? It doesn't have any stains."

"But it feels sticky. You can feel it's dirty with your bare feet."

PIECE 42 — TERMINAL

Our flight home at Thanksgiving was stressful. Daniel seemed to be overwhelmed in the Orlando airport terminal. He didn't want to find the *best* (quietest, least crowded, well-lit for reading) place to sit. He sat down in the *first* place we came to, the dark, cavernous, central lobby. He did speak up for himself, though. I asked him to please stay with my suitcase so I could walk around with free hands. He said he didn't want to be stuck there, not knowing when I would return. I found a cart, put my bag on it, and said I would be back in 30 minutes. He agreed to stay with the cart, since he could get up and push it.

Our late night flight was cancelled. Daniel doesn't handle change very well, but he managed okay. He slept on the airport floor for two hours, and then he followed me to the shuttle bus to our hotel by 2 a.m. While I was negotiating compensation and re-routing with the airline, Daniel had a good idea that was helpful. I was trying to get the absolute first possible flight out the next day. Daniel suggested taking the later nonstop flight at 3 p.m., so we could get a full night's sleep and not arrive home grumpy. I never would have thought of that. We both slept hard and well.

After the endless travel day Wednesday, including sleeping on the airport terminal floor, and a long night's sleep at the hotel, and anticipating another long travel day, Daniel refused to get a shower. I couldn't believe how disgusting that was. What could I say to convince him? Oh, why is everything so difficult?

"I don't want to look at a greasy Daniel. I want to look at a clean Daniel."

[Nothing.]

Calmly, I insisted, "I'm not leaving until you shower."

He protested, "But I'm hungry!"

We hadn't eaten in 15 hours. My stomach was rumbling, too. "The sooner you shower, the sooner you'll get to food."

He showered.

Going Backwards

On the drive to Orlando after leaving The Program for Christmas break we stopped at a highway exit. While we ate lunch, I checked with Daniel to be sure he had followed through on a task his advisor and I had both reminded him several times to do: "Did you take the note to your psychology professor about missing your class next Monday?" When he didn't answer me, I knew the answer was no.

He had the note with him in class last week and was supposed to have taken it to the teacher last Monday. That night I asked him on the phone if he had taken the note. He hadn't, so I asked him to walk it across the street Tuesday. He said he would take it to class on Wednesday. He didn't.

I took a deep breath, and exhaled in an exasperated sigh, "We're going to drive all the way back now and take it."

"He's not there now. The school is closed for the holiday."

"You will have to slip it under his office door." Thirty-five highway miles later, I pulled into the school parking lot. I handed him a pen and paper and helped him compose a note.

"I'll wait here while you take it in." I was learning. In this case, I didn't give him a choice. I didn't get emotional. I didn't let him off the hook. We simply went back and got it done.

PIECE 43 — GIVING THANKS

We missed the big family gathering Thursday, but there was a picnic planned Saturday for the extended family. Daniel refused to be flexible enough to ride together with Steve and David and me a half an hour early. He said, "Too bad, you said 12 to 1." He said he would drive over on his own.

"Well, then, please be there right at noon." He showed up (that's the good part—everyone was so glad to see him!) but not until 12:30. We had all been waiting and waiting for him. He missed the group photo, though it was important to my parents to have all 13 grandchildren in their Christmas card. Here are the good things that happened over the holiday:

- Daniel woke up at 10 a.m. daily, as I had requested, even though I had to wake him up.
- He went to sleep at a decent hour each night.
- He cut back on computer time—no more than two hours per day.
- He cut back on soft drinks & substituted water.
- He took his medicine daily.
- He cleaned out his closet of stuff that had been thrown helter-skelter when he left here in a rush last summer. He threw out loads of old papers. He made two stacks: a giveaway pile and a storage pile.
- He went to his appointment at TEACCH today, the first step in getting an evaluation/diagnosis of autism. Daniel explained The Program to the psycho-educational analyst and answered his questions honestly.
- Daniel helped with the dishes once or twice.

- Daniel offered to cook dinner once (the famed "barbecue cups" Mack had taught him to prepare.)
- He called his grandfather to invite him to lunch with him and his dad.
- We laughed a lot, especially at our silly dogs!
- Daniel went to the science museum with Steve and me with two younger cousins, ages 15 and 16. Daniel was intrigued by the wooden puzzles, by the 6,000 pound granite sphere fountain that could be moved by a finger, and by the swimming, flipping otters. We enjoyed a planetarium show.
- Daniel liked going out to eat at our favorite places, a drive-through, greasy hamburger place, "Cook Out," (we pronounce "koo-gowd") and our traditional Chinese restaurant.
- Daniel's brother David is good with math. He helped us calculate how much The Program costs per day. Daniel couldn't believe it comes to $258 per day, including $258 for Saturday and $258 for Sunday, even. I hope his shock at those figures help Daniel to make the best use of the rest of his time there.
- Daniel played Parcheesi with Steve, David, and our neighbor Fred.
- Our family plus the two dogs walked and let the dogs run wild in a field.
- Steve, Daniel and I hiked two hours at the park Sunday with the dogs, in the woods and through fields, up and down hills, crossing streams.
- Daniel and I went to church Sunday. When we walked in, an old friend, Daniel's first grade teacher, who had also been his "nanny" one summer, came up to us and teased Daniel "You are going to be speaking in 30 minutes, when I give you the signal." Daniel smiled.
- Another of Daniel's friends, who had met with him weekly for lunches/informal pastoral counseling, was the one

preaching. Daniel ordered sermon cassette tapes to be mailed to him at The Program.

- Daniel was laughing and talking in his sleep. That's a first!
- He told his grandfather at lunch that he likes it at The Program. (Not qualified or hesitantly, "It's okay," not a compliant shrug of the shoulders; but that he likes it!)
- Daniel told Steve that next year there will be girls at The Program and that they're getting a house for students like him (Daniel) and the first year students will take over their apartments.

Steve's Review of Thanksgiving Vacation

I didn't notice too terribly much change in the usual Daniel but he did stay off the computer for most of the time. Yeah!! I guess that is a big thing. He skipped out on one social event but made a promising show at another, though it seemed hard for him, but he gets high marks for going and being there. He loved a 'nature' museum we went to, he didn't want to leave due to the many interactive puzzle solving things. He showed determination and solved many hard 'puzzles.' We had a wonderful 2 hour hike with his mother as well and 2 dogs. He was probably at his best then, a beautiful day, fresh air and exercise is key. Steve

PIECE 44—BAREFOOT

Before the December holidays, Steve and I flew down for our annual review of The Program, with their entire staff. Daniel didn't show up at the appointed time and place. Someone had to be sent to find him. Daniel walked in barefoot. Dr. Michael asked him to leave the room. Apparently, Dr. Michael had told Daniel he could wear anything he wanted, he just couldn't be barefoot.

Dr. Michael went outside to talk to Daniel. Dr. Michael came back in the room, red-faced. He seemed embarrassed by Daniel's behavior, as if it reflected badly on Dr. Michael that he couldn't get Daniel to follow a simple instruction. The whole staff appeared flustered by this disruption of our meeting. I was surprised that Daniel picked such a silly thing to protest, but I wasn't as shocked as the staff seemed to be. I had experienced a lifetime of such mysterious shenanigans.

As Daniel waited in the next room, some of the staff shook their heads and took turns trying to figure out how to handle this kink. The pressure was on: the parents had flown down especially for this one-hour meeting. The psychologist tried to interpret what was in Daniel's mind.

I broke the bewilderment by announcing that I thought this was a sign of great progress, that at least my passive son was actively making a statement. Even a strange protest was better than no involvement at all. I don't know whether the staff was more shocked by Daniel's lack of shoes or by my inside-out attitude.

Daniel's Answers (Age 29)

[Do you remember why you did this?]

"I don't remember why it was important. I probably didn't plan it. I was probably already barefoot, and then Dr. Michael said to put on shoes, so then I realized I could mess with him. He and I were like that, we could mess with each other. I knew they wanted to present a certain image for the parents so I wanted to make it so they would have to address some of the issues. I knew they would only tell the parents the best things. I just didn't want it to be perfect for the parents and then go back to the way it was after they left. It's sort of like, when you are kidnapped and you don't want to yell out, but you send out a signal and see if they'll pick up on it."

PIECE 45 — "HURRICANE NILLA"

Besides the usual challenges inevitable to any first year of operation, The Program had dealt with unimaginable events: four hurricanes in one season. But they had another "hurricane" to deal with yet: me—Nilla—a mother advocating for the best possible outcome for what seemed to be the last chance attempt to reach her deserving son.

In one of our program review meetings, the director teasingly characterized me to the others as a "pit-bull." If you knew me you may have been confused because I am as quiet and mild-mannered as my son is. I am tender-hearted. I try to be diplomatic and to soothe everyone's feelings. I want to be a peacemaker. My goal is always to defuse conflict. But when it comes to protecting my son's best interest, I morph into a ferocious mother-bear. I had lived a lifetime of trying to protect my son, to arrange circumstances for his benefit. I was trying, at a great distance, with zero power, to control my son's environment.

The other families of guys participating in The Program had been dealing for years, some decades, with this diagnosis of Asperger syndrome, but this was new territory for our family. Daniel wasn't even technically diagnosed yet! My emotions were raw with grief and concern. I was desperate. I needed to learn how to separate from my son, but the usually difficult process for any parent-child was unimaginably complicated due not only to his Asperger syndrome but also to my own root weakness of "co-dependency."

When Daniel's brother David and I were in Florida during David's spring break we took Daniel and Sam out for dinner with us. They laughed a lot and seemed to enjoy being together. It was wonderful to see Daniel looking so happy and relaxed in a public setting for a change!

Since the beginning of The Program I had had concerns about Daniel rooming with Walker. I'd mentioned it in every meeting I had with the staff. Originally Dr. Kathy said she thought Walker might bring Daniel out of his shell and Daniel might help Walker set limits. Dr. Samson explained at our December meeting that it had been useful for Daniel to learn assertiveness with Walker. I am sure Daniel benefited somewhat from such learning experiences but I think most aspects are minuses. I agreed that was a good try and that that experiment had served its purpose though I think Daniel's living situation detracted from his progress.

Walker stepped over socially appropriate boundaries to reach out to Daniel. His exposure to Walker had a good shock value, to have someone step into Daniel's territory uninvited, to ignore Daniel's withdrawal. But it annoyed Daniel and was stressful for him so that he had to protect himself from Walker. Daniel mostly hid out in his tiny bedroom, isolating himself further.

Daniel needed to learn to interact with more socially normal roommates. He needed to be safe in his entire living space—in his living room and kitchen too. He needed to fully occupy an entire apartment, not only a walk-in-closet-sized hole of a bedroom.

Walker would not eat what Daniel cooked. This was discouraging for Daniel, and was detrimental to his learning about "life skills" planning and preparing meals. When I first saw their menus on the refrigerator back early in the fall there were real meals listed. Daniel talked to me about cooking. Toward the end of the school year, their menu on the refrigerator was a pitiful joke: "leftovers," "pizza," or "cabinet items."

Walker had violent temper tantrums while on the phone with his parents and with his girlfriend at night. Literally for hours he would slam things, throw things, stomp his feet and scream vile obscenities at the top of his lungs. The night I slept on Daniel's floor I told him how upsetting this was for me to overhear.

Calmly he said, "Oh, that's because it's your first time."

My heart sank. "Does he do this often? Does he need medication? Shouldn't you call Mack to come over and help deal with this?"

Daniel wouldn't answer my questions directly but after a few minutes he replied something like, "It happens often. Walker's moods change within minutes. I don't know about his medications. Last time I called Mack, he told me not to bother him again."

Experiencing this was the last straw for me. It was NOT acceptable for Daniel to be living in this abusive environment. I asked Daniel for his thoughts. All he would say was, "I don't know." Three little words, compared to my hundreds (577 words, to be exact... I asked the computer to count them.) I couldn't know his thoughts. No one could know his thoughts. Maybe Daniel didn't know his own thoughts, or didn't want to share them. What I did know was what I had observed. I'd been around Daniel interacting with Walker in the apartment and it was obviously not good for Daniel. Daniel clearly didn't like it.

I was frustrated that Daniel responded to my questions, "I don't know" when I expected him to say, even if quietly, "I don't want to room with Walker any more. I want to room with Sam." Everything else about Daniel (except for his three little noncommittal words) when I'm around him screams "GET ME OUTTA HERE!"

Maybe Daniel is hesitant to leave because he doesn't like change. He would rather stay in a toxic environment than to change to a better one. Daniel needs help learning to figure out what he wants and needs. He needs help figuring out how to advocate for himself preferably without my help.

Daniel's Answers (Age 29)

[Can you explain why you didn't ask to change roommates when it was such a difficult situation?]

"That was not really the point of The Program. Focusing on that as a problem was a distraction."

[You mean the roommate aspect was a distraction?]

"You could take all kinds of angles on it, like 'how to express yourself,' or 'how to deal with conflict,' that would have been fine, but making it go away, changing the situation, avoiding the problem

would just be a distraction."
[That seems like a very mature perspective.]
[Shoulder shrug]

STEP FOUR
FINDING EDGES

Nilla's Method for Completing a Jigsaw Puzzle
1.   First, I turn all the pieces out of the box
2.   I plop the pieces onto the table into a big jumbled pile.
3.   Turning over each upside-down piece right-side up, I begin to see what I have.
4.   **Next is finding edges—pieces with straight edges form the outer border.**

Pieces with flat edges are prized. They represent the boundary line of what fits inside. Matching straight to straight is easier than accommodating the many varieties of curves, inner or outer, on each puzzle piece. Straight edges usually give away their orientation, whether top, bottom, left or right side. And the four corner pieces are keys to connecting horizontal and vertical.

Get off to a good start with your jigsaw puzzle by finding your outline. A completed edge will then provide a stable frame for the rest of the inside pieces.

Ancestors form the outer edges, the framework for our lives. Family, our given kin, and friends, our chosen kin, provide structure for us to follow as we place the pieces into our lives. They are our models for community, for relationship. They guide us as we find our way in the world.

PIECE 46 — FAMILY TREES

Steve's mother grew up a tomboy who loved to climb trees in Culloden, a tiny town in southern Georgia. She was a sweet brunette with dark eyes who sheltered herself inside her home and garden or her Sewing Circle. She spent her free time reading the *Bible*, *Guideposts* and *Reader's Digest* in their dark-paneled den with the green shag carpet. She preserved her formal front room with its credenza and prized her dining suite, with its china cabinet filled with glass compotes and porcelain dishes. She served a full, home-cooked dinner every night. As a good Southern Baptist, she did not allow alcohol in her home. She loved words. Later in life, she worked as church secretary for Wieuca Road Baptist Church.

My mother grew up in Fort Pierce, on the east coast of Florida. When she was a teenager, her grandmother took her on cruises around the world. My mother was a sophisticated blonde with blue eyes, a model look-alike who was sometimes confused with celebrity Grace Kelly. My mom was a leader in the community. Later in life she became a local television personality.

Some of my New England ancestors were famous enough throughout the past century to appear on the front page of the *New York Times*. My great-grandfather George Putnam (of G.P. Putnam and Sons Publishing) discovered, promoted, and then married Amelia Earhart. Other ancestors appeared further back in the business section of the *New York Times*. My great-great grandfather Edwin Binney and his cousin started the company which invented Crayola Crayons. My parents' double wedding was featured as a society event in a photo essay in *Look Magazine*.

My father, tall, dark and handsome, grew up playing tennis. He was a college basketball star. He became a physician and a community leader. His father, a bank president, and elegant, beautiful mother were socially well-connected.

Steve's father kept his xoyzia grass lawn immaculately tended. He was an up-and-down entrepreneur. He started businesses, which he pronounced "bid-ness." Some of them succeeded, some failed. Both of Steve's grandfathers were mail carriers in southern Georgia.

My family's social milieu was the country club, cocktail parties, luncheons, volunteer boards, private schools, and summer resorts. I was invited by the Debutante Committee to make my debut, though I declined. Steve's family's social world was their church Sunday school class.

Related to economic status, Steve's family was well-off for a time. When his father's business was thriving, they were able to buy a boat and build a sturdy brick ranch house on two acres of land. When his father's business was struggling, he had to declare bankruptcy and, sadly, they had to move out of the lovely home.

My father had a more steady income, not as prone to risk. My mother worked with an architect to design a beautiful, three-story five bedroom home with cathedral-ceilinged living room. She hired a professional decorator to furnish the living room, den, guest room, and play room, with custom drapery and upholstered furniture. Past the two story foyer and stairwell, between the dining room closet stuffed with sterling silver and crystal stemware, and the living room overlooking a wooded lot, was a full wet bar, well-stocked for the next party with socially-required libations.

I was privileged to enjoy many advantages, including attending private middle school and high school, summer camps, swim and tennis lessons at the country club, dance lessons, and piano lessons. My mother had full-time help with housework, laundry, babysitting and cooking. Weekly, we had milk, butter, orange juice, eggs, cases of beer and bottled coca-colas delivered to our home.

Steve struggled throughout school, from elementary all the way through seven years of college. He doesn't remember his parents reading a book to him.

My parents read books to me from an early age. My mother sang lullabies to me. Our home was filled with shelves of books and dictionaries and encyclopedias. Informally my father improved my spoken grammar. When I said, "Me and Dolly are going to…" he corrected, "Dolly and I are going to…" My parents modeled conversational styles at the dinner table and formally introduced us to people as we met them around town. They taught us to shake hands and smile. My father taught me about classical music and Broadway musicals as he listened to his extensive collection of record albums. I grew up in an enriching environment, full of intellectual stimulation. I succeeded in school academically. I loved going to school.

Our two families attended churches of different styles. Steve's family belonged to a large Southern Baptist church with conservative beliefs. My family belonged to a large Methodist church with liberal beliefs.

For recreation, Steve's family enjoyed family meals and watching Steve's high school football games. On holidays, Steve's mother cooked a big dinner and they all sat around the den and watched the parades or football games. Steve's father often grilled out and they churned home-made ice cream in the back yard. The most noticeable thing about Steve's extended family was that they accepted each individual as they were, "warts and all." Everyone was welcome to stay for dinner, which would be served "family style" with all the food on the table.

My mother didn't like the chore of cooking daily meals. If we were not traveling over Easter or Christmas holidays we dressed formally and ate at the country club. After the heavy meal, my father got everyone outside to walk around the block, ride bikes, or play tennis.

Our families were certainly different. On the surface it would seem that Steve and I had nothing in common. But we did not necessarily share all our parents' views. When it came to deeply held moral, political and spiritual beliefs, Steve and I shared the same values. Aesthetically, we have the same taste in art and furnishings. Once, Steve and I separately chose only one item we liked, an identical upholstered armchair, in a huge five-story warehouse. We enjoyed the same kind of recreational activities, usually outdoors in the fresh air and sunshine. We appreciated the same kind of beauty and were both in awe of the magnificence of nature. Steve and I agreed on the things that were important to us.

PIECE 47 — CHILDFATHER

Steve's mother said he was an easy baby, a happy baby, always smiling. Steve fondly remembers his favorite teddy bear he named "Happy." Steve had a stable home base where his mother was reliably in the kitchen cooking dinner or in the laundry room folding clothes or sitting in her rocking chair in the den stitching up a hem in the evening.

Steve has two older brothers. He always fought with his oldest brother Mike and never seemed to have much in common with him, but Steve is as close as an identical twin with his middle brother Kirk. The two of them and a bunch of neighborhood guys wandered in the woods behind their houses, swam in their two-acre neighborhood lake, made forts, dug tunnels, climbed pine trees, threw M-80s in the lake, hiked 15 miles to a state park, and directed dramatic home movies. What a great life of freedom and adventure for a rambunctious boy!

As for school? Steve *hated* everything about school, except for recess. "During class, I sat by the window so I could look outside and hear other kids at recess. I was the *fastest* kid. No one *ever* hit me in dodge ball. I was the *best* at pull-ups, well, except for this chunky kid who was built like a Mack truck, but that doesn't count. And I hated my bus driver—we called her 'The Wicked Witch of the West.' In the morning, my mom would say, 'Hurry up, Stevie, you're going to miss the bus,' and I would be panicky, looking around for my backpack and my lunch sack. I would put my shoes on and run to the end of the driveway, which seemed like a mile away. Sometimes the bus driver would wait for me and sometimes she wouldn't."

When Steve was in first grade, his older brother Kirk invited a buddy, Rich, for a sleepover. Steve still remembers listening in awe as Rich read a book aloud. Steve even remembers the title of that book: *Ghosts, Ghosts, Ghosts.* He was impressed that a nine year old could read!

"In seventh grade, I liked girls, and they liked me, but I didn't know how to be liked. In eighth grade my girlfriend was the most popular cheerleader, but I wouldn't kiss her because I didn't know when you were supposed to kiss, so she broke up with me."

"I was really good in football. As a freshman I was the starting running back, until in a pre-season scrimmage I broke the quarterback's arm. That was the end of the team that year. The next year, I was the starting running back, until Coach Allen used his cigar to burn a hole in my 'long' hair (short by today's standards—it was 'all' the way down to the nape of my neck—as long as the Beatles' hair) and I quit the team right then and there."

"When I was about 15 years old I discovered art class. The teacher said I was talented and he encouraged me to continue drawing and painting."

"In high school I led a weekly Bible study in the morning before school. The principal asked me to speak at the Baccalaureate but only if I would shave my beard, which I refused to do on principle, so I didn't speak at the Baccalaureate. I was not allowed to attend my own high school graduation, because I had a beard."

"My mom took me to doctors to try to figure out why I was having so much trouble with gas and cramps and diarrhea and constipation. I remember being *so* embarrassed when they told me I had a *spastic* colon! I didn't even mind all the pain. I just didn't want to have to admit to anyone that word—spastic!"

By the time I met Steve, he had spent a year out of high school living on his own. The day he and his steady girlfriend arrived in California to attend art school together, she broke up with him. On the first day of art school at the California College of Arts and Crafts in Berkeley, the first teacher of his first class asked him what his astrological sign was. Steve answered, "I don't have a sign. I don't believe in that stuff." The teacher cursed him with the foulest language Steve had ever heard. Steve got up and walked out of the class, never to return. He found a few friends in a local church but for the most part he was achingly lonely.

Steve, Writing in Nilla's Diary March 16 (Daniel Age 5)

Daniel, your 5th birthday will be next month. That makes me feel old. I just turned 30, 2 month ago. This week you are on spring break. Your first year at school You like it. So do I. You definitely have a mind of your own. You a extremely intelligent and started readed whole books about 2 weeks ago. The 1st thing you did when granddaddy came to visit this weekend was to read the whole book of Hop on Pop to him. You have always been an incredible athlete and you like to say no a lot and do things your own way. You remind me a lot of me. At this very minute you are swinging on a rope swing I made for you. You love to swing. Your love to paint and draw now. You love to tinker with things and try to figure them out. You always need to know how things work. I am glad I've worked at home all these years and feel sorry for those dads that can't "grow up" with their sons. Sometime I just want to spend all the time with you and do things like pitch the ball camp hike etc. You actually use to be a better hiker at the age of 2 & 3 than you are now. I hope things change. I'm looking forward to when your older, too, so we can ski hike etc. together. I love you Daniel. Your dad.

Steve, in Nilla's Diary January 2 (Daniel Age 7)

Dear Daniel, I see so much of me in you. You remind me of me. Everything you do brings back memories of my childhood. Though I could not read at all at age 6 ¾ and you can read everything by yourself. You are the greatest athlete ever born. We throw the football a couple of times a week and you drop less than I do. You never miss the baseball when I pitch. You love your brand new "Old Time" pocket knife Santa brought you. So proud of it. Your often stubborn as a mule and gentle as a deer. You helped your mom and me last week at church in the nursery and were so sweet to the babies. You help us today at our new church building scraping and sanding paint. You always want to help. You love to do things with me and I love to do things with you. I love you Daniel. Your Dad

PIECE 48 — MOST IMPROVED

Steve and I finally seemed to be getting a handle on Daniel's behavior problems, but before we could savor any lull in the eye of the storm, Daniel handed off his relay baton to David, who raced ahead of us into his "terrible twos." His fierce toddler tantrums resisted every method of discipline. We were forced to implement "time outs" but David threw shoes and banged toys and slammed books against his bedroom door for hours and hours and never gave in.

The little wild man took joy in escaping my grip in parking lots. To protect him from cars, I had to restrain him, so I circled my arms around him and clumped down onto the curb with him in my grasp, in spite of other adults' critical glares and stares.

David lived every day with exuberance, with a mischievous way of making people laugh.

His kindergarten self-portrait featured his smile lined meticulously with rows of grinning teeth. In second grade, David loved playing at recess with his many friends, but complained the school work was too hard. His teachers suspected a learning disability. I was indignant. I blamed their weak teaching methods, which I assumed must bore my exceptional child. I took him to a psychologist for testing to prove my son was fine, which would prove the school was the problem. David's IQ scores were extremely high, so I was right that he was gifted, but his disorganization and frustration proved the school was right. The discrepancy between ability and performance indicated he qualified for disability services.

I threw myself into PTA-perfect-mother-mode. I thought if I were more involved in the classroom that David's experience would be enriched. I volunteered to teach art lessons and led tours of the art museum. I brought in watercolor paints and clay and challenged the second graders to imitate master artists and sculptors. I brought in real-life food pyramids to illustrate nutrition week, and demonstrated a model of the DNA helix on the anniversary of its discovery by Watson and Crick. I created elaborate bulletin board displays. I was an obsessed mother.

I encouraged David to enter art, music and science contests. I recorded David's musical cacophony with pots and pans and wooden spoons from our kitchen cabinets to imitate composer John Cage. When David won first prize for creativity, I insisted that he stand at the front of an auditorium full of parents and students to perform his original composition. At the time, I believed I was encouraging him, but in hindsight I realize I humiliated him and embarrassed myself by exhibiting my pushiness.

In the third grade, David developed a fear of germs, which I later realized coincided with the week that the prudish teacher warned the class about the AIDS virus. At first we thought it was a temporary phase but it continued for weeks, then months. David wouldn't eat around other people. He required that I prepare his food separately, under his supervision. If I talked, I had to start over again. He wouldn't eat at school or in a restaurant. His phobia developed into a serious case of obsessive-compulsive disorder, and he began to lose weight rapidly. David began seeing a counselor and taking medicine. Steve and I went to counseling and implemented methods to assuage David's anxiety. His mood improved gradually over the next year.

When David was in fourth grade, we moved to a suburb of Atlanta. New everything: new home, new friends, new school. I let out a sigh of relief when he seemed to bond well with his very structured teacher, until suddenly she switched schools after only two weeks. David seemed to have trouble right away with the next teacher. I wrote a scathing letter to the principal. I was angry about the switch and I complained about the many ways the teacher was failing my son. The school called a meeting, where I humbly discovered there were two sides to the story. Gradually I developed respect for his teacher and began to acknowledge that my son needed help. I found a specialist who evaluated David's thinking styles and learning needs. He diagnosed David with ADHD and referred him to a psychiatrist who prescribed medication. The specialist wrote the most thorough, accurate, insightful report which proved to be extremely valuable throughout the next ten years of David's schooling.

After one year we moved again. David made good grades in math as long as he didn't have to "show his work." He saw the correct answers in his mind, though he may not have followed the same process as the teacher. David made friends easily, acted in school plays, and became involved in the church youth group. At football tryouts, he didn't make the cut, but David refused to give up, regardless of what the coach thought. First he became the water boy, and then the team manager. One day, when he was allowed to participate in practice, the coach realized he was a good player and asked him to join the team. David scored a number of touchdowns that season and was recognized at their awards banquet as "most improved." The same pattern repeated across several sports, where he initially didn't make the team, but persisted until he was successful, and received recognition for "most improved."

As academics became more demanding in middle school, David seemed to complete fewer and fewer assignments. His backpack contained an atrocious conglomeration of crinkled papers crammed in since the first day of school. He began bringing home more and more failing grades. Steve and I didn't know what to do with our son. At the beginning of David's eighth grade year, my father and stepmother recommended boarding school. We were grateful but politely explained we couldn't imagine sending our child away for ninth grade—he was still so young.

By the middle of David's eighth grade year, we agreed to visit the boarding school campus and to give it fair consideration. Immediately, I was bowled over by McCallie's strengths. Not only were they accustomed to helping students academically, they understood what motivated boys. Not only could they provide David with the help he needed in the tutoring lab, they were also dedicated to building the guys' character. I was "sold" when, in the cafeteria, our tour guide told both Daniel and David, "Gentlemen, get your mother's tray for her." Wow. Yes, this was the place they needed to be, if for nothing else than to prepare them for life. Living in dorms would be a great way for them to learn to get along with others. David entered boarding school ninth through twelfth grade and Daniel attended his senior year only.

When the terrorists struck the World Trade Center September 11th, I worried about how David was handling the devastating news, while he was so far from home. At that moment, he began planning his route to the U.S. Marines, determined to do his part to protect our country. He enlisted his senior year, but his admission was ultimately denied, due to a dislocated shoulder he injured while playing lacrosse junior year. David was devastated by this roadblock. His own surgeon had given him a clear go-ahead. We tried everything imaginable to get the military physician's report overturned. David kept "throwing shoes at the door." He contacted his senator and pursued his objection all the way up to the Surgeon General. Nevertheless, he was not accepted into the Marines. David was devastated for years by this definitive end to his dreams. He began playing online poker Texas Hold 'Em style, and won an all-expenses paid spot in the Poker World Championships in Aruba, but lost in the early rounds there. His life was at loose ends, until he began listening to the Dave Ramsey radio program that taught how to get out of debt. He transformed his life by canceling credit cards and going to a disciplined, all-cash envelope budget system. David persisted until he was debt-free and began to pester Steve and me until we did the same.

David transferred colleges and focused on his strength in math and accounting. He majored in finance, obtained a professional certification, and was hired by a bank and then an investment firm. David met the woman of his dreams and told her after only two weeks that he knew they would be married. She loved him and appreciated his leadership style, and recognized he would never give up on her, so two years later they became husband and wife.

Once again, David was "Most Improved."

PIECE 49 — TAPESTRY

Early one morning as I was sclathing (one of my favorite words!) in bed, Steve came in to remind me it was time to wake up. "Nilla, you said you wanted to wake up at 7 o'clock today. Do you still want to get up now or are you going back to sleep?"

"Oh yeah, I need to get up. Thanks."

He stood in the doorway for a while to make sure I got out of bed. He leaned against the wall, staring out in the hall at a tapestry I wove thirty years ago and said, "That brings back great memories."

Groggy from sleep, I asked, "Memories of what… visiting my weaving studio when I was a college student in Atlanta?"

"No. Memories of visiting your family in Florida."

The small, colorful, cartoonish tapestry he was staring at represented my grandparents' Colonial-styled home in Fort Pierce, Florida, where my mother grew up, with its wraparound porch overlooking the Indian River. My great-grandmother Dofry lived ten miles inland in a large Spanish styled estate set within a "hammock," an oasis in the middle of citrus groves. When Steve and I were dating in the '70s my family invited him to join us on vacation for a week.

"What about it? What do you remember about visiting my family in Florida?"

"It was like going to the moon."

I listened, waiting for more explanation.

"I had never experienced anything like your family. It was another world. I may as well have been on the moon." Steve walked away to the kitchen to pour his coffee, and my mind lulled back decades to my childhood visits with my grandparents. During the drive down I-85 south, the first time we took Steve to meet my Great Grandmother Dofry (nickname for Dorothy) we told stories about her to prepare him for the visiting-Dofry-routine. My mom warned him ahead of time, "She's going to give you money."

Steve: "What? What are you talking about?"

Nilla: "She's going to shake your hand and leave a $20 bill in it."

Steve: "Well, I'm not going to take it. I won't accept it."

Mom: "Yes, you have to. She does that to everyone."

Steve: "I'm not going to take money from anyone for visiting them. That's crazy."

From the driver's seat, my dad turned his head to the side and affirmed, "Steve, I know what you mean. It sounds strange, and I felt the same way you did when I first met her, but over the years I've learned you just have to take it. It would cause too much of a fuss to turn it down. She just wants to help out with the cost of your traveling to see her."

Steve shook his head with a puzzled look on his face.

We did have our typical visit with all the usual laughing and one-ups-man-ship. Dofry held court from her Mayan hammock, swinging on the screened porch off the upstairs loggia. We introduced Steve, a college student, as a budding artist. Dofry did shake Steve's hand and did slip the $20 bill in his palm, just as we had predicted. She asked her live-in help, Peg, to bring fresh-squeezed orange juice for us. She whistled bird songs to teach us to identify them, pointing out the colorful, male painted bunting on the feeder. My dad described the book he read that week. My mom told about her latest volunteer project with the Junior League. My sister recited a poem. I played my original composition on the piano. Then Dofry interrupted, "Now, dear, it is time for you to go for a swim."

I put my reminiscences aside while I turned my heavy, middle-aged body out of bed and joined Steve in the kitchen for a bowl of cereal. Crunching on Cheerios, I questioned him. "So now, over thirty years later, you're telling me that visiting my family was like being on the moon? I always knew our families were different, but I don't think I ever realized quite the impact it had on your life."

Steve explained, "It's just that I had never been around country club-sophisticated types. Your family had all these stories from the past. My family didn't have any stories. I mean, maybe 'Uncle Trevor died in a car crash,' but that was the extent of it. "And at your great grandmother Dofry's home I would admire a painting in her living room and she would say, 'Oh, that's by Beanie Backus,' and she would pick up the phone and call up the artist, then hang up and say, 'We're going to go see him in his studio tomorrow.' I had never seen such access, connections to people. It seemed like they knew everyone. And I had never been around alcohol either, people having a cocktail every evening before dinner and regularly serving each other scotch or vodka.

"I was in my own world. I had lived a very sheltered life—well, not sheltered—but I had lived my own interests up to that point, and then I was learning about other people and other families."

"What do you mean? What do you remember as so different about our families?"

"When I first met your family, I remember being uncomfortable and comfortable at the same time. They were very friendly and welcoming to me, but I was uncomfortable because I felt like an outsider, like a... um... little kid maybe... or immature... or unsophisticated. Even though I considered myself middle class, around your family I felt lower class. It was partly because I wasn't sophisticated in the sense of knowing things that your parents knew, like they might ask me a question and I wouldn't know it.

"Like, I remember standing in your kitchen and your mom asked me, probably since I was from Georgia too, 'What do you think about Jimmy Carter?' back when he was running for president. I said something like, 'He seems like a good guy,' but I didn't know anything else to say. Your dad always talked about the latest thing, what was in the news, that kind of stuff. My family didn't talk about politics or world events. I just didn't have conversations like that with my parents. Usually my dad wasn't there for dinner anyway."

I rinsed our cereal bowls, loaded them in the dishwasher, added detergent, pressed the "Normal" cycle, and then sponged off the counters. A clean kitchen sink in the morning makes for a good start to the day.

PIECE 50 — PEACE MAKER

Nilla's Diary March 3 (Nilla Age 9)
Mommy and daddy get in bad fight. Daddy says "Mommy is a greedy little person" And Mommy says "I'll hit you with a brush" But They make up. And go to two partys and an opera.

I was born a peacemaker. Over the years my parents would repeat to me the story of when I was a baby and I had a horrible case of whooping cough. My parents were arguing, and the argument evolved into their debating whether or not to take me to the doctor. I quit breathing. Immediately, they stopped arguing, grabbed the car keys, and sped me to the hospital.

After the passage of fifty years I now put a layer of meaning over that story to interpret that I would give my own life, my own breath, to stop an argument.

My parents told me that when I was two or three years old, they woke up one morning to find that I had made green Jell-O for the family dinner that night. Apparently, while they slept, I had pulled a chair over, crawled up onto the kitchen counter, found a box of Jell-O powder, and, as I had watched my mother do many times before, emptied it into a bowl, stirred in a measuring cup full of hot water, and put it into the refrigerator to chill.

The fifty year old interpreter (me) now says this was my way of alleviating my mother's stress. She hated to cook and she hated the cold weather in Wisconsin, where we lived at the time. Maybe I was hungry, maybe I was bored, or maybe this was my way of taking care of her.

When I was five years old, my best friend Annie Bananie lived in the house behind mine. We went to the same school, summer camp, dance classes and belonged to the same Girl Scout troop. We spent all our time together, running back and forth between houses, dressing up dolls, playing "Mother May I?" or "Red Light, Green Light" on the sidewalk, riding our bikes around "The Circle," or making potions out of mud and earthworms and hand lotion.

When either of us was mad at our parents, we would pack our bags to "run away from home" but usually ended up at the other's house for a few hours or until dinner. I had two younger sisters, who were trouble enough, but she had two younger brothers, who were mean. They fought, they yelled, they cussed. I had never in my life heard such high volume voices or such "foreign" vocabulary as when I was at her house.

Annie Bananie's mother told me that one day, when Annie and I were five, when the brothers and Annie were all yelling at each other, I turned calmly to her and said, "Mrs. Garner, speaking of astronauts…" although no one had been speaking of astronauts. I was trying to change the subject, to stop the fighting in my own feeble way.

When I was about nine years old, I walked to my piano teacher's house for my weekly lesson. I always dreaded walking past the house on the corner in the neighborhood behind ours, where a mean little boy shouted at me and threw rocks. Every week, I hoped he wouldn't be there. I tried to sneak past him unnoticed. If he spotted me, I would run faster to the other side of the road to dodge the gravel hurled through the air. All the neighborhood kids talked about how naughty he was. No one liked him. I felt sorry for him. When my Sunday school teachers taught the Bible lesson to "turn the other cheek" to our enemies, which I recently identified as Matthew 5:39 "Do not resist an evil person. If someone strikes you on the right cheek, turn to him the other also." I applied the lesson to my life, and identified the naughty little boy who had thrown rocks at me as the "evil person" in my life at that time. I inferred that the Bible was instructing me to do something kind for him, though I couldn't figure out what that would be. I wasn't going to stand there while he threw rocks at me. Next time I went to Woolworth's with my mom, I looked through the toy section and chose a bag of toy soldiers as a gift for the naughty boy. I took the bag to the register where my mom was already in line and asked her if I could buy them. She knew I didn't want to play with toy soldiers, so she asked me why I wanted them. "They're for the boy who throws rocks at me." Her expression could have scalded my face from the steam of irritation that spewed forth to accompany her solid, "No. Go put those back." She never asked me to explain my reasoning.

PIECE 51 — LIVING LIKE DOGS

Malone is my friend Jennifer's sleek, hulking, black Great Dane. Malone seems much too big for the small home she shares with her human family. Malone alone covers most of the brown-shag-carpeted living room floor, while she lazily suns by the picture window. Her wagging tail is dangerous, flailing like a lethal Billy club. Once she snapped my sunglasses and crushed them with her oafish paw. In spite of her clumsy power though, she is no menace. She is quiet, pleasant, and unobtrusive except for her physical size. She is a graying eight dog years, and even-tempered. Malone is a visually ominous watchdog but politely welcomes anyone into the unlocked house.

My friend Jennifer, Malone's human, is a neat, petite, lean white woman. She lives in her small home with her friendly humming husband John, their three kids Jacob, Jaron, and Jordan, their dog Malone, and their scruffy black cat Messiah. Jennifer is busy, bubbly, and a compulsive housekeeper. She loves being at home; circling around, circling around, circling around to curl up in a cozy spot. She hates to cook and is a finicky eater, but is contented by a plate mounded with bland mushy micro-waved foods like cottage cheese, leftover corn kernels and couscous.

Jennifer befriends everyone, animal or human. She picks up scraggly strays that others conveniently ignore. She fosters abandoned dogs until they find homes. She fosters humans new to town until they feel at home. Her home is full of warmth, comfort and universal acceptance. Neighborhood children congregate at her home, which is always buzzing with needy ones. Jennifer majored in physical education. She is constantly stirring up fun and arranging activities from board games to flag football to scavenger hunts.

Tragedy rolls off Jennifer's back the same way raindrops drip off Malone's slick, thick fur. A neighbor's dog bit her son Jaron in the face, resulting in many stitches and plastic surgery. Jennifer handled the situation calmly, almost seeming to lack the anguish I felt even at a distance. I went grimly the next day to visit them and found Jennifer cheerily chatting with the dog's owner and Jaron bouncing around playing with a friend. No mourning at that house over a serious accident.

Jennifer births her babies at home with a midwife's help (if the midwife manages to arrive in time). She distrusts doctors and relies on home remedies and folk medicine. Instead of having her plantar warts cryogenically frozen off by a physician, for example, she asked her roommate to burn them off. Jennifer gouged her hand while fixing a craft. She severed a nerve that required emergency treatment and later, specialized surgery when she lost feeling in her fingers. The night of the surgery she refused to cancel prior plans to host a party and the next day insisted on serving Christmas dinner in her home for a guest family as well as her own. That night I found her vacuuming her stairs, a thankless job that I somehow avoid doing for months at a time in my home. Jennifer planned to ride the city bus to her doctor's appointment, claiming it would be too much trouble for me when I offered to drive her. Jennifer just goes on about her routine, not requiring any pampering or accommodation.

Whereas my own life seems dominated by chaos, self-pity, confusion and anxiety, I am learning from Jennifer to live more like a dog—the simple life of survival—consisting only of food, rest and play.

I am learning by observing Jennifer how to discipline my own children calmly, consistently, matter-of-factly, as though they are animals needing to be tamed. When Jennifer's newly crawling one-year-old daughter nears their stairs, I panic and run to grab her away, to rescue her from a terrible fall. Jennifer explains quietly that I should leave her, that the baby is learning to "respect" the stairs. I watch, amazed, as Jennifer's method does indeed work. The baby stops, feels the empty space and turns around. Instead of overprotecting her child, Jennifer is teaching her early independence, letting her experience natural consequences, yet keeping her ultimate safety in mind.

I appreciate Jennifer's loyalty, her trustworthiness, her even temper. Watching her cool lack of emotion or worry pulls me out of my own intellectual arrogance and narcissism. Those times when I wonder if she is simply as dumb, shallow and naïve as the animals she cares for, I remind myself that I am one of those scraggly, homeless strays she has sheltered from this threatening world. My heart begins wagging as I am learning from my friend to live life more like a dog.

My learning how to care for my children indirectly from Jennifer reminds me of the way Daniel has learned to interact with people and to decrease his anxiety from observing TV's "Dog Whisperer" by modeling the way Cesar Millan handles his "pack."

PIECE 52 — "PITCH"

Steve developed his own language:

- "Pitch" describes anything cool or intense or extreme, possibly originating from the phrase "pitch dark?" Pitch also means affirmative in the extreme. Pitch is a one word equivalent of an entire sentence—to save words.
- "Duh" is his affirmative response to any question.
- "Stupid" is his negative response to any question.
- "Jacker" means good friend or girlfriend.
- "...and them" is appended to his brother's name to include his wife, ex: "Kirk and them" means Kirk and Sharon.
- "Fittiwunhunrtremmlroe" is how he pronounces his address, in a mumble, all words running together, consonants disappearing into stretched out vowels. He barely moves his lips when he talks. Is it laziness? Is it his southern accent?
- Place names and people's names are never preceded by articles such as "the," as in: "We're going to Tetons with Abbotts."
- "Best" Steve couches everything in hyperbole, always in superlative terms. "This is the BEST dinner EVER!" or "I have NEVER seen a sunset as beautiful as this one."

"Number"

Daniel laughed at how often Steve repeated certain observations. We came up with a numbering system to save energy. When we heard Steve beginning one of his usual statements, we could substitute a number, and then we would all know what he was going to say and he could save his breath. Now, when we recognize a Steve-ism, we just shout out, "NUMBER!" in the same way children punch each other when they spot a Volkswagen Beetle.

1. LEAST "These are the LEAST people I've ever seen here. How can they stay in business?"

2. MOST "This is the MOST cars I've ever seen in this parking lot. This place is packed!"

3. ALWAYS "What?! You didn't buy buns? You ALWAYS have to eat hamburgers in buns!"

4. NEVER "Nilla, why do you NEVER cook dinner?"

5. THIS REMINDS ME OF... Steve never seems to encounter a new event or person.

6. LOOK AT... Comment on a stranger's appearance. "Look at those pants down to his knees."

Out of a sense of fairness; equal opportunity including the whole family, Daniel added to our list:

7. Mom mocking Dad, like when he leaves the stove turned on high.

8. David finding "ALL-INCLUSIVE!" bargain deals.

Visionary

Steve dreams in living color, like a rolling motion picture. When I visualize my dreams, it seems they are in black and white, or at least I don't remember vivid colors. I "see" more in ideas or symbols. For example, if a color, like red, is significant in my dreams, it's almost like my mind labels it red and I interpret it as red, but it is symbolic red and not the visual appearance of red. When I see grass I label it green, but don't really "see" an image.

Steve asked me to explain. "Can you remember friends' faces, or, say, your dad's face?"

"No, I don't have images of them stored up, only symbols of them, vague shapes, and probably mostly words describing them, maybe like the letters "D-a-d" or "S-t-e-v-e" superimposed on an oval form for the face with symbolic shapes for nose and eyes and hair, like a child's drawing."

"That is so sad."

I asked him, "Why? What do you see?"

"I see pictures of people's faces, as though they are right there in front of me. I see them in different poses, angles, and expressions, specific to certain moments."

"Describe what you see when I say 'mountains.'"

Steve clarified, "Which mountains?"

"Like the Tetons."

"That depends on the time of day and the view."

I tried to keep him talking. "Well, pick a time of day and a view, and describe it."

Steve described explicit color names, like aspen glow, sienna, and ochre—against a cerulean sky, with an overlay of alizarin crimson—to explain the kind of glow of sunlight.

I gave him an example to contrast his. "When I imagine 'mountains' I see jagged lines; an abstraction. If you ask me to visualize the Tetons, the only thing I can picture is a photograph I remember of our family posed in front of our Suburban, with the Tetons in the background."

Hmmm… I wonder. Maybe I can only affix a visual memory if it has already been 'translated' for me (like in a photograph) into a flat, still, two-dimensional format. Steve can imagine and visually re-create anything he has seen, and remembers it in moving, three-dimensional space.

Steve was so saddened by this new realization. He thought everyone in the world saw and thought like he did. He was not aware of such fundamental differences. He was grievously sorry for me and I am sorry he cannot know the joy of words, the depth of ideas and concepts that I know, the complexity of emotions that I feel.

We are all so different. We must be the most fascinating jigsaw puzzle for God. I think He delights in fitting together His plans for us. We each see the world in such unique ways—only God could possibly understand us all.

PIECE 53 — OTHERS, PUZZLED

L ate Christmas afternoon, Steve, Daniel, David and I went to my dad's home to visit him and his wife for the holiday for our annual gift exchange. Two of my sisters, Dolly and Sally, and Sally's husband Kevin joined us. Everyone sat around chatting in different rooms.

My sister Dolly and I were in the kitchen assembling a complex new coffee machine we had given my dad. When we figured out how to operate it successfully and brewed a single cup of cappuccino, we went into the family room to join my dad at the table where Daniel seemed to be working on a jigsaw puzzle.

Earlier in the month, I had given my dad the 1500 piece "Proverbidioms" jigsaw puzzle for his birthday. I had searched for and found it through the internet. I had seen a poster of the same image at The Program. They used it with the guys a few times to discuss illogical phrases, such as: "The way to a man's heart is through his stomach" (The puzzle image pictured a woman literally reaching inside a man's ribs with her arm in up to her elbow.) It illustrated hundreds of other idioms that are especially difficult for people like Daniel to process.

Dad seemed to love the puzzle, especially its subject matter of the proverbs and idioms. It was a hit at his birthday party, all of his thirteen grandchildren gathered around the image identifying phrases from the little scenes. My dad, my sisters and I enjoy working jigsaw puzzles together; it's the only activity I can think of that keeps my sports-loving, always active dad still for an hour so we can actually get in a good visit with him!

I felt pressured to get that puzzle completed ASAP. We were overwhelmed by a puzzle of 1500 pieces; I usually preferred simpler puzzles with 300 or 500 pieces; 750 at the most!

My sister Dolly had spent Christmas Eve at dad and Babe's house. Maybe Dolly had also felt the unspoken pressure to help complete the jigsaw "chore." She and Dad had already spent hours on the puzzle. The two of them had laid out about half the pieces in a determined arrangement. They had placed the straight-edged pieces around the outside border, the dark pieces to the left, light pieces to the right, and pieces with recognizable images near the top. It was obvious there was an orderly plan underway.

After 15 or 20 minutes of our idle chit-chat, Dolly suddenly realized that the puzzle-in-progress looked substantially different than she had left it. She noticed that Daniel, instead of collaborating with the team and contributing productively to the process, had decided to start from scratch and apply his own idiosyncratic method. He had removed most of the pieces from the table and combined them back into the box to sift through, along with the other 1000 loose pieces. He was starting a fresh mound of what he considered to be significantly identifiable images.

Dolly's cheeks flushed; she was livid. She stood up, speechlessly gesturing and stammering, attempting to explain the perfect logic of what their intended method had been. She gasped and exhaled in frustration at the destruction of her efforts.

Daniel, never glancing up, showing no remorse, said "I probably messed it up." He continued with his sorting method.

My instinct was to calm Dolly, to soothe her, to gently rub her shoulders and say, "That's all right, there, there. It's just a game. It's just a puzzle. Don't get so upset." At the same time I realized I felt as aggravated as she did. How idiotic Daniel had been! How stupid he was to change what someone else had started without asking permission or even announcing his intent to sort through the puzzle.

Dolly stormed out of the room, furious, obviously needing time to seethe. I felt embarrassed, exasperated, and responsible for making it all better. I wanted to "fix" it. I wanted to say "I'll stay all night and put it back the way it was." I wanted to heal the wounds. My habitual response was to play the family peacemaker. Instead, I watched myself practice my newly learned behavior of "staying out of it;" of "minding my own business." I didn't say a word to try to intervene or to manipulate. I just sat there feeling sheepish. The room was quiet. The only sound was Daniel rattling pieces as he shook the puzzle box.

After a while, Steve wandered in from the other room. He sat down at our table. I was flipping through a magazine. Dad was reading his book. Daniel was arranging puzzle pieces. I explained to Steve that Daniel had changed the puzzle as it was in progress and that Dolly had left the room in anger.

Steve (Clueless Character #2), instead of parentally correcting Daniel's errant childish behavior, laughed aloud! He joked about how that's how jigsaw puzzles should be... everyone comes in and revises what the last person has done. He rambled on and on, inventing rules for his creative new game. I wanted to punch him in the nose.

More time passed with everyone doing their own thing. I continued to feel awkward until it was time to go home. Steve and Daniel said goodbye and waited for me in the car.

I apologized to Dad. "Sorry about the puzzle. I don't know why Daniel did that."

He shook his head quietly, "Oh, that's okay, no big deal." He kissed my cheek and hugged me goodbye.

When the three of us, Daniel, Steve and I, sat down for dinner that night, Daniel told Steve, "Wow, Dolly was *really* angry at me. I might need to make some sort of peace offering."

Steve asked incredulously, "Was she really mad?" Again, I resisted the impulse to punch Steve in the nose.

Inside, I was pleased, no, relieved, that Daniel was actually aware of Dolly's emotional response and that he comprehended somewhat the intensity of her anger. I was glad that he mentioned he should take a step to make amends. I suggested, "Daniel, you could just apologize to her."

He shook his head firmly and said, "No. I'm not going to apologize." He gave an adamant stare and continued to eat.

Puzzled, I dropped the subject. The conversation changed, but I continued to wonder... What did Daniel mean "make a peace offering" if it didn't include an apology?

The next day when I saw Dolly I asked her how she was doing.

"I'm tired. I didn't sleep very well."

"You didn't? I'm sorry to hear that. Was it the bed?"

She shook her head no.

"Was it being away from home, in an unfamiliar room?"

"No."

"Was it something you ate for dinner last night that upset your stomach?"

She muttered "no" and hung her head. Eventually it came out that she had tossed and turned about the puzzle incident. "I know I shouldn't have gotten so mad and I shouldn't have been so angry toward Daniel. But all during the night I was thinking about you and how what happened with the puzzle was only a tiny fraction of what you've endured."

"Yup, that's my life."

It was as if a metaphorical light bulb had appeared above her head powering on her understanding of Asperger syndrome for the first time. It was like she finally had a grasp of what this condition is about.

She continued to mumble about it, trying to put words to it... "But he's so intelligent. It's not that he's retarded."

I said, "Yes, in some ways he is retarded, if you are using the word in its literal meaning—which is 'slow.'"

She said, "Well, I mean, he doesn't have a low IQ, like, he doesn't have a mental handicap."

I said, "Right, but he's both. He's intellectually gifted *and* he's socially disabled."

Over the last few years, I had spent hours and hours trying to explain Daniel and Asperger syndrome to Dolly. She doesn't have any children of her own, but she is a devoted and very involved aunt. She adores her nieces and nephews, including Daniel and David. I always assumed she understood. I have given her examples. I have explained things in detail. She listens attentively. But I realized she still had no idea what I meant until an incident happened directly to *her.* It was like all the language in the world had floated by her without impact. It took a personal experience for it to make sense.

Isn't it ironic that all this came about because of a jigsaw puzzle, which is a symbol commonly used to represent autism?

Daniel's Answers (Age 29)
"Her response was blown out of proportion. I mean, it's a *game!* Not even just a game, but a puzzle, that there is no right way to do it. It's the only game that doesn't have rules, and yet we have to impose rules on it! It's the only board game you can purchase that doesn't have a set of rules that come with it."

[Why do you think you didn't want to apologize to her later?]

"This is another example of instead of not talking about stuff, to just talk about it."

[When it happens.]

PIECE 54 — CHARACTER

After finishing his first year at art school, Steve spent one summer living with his brother Kirk out west. The sun bronzed Steve's skin to a dark brown. He wore his waist-long hair in two braids that fell down either side. He learned to bead and crafted a blue and brown neckband tied with leather straps. Steve found a job mopping floors for a bakery, which meant he began work at 5 a.m., but also meant the rest of his days were free for hiking in the mountain canyons, calling to crows and stalking wildlife along the river.

Steve anxiously chews the inside of his cheek. The dentist says he grinds his teeth. I can hear Steve coming from a distance because I recognize his signature throat-clearing noises, his constant sniffing, and the familiar sound of his slippers shuffling down the hall, "swoosh, swoosh, swoosh." He draws out his yawns, ending with a distinctive "kh-kh-kkh-kkkhh" repetition.

When he feels too much sensory input he waves both his hands, fingers spread out, circling at his temples, like he's trying to clear away cobwebs of confusion. The frantic movements seem to illustrate the term "scatterbrained."

I've never seen anyone else pull off their shirt the way he does: both hands go to the back of his neck; all 10 fingers shuffle rapidly, gathering the fabric into accordion folds. He says this way is ingenious because it keeps the shirt right-side-out, ready for wearing the next day (and the next day, and the next day.)

Steve has learned over the years that his organizational skills are lacking. When he needs to remember something, he pre-scolds himself, "I won't remember." Then he writes the reminder on a Post-it Note and sticks it to a glaring surface so he won't forget. He writes notes while he is driving and while he is sleeping. One time he woke up feeling what he thought was a scab on his face until he picked at it and realized it was a Post-it Note that he had written during the night and rolled over in the bed and had stuck to his face.

Finest of the Fine

Steve doesn't drink, smoke, gamble, or spend every weekend playing golf. He doesn't overspend, he doesn't overeat. He is not a couch potato. He is not a chauvinist. Steve is honest. He never tells a lie. He is loyal. He is frugal. When I first met him, he was a potter. He is as grounded as the slab of clay, as centered as the pot on the spinning wheel, and as focused on what is right in front of him.

He is inventive. He invented a backpack-carrier out of two brooms. He invented a steady cam and an overhead extension for his professional movie camera for the cost of only five dollars in materials. He is resourceful. He figures out how to use what he has.

He is responsible. He is *always* on time. Like clockwork, he shows up on the exact minute he is expected to arrive. If I ask him when he will be home, he doesn't tell me in 5 or 10 minute increments, he tells me he will be home in two or three or eight minutes. His being on time is a rule that cannot be broken. He does not understand how our friends can show up chronically late by 15 or 20 minutes.

He expects other people to be as dedicated and devoted as he is. It is a good thing he works for himself. It is difficult for him to depend on other people because they usually let him down. He is usually disappointed that people do not meet their own deadlines or don't follow through with what they say they will do. Steve is a hard worker and plays hard too. He is persistent, determined. When he sets his mind to something, I know he will get it done.

Steve is athletic. He can catch any football a quarterback can throw. He can sprint at top speed to catch a Frisbee thrown across a field. Playing tennis, he can run down a drop shot that barely dinks over the net; he will flip and whirl and spin around like a top to pop back a deep lob. He can pick up a new sport he has never tried before and master it quickly. Despite his fear of swimming, he overcame it to learn to swim and then to train and to eventually complete an Ironman triathlon.

Steve is a visual and spatial genius. His perspective is unique. He helped me study for astronomy class in college because he could easily imagine the relationships of planets in space while I could not.

He is stable. He likes routine. He does the same thing every morning, eats the same thing, and makes the same lunch sandwich—always with chips and sweet tea—for himself every day. He goes to bed at the same time every night.

He is funny. He doesn't mind when I giggle at him when he can't find the butter or when he forgets a familiar word for the fifteenth time.

Steve is totally fun and makes me laugh. He plans all our leisure activities and has always taken the boys camping, backpacking, skiing, hiking, biking—anything outdoors. Steve and I have grown up together. I love him. He is my family. He is my best friend for life.

PIECE 55 — "YIDDL' BRUZHER"

I felt energetic and vibrant during all nine months of my pregnancy with Daniel's little brother David. I swam laps regularly at the YMCA. Glowing with good health I was able to decline anesthetic during his birth, which came two days earlier than the doctor had calculated.

Nilla's Diary for Daniel February 21 (Daniel Age 3)
Your "Yiddl Bruzhr named Day-vid" was born this morning. You were very quiet when you saw me in the hospital. I was very worried about your reaction to David. I didn't want you to be jealous. You love your little brother and are proud to be the big brother, but I know you miss me while I am in the hospital. I miss you very much and don't want you to be lonely.

Nilla's Diary February 24 (Daniel Age 3)
I come home from the hospital. We pick you up from daycare where you play with Jessica, Brandon, Ashley and Chad. You touch David's head softly with your finger. You seem very proud of him.

David was a sweet, snuggly baby. He loved being held and cuddled, curled up in any lap. He had beautiful, soft skin, symmetrical features, big blue eyes, long eyelashes, and a huge smile. Our neighbor insisted that we have him try out as a child model (we didn't.) His fuzzy blonde hair feathered out in wisps like a halo emanating from around his large head.

Nilla's Diary March 4 (Daniel Age 3)
When I told you "I love you" today, you said, "You do NOT! You love Day-vid!" It made me sad because I love you so much.

Nilla's Diary April 3 (Daniel Age 3)
You are so proud of and love your little brother—hold his hand, tell him you love him, pat his back so he'll burp.

Nilla's Diary April 29 (Daniel Age 3)
You are getting rough and sometimes mean to David. It makes me sad when you tease him.

David lived his little life with gusto. He ran full speed ahead until he collapsed in exhaustion. We have photos of him asleep in his high chair, head clonked down into a plate of spaghetti; another of him sleeping soundly, stretched across a staircase. We found him wearing only a diaper, asleep on the cold linoleum kitchen floor in freezing winter temperatures—he had "escaped" his warm, carpeted bedroom so he could sleep with the dog.

Daniel's Answers (Age 29)
"My general impression of this book is that I did a lot of things wrong but I don't see what you did wrong. It comes across as you always trying to help."

[Here is your chance to point those things out.]

PIECE 56 — CONTROL

I used to have panic attacks when I attended church women's fellowship events. That probably sounds odd because panic is more often associated with fear of enclosed spaces, fear of flying, or fear of heights. I couldn't figure out why I felt panic. I didn't think anyone meant harm to me. I didn't feel judged. It didn't make sense. All I knew was that my heart started racing, my face flushed hot, my ears burned red, and I felt so much anxiety that I had to leave the room immediately and walk around the block a few times.

Years later, I realized why I might have felt that way. *I had felt responsible for every woman in the room.* The more women in the room, the more responsibility I felt. Whether there were 10 women or 80 women, I felt I had to greet each woman with a smile. I had to be pleasant, I had to appear happy, and I had to do whatever I could to be sure that each one of them was happy. It still doesn't make sense because no one was asking me to do those things.

I had spent a lifetime being thoroughly indoctrinated to be a caretaker. I was the first-born, the oldest of four girls. My youngest sister was 10 years younger than me. I became like her second mom and carried her around on my little hip. I babysat frequently for my own sisters and for neighbors and friends.

One time when my parents were out of town, we girls were outside with all our neighbors riding our bikes around "The Circle." My sister wrecked her bike into the telephone pole and broke her nose. I didn't think the adult neighbors were responding quickly enough, so I threw my bike down and ran over to help her. Unfortunately I tripped over my bike handle bars getting there and skinned my own face raw. The babysitter had to take my sister to the hospital for x-rays. My sister and I spent the next day out of school eating pudding and watching cartoons in our parents' bed, laughing in spite of our cracking scabs.

My parents trained me to be obedient and helpful. Their praise for my "good" behavior was the way I tried to convince myself they would keep on loving me. I enjoyed doing nice things for my parents. I loved to pretend I was a waitress and write their order on a little notepad and bring them breakfast in bed.

I was the community empathizer. I was highly skilled at figuring out other people's motivations. This talent earned me my favorite job as a creative product editor at Hallmark Cards. My job was to figure out how people wanted to communicate their feelings to their loved ones and friends through greeting cards. Woohoo! Now I could definitely apply my overactive care-taking glands not only to my family and friends, but to people across the entire nation!

In public I feel compelled to correct grammar and spelling on signs. I am the one who flattens the kink in the rubber door mat at the grocery store entrance so no one trips. I pick up litter. I put fallen items back on the shelf. When a woman turned her car in front of mine and wrecked my car, I hugged her and patted her back because she was stressed and crying and distraught.

There is nothing wrong with being thoughtful and caring. What I later learned WAS toxic was my extreme approach to "care-taking." I lived my life inside out. Instead of feeling like a self-contained individual, it was like I was walking around without my skin on, absorbing other people's feelings rather than experiencing my own emotions.

With a lot of help from counselors, fifteen years of medications to help with anxiety and depression, regularly attending "twelve-step" meetings, reading about "co-dependency" and "enabling" patterns often ingrained in addictive families, and learning how those patterns had a hold on my life, the panic attacks have subsided. I am beginning to feel comfortable in groups again. This year I noticed enjoying myself at art galleries and parties.

After a lifetime of training to be the solver, the fixer, the comforter, I finally figured out that I am not the ruler of the universe. After thirty years as a Christian, I realized it is not up to me to take care of everyone—that's God's job. I thought I was being good and helpful, but I was actually acting arrogantly.

Many of the things I tried to "fix" ended up being tangled, gummed up messes. My well-intentioned but misguided interference caused pain. I cringe when I think of the negative effects my meddling has had on the people I love the most. I feel regret. I want to re-wind time. I want to re-do and correct my wrongs. But time doesn't go in reverse.

What I am beginning to learn to do is to trust God; to cry out to God; and to ask Him to help me. I am learning that just because I notice a need does not mean that I have to be the one to solve it. I am beginning to learn to "Leave it!" like the sharp command I give my rascally dog when he has a sappy pine cone in his mouth and wants to bring it inside to tear it apart on my carpet.

Slowly, I am learning to take responsibility for what is in my "circle of control" and to leave the rest to God. Sometimes I have to envision a hula hoop around my waist, to remind myself that I belong inside that imaginary three foot circumference and my responsibilities end there. I need to remember to "mind my own business."

I am practicing letting others live their own lives, feel their own feelings, make their own mistakes, and to be proud of their accomplishments. I am learning that overly caretaking for people not only wears me out, but it can interfere with them learning their own lessons, solving their own problems, and even them turning to God for help.

The most ridiculous aspect of my trying to control other people's lives is that my own life is nowhere near "under control." I neglect my health by overeating and under exercising. Until recent years I spent too much money thinking a short-term purchase could lift my spirits and make me feel better for the moment. I also loved giving gifts to other people, even when they were not expected, even when we could not afford my flawed generosity.

PIECE 57 — BULLIED

itch Hiker (Daniel Age 20)
Back home one day Daniel was driving downtown and picked up a hitch hiker. The guy took Daniel's wallet, which he had left out on the dashboard in plain view. Daniel told the guy to give it back to him. When he wouldn't give it back, Daniel refused to stop the car. The guy jumped out and ran.

Daniel called his dad from a pay phone. Steve and David met Daniel at the police station. The police officer *lectured Daniel* about how Daniel *could have been charged with kidnapping* for not letting the hitch hiker out of his car.

The police knew who the guy was from Daniel's description and quickly arrested the habitual criminal; and they recovered Daniel's wallet in some woods.

Park after Dark (Daniel Age 22)

I helped Daniel move into his dorm room. After a long day of unpacking and getting him settled in, we went to Wal-Mart to buy a few more things he needed. We took our tired selves out for dinner, and afterward he wanted to show me a park nearby, even though it was already dark. He drove slowly through the small park, circling a few times, pointing out a petting zoo and a picnic area.

A police car with lights flashing pulled him over. The officer approached the driver's side cautiously. She asked for his driver's license and registration and shined a blinding spotlight into Daniel's eyes as she questioned what he was doing in the park at night.

"Driving."

I tried to fill in the blanks. "He is a student at UNCA. I helped him move him into the dorm today and he just wanted to show me this park. I am his mother."

The officer still seemed concerned about Daniel's appearance. His face was blank. He wasn't looking at her. Maybe she was wondering if he had something to hide, like whether he had been drinking or if we had been in the park to deal drugs?

The officer let Daniel go after reviewing all his documentation, but she never seemed to relax her guard. She couldn't hold him there because he hadn't done anything illegal, and all the papers and car tags were in order. Even though there were no signs saying the park was closed at dusk, she told Daniel to stay away from the park after dark.

Security Bullies (Daniel Age 27)

Daniel had a class assignment he needed to research. His community college has a library exchange agreement with five other local colleges and universities that any student may use the library of any other institution.

One afternoon, Daniel rode his bike to Salem College. The small, private, women's school campus is set in the middle of Old Salem, a historic tourist attraction. There are hundreds, if not thousands, of people of all ages, who walk all over that campus throughout the week, day and night. The library is set on a public street.

Daniel parked and locked his bike and helmet outside the library entrance and walked into the library with his backpack to do his research. He spoke with the reference librarian and found the information he needed. When he walked out of the library, there were two college security guards waiting for him.

"Excuse me sir, will you step over here please? Do you have any identification?"

Daniel handed them his driver's license.

"What are you doing on campus?"

"Going to the library."

"Do you attend school here?"

"No. I go to Forsyth Tech."

"What are you doing here?"

"We have an exchange and I needed to pick up something here for an assignment."

"We had a report that you were sitting on the steps of that residence hall over there."

"I wasn't sitting anywhere. I rode my bike here and went inside the library."

"Well that is different from the report we have from a female student."

Meanwhile, the two other officers who had been called arrived on the scene. Now there were four armed, uniformed officers interrogating Daniel. Daniel is a quiet, good looking, calm guy with a boyish face. There is nothing about him that appears menacing or ominous.

Daniel explained to the officers that this would be a great story to use for an example for his paper, which was to be written about prejudice, bias, or discrimination, related to the recent popular movie "Crash."

By this time the security department supervisor had arrived. Now there were five armed, uniformed officers standing around staring at Daniel as if they were prepared for trouble, as if he was some great safety threat to the campus.

Daniel rode his bike home and told us what had happened. Steve and I were furious that he would have been surrounded like that and intimidated. We felt protective of him. By this time, it was late Friday evening, but we wanted to get an explanation anyway. No one answered the phone in the campus security office, so Steve and I went down to the college. Even though it was after dark on a weekend night, the prime time I would think the college would have extra guards on duty, no security officers were to be found. We went to the security office. None were on duty.

Daniel's Answers (Age 29)

[I was apprehensive when the police stopped you after dark in the park, that they might charge you with something you didn't do, because they seemed so suspicious.]

"I just figured it was them doing their job. They are trained to treat every traffic stop as serious. They treat every single one with the same amount of gravity."

[Whenever I've been stopped, I've never felt anything that serious.]

[Shrug.]

[What did you think of the Salem College campus security? That made Dad and me SO MAD!]

"I thought that was hilarious! All five of them, or whatever. It was the stereotypical security guard, with nothing better to do except intimidate someone. They just wish they were real police officers. I was telling them, 'This will be perfect in my paper I'm writing!' but they obviously didn't think it was funny."

PIECE 58 — MAKE A WISH

Scott and Daniel were best friends, like brothers. Their grandparents were good friends. Daniel called Scott "S." The boys were in the same class at The Summit School and on some of the same sports teams. Between play dates and sleepovers, they were constantly together, either at our house or theirs. Both of Scott's parents were attorneys who worked long hours, so they had a full-time housekeeper who cooked, cleaned, and stayed with the children. Scott and Daniel each had a younger brother. David always hoped he would be invited over too, because they had the best video gaming systems and the latest, most popular games.

Scott's family lived in the house next to the country club. Both families were members, so once the boys were old enough, they were allowed to walk down to the tennis courts or the swimming pool. They were allowed to charge a lemonade and hot dog from the grill for lunch.

Scott went to the same summer camp in the mountains an hour away from our home and was in the same cabin with Daniel. Even after we moved out of state, Scott's family let him travel for a week in the summers to visit us, every place we lived, and let him go to summer camp with Daniel in the Idaho Sawtooth mountains. They were the kind of friends that each time "S" visited us the boys picked up right where they left off and had a great time together. It was always fun to have "S" around. We would go hiking, swimming, eat out, go to movies, play miniature golf, tour the "Amazing Maize Maze" or whatever entertainment the guys chose.

When we lived in the Midwest, we heard the bad news through the grandparents that "S" had been diagnosed with cancer. I considered Scott to be like my third son and was devastated. I tried to explain it to Daniel, and found a card for him to send to "S" in the hospital, along with a table-top Christmas tree with miniature ornaments and tiny lights with a motorized train circling the base for "S" to have to brighten up his room. We sent a teddy bear monogrammed with the initial "S" and had an identical bear with a "D" for Daniel so he could keep his friend in mind.

A year later, we had heard "S" was doing really well and that the cancer was in remission! "S" had missed a year of school due to the aggressive chemotherapy treatments so he would have to repeat the 10th grade, but that was insignificant in the scheme of things. Scott was getting stronger and healthier every day.

Scott's mom called me out of the blue and said she had something important for me to consider. I wondered what it could be. "Part of Scott's recovery process has included an offer by the Make-a-Wish Foundation for Scott to choose what he would like most in the world once his treatments are over. Part of the mission of the Make-a-Wish organization is that during the grueling treatments it is therapeutic for the patients to imagine wonderful ideas, to consider their grandest dreams. Each patient chooses specifically what is most important for them. Scott's choice is to go this summer on "The Western Tour," an organized five week bus tour with about thirty other teens from our area. They will travel a large loop around the U.S., visiting landmarks like the St. Louis Arch and the Golden Gate Bridge, drive through the Colorado Rockies, visit Disneyland in California, and national parks like Yellowstone and The Grand Canyon."

I was glad to hear from her and felt honored that she was sharing this, but I still didn't understand why she had called me. "Part of Scott's wish is that Daniel would be invited to go with him." Tears welled up in my eyes. "All expenses would be covered by the Make-a-Wish Foundation. Will you please explain all this to Daniel and you all consider it for a few days? Let us know what you decide."

Choked up, I stammered, "Thank you. That is amazing. I have never heard of anything so moving. We are all so very happy that

Scott is doing well now. I am touched that Scott would involve Daniel in this important choice. I am sure he will want to do this, but Steve and I will talk it over with him and let you know."

Of course, Daniel said immediately he would like to join "S" on the tour, so we proceeded with the plans. I was honored that our lives would connect in such a special way by an organization I had always admired. Now I could witness its powerful effect up close. I realized that Scott's parents could easily have afforded to send him on this trip, but that was beside the point. That gesture would have been meaningless to Scott, because his parents routinely paid his expenses. I am sure that since that time, Scott's parents have donated to Make-a-Wish Foundation many times more the value of Scott's trip. The financial aspect is insignificant compared to the central purpose of Make-a-Wish, which is to give the sick child a reason to live. Drawing their attention away from the painful treatments and miserable needle sticks, distracting them from the nausea, Make-a-Wish re-directs the child's attention to imagining the most wonderful options. They can fantasize with no limitations. What would they like most in the world? Meeting a movie star or sports celebrity? Riding a roller coaster? Meeting Mickey Mouse at Disney?

Altruism was central to Scott's wish: making the trip possible for his friend Daniel, who wouldn't have been able to afford to go otherwise.

Daniel's Answers (Age 29)

[Whatever happened to your friendship with "S"?]

"Moved."

[Yes, we moved all over the country, but he visited us everywhere we lived.]

"Moved."

[But it seems I remember it was only after we moved back here that you and "S" stopped being friends. I know we moved a lot, but I have kept up with my friend Annie Bananie, even though we haven't lived in the same town since we were nine years old.]

"Maybe so, but that is unusual. You have worked to keep that up. It takes work to keep up a friendship."

PIECE 59 — STRANGER DANGER

On a Thursday night Daniel called to see if I would keep Jada for the weekend. "Sure! I'd be glad to. What are you doing? Something fun?"

"Volunteering to work on the A.T."

"Wow! That is cool!" This was out of the blue. I went into protective mother mode. "Be sure to take sunscreen and mosquito repellent, and wear long sleeves and long pants so you don't get chiggers or poison ivy."

[Silence.]

"How did you find out about doing trail work? Are you going with a group?"

[Silence.]

"Who are you going with?"

"This guy from my classes."

Worry antenna—zing! "Hmmm... Okay.... Well it would be good if you would give someone, like Jimmy maybe, some contact information."

[Silence on the phone.]

"That's just a good idea to do. Dad and I do that. When we go out of town we give each other our contact information, just in case there is an emergency."

[Pause.]

"Seeya."

I thought a quick prayer, "God, please protect my son," before calling Steve to pour out my anxiety. "What if the guy chops him up? We don't know anything about this guy, and we don't know if Daniel has the skill to evaluate whether or not someone is safe."

To my great relief, the next day Daniel emailed us the guy's name, phone number, address, and directions to the place they planned to start. I felt much better after that, just knowing some kind of data.

Daniel returned Sunday afternoon. He came to our house for dinner.

Nilla: "So, tell me about the trail work you did."

[Silence.]

Nilla: "Did you work on the trail?"

Daniel: "Painted trail markers."

Nilla: "And was the guy you went with a student in your computer basics class or was he an instructor or helper?"

Daniel: "Student."

A while later, after we had finished dinner and I was cleaning up the kitchen, I mused, "I'm trying to figure out how your conversation went from computer basics, like using a mouse, to let's work on the Appalachian Trail this weekend."

[Pause.]

[Thinking.]

[Facial grimaces.]

[Eye squints.]

Cutting up papaya he had frozen in a Ziploc bag, Daniel asked, "Who wants some papaya?"

Nilla: "I'll have a taste."

Steve: "I'll try some. I don't know if I'll like it."

After a while, I repeated my question, "So, like, how did your conversation go from mouse to trail?"

Daniel: "I think he took one of my first classes back at the beginning, like last fall. It was internet basics, and he wanted to know how to follow his trail buddies, to send and receive messages with them. So, from there, he showed me his group's website. And I told him I had done some hiking. He said, 'If you ever want to go with our group and do some trail work, let me know.' And then I didn't think about it for a while because it was winter. And then recently I wanted to get outside and hike. I wanted to give something back because there are other people who have prepared the trails for me so I wanted to do something to contribute. So I called him and asked him if there was anything coming up. And he told me about this weekend, about some land in Virginia where we could camp out and do trail work on the AT."

Nilla: "Oh, the internet. That makes a lot more sense to me that that would make a connection, rather than just how to use a computer."

Daniel's Answers (Age 29)
"The way you tell it, it comes across that it doesn't acknowledge you're doing anything wrong here. You're getting worried about something you don't need to worry about. It sounds like you're doing everything right and I'm doing everything wrong. You should acknowledge both sides. Yes, maybe I should say more, maybe you shouldn't step on my toes. Yes, your response is understandable, but not as the only response, or not as the first response. It becomes like an interrogation, like you have to get all the details to find out if it's safe. It's not fun telling you if that's the way it's going to be. I mean, if that's your default response,"

[You mean, you'll just shut up even more?]
"Yeah."

PIECE 60 — HIGH TENSION

As I have reached out to other families for support, I have observed that almost all of "us" are quirky, each in our own way. Although the etiology has not been established, it seems obvious to me that Asperger syndrome has genetic components. Many of us mothers in our monthly Parent Support

Group are socially awkward. Some talk endlessly without the usual pauses to allow someone else to give their opinion. Others are zealots about miniscule topics. Certainly all are affected by a stressful environment at home.

Email, Nilla to Sharon October 21 (Daniel Age 25)

Rosie was at the Autism Parent Support Group meeting today. Sylvia had given me her contact info at our last meeting, so I invited her to come today. I like Rosie. Her son Jimmy is 24.

There was a good sized group today, about 12-15? It was better organized... one minute introductions around the room to start. But then it spiraled down. The rest of the meeting focused only on IEP meetings, mostly those at one particular school. Lauren brought us back into focus, but then the meeting reverted back to the same subject. It may be helpful to those who are going through battles with their schools, but I wonder if they should have their own meeting about that topic exclusively.

I picked up on heavy tension in the room. The discussion was peppered with entitlement, manipulation, control, and strategies for adversarial stances against the school system. It was unpleasant to hear, and I could see how going into an IEP with those attitudes would make any meeting confrontational.

Today I did not sense much compassion for teachers and schools. I can remember so many times that I felt that same judgmental way toward my sons' teachers and schools. I wish I had then the perspective I have now. Now I think (hope?) I would demand that my child receive the services he needs while also expressing empathy for the providers. Maybe not, maybe it depends on my own circumstances since Daniel is beyond those tender years?

Today there seemed to be such a heavy layer of darkness. I sensed intense fear and anxiety in moms new to autism (of a three year old) and those facing IEPs for the first time. I wanted to say a prayer, to ask God for peace. Before the meeting ended, I spoke up that I wanted to say a word of comfort... "I've lived my whole life with fear and anxiety, believing that if I did something right my child would be okay; and if I didn't do everything right, my child would not be okay... I want to say something to ease everyone's burdens and say... do all you can, learn all you can... but then take a deep breath and know that it will be all right." That seemed to release a lot of tension in the room.

I don't know if I can sit through another meeting like today's again without an initial "blessing." Maybe I'll write a non-denominational mother's blessing that I offer to the group to read aloud or silently before each meeting. Next time I will at least go early, say my own prayer before it begins, even if it's just me by myself. I am accustomed to church groups that ask for God's help in our lives. I don't intend to push my faith onto others, but even twelve step support groups acknowledge the need for a "higher power."

If I didn't believe that God made Daniel this way for a reason, I couldn't cope with Daniel's disability. I may not know or understand God's purposes, but I do know He is in control of Daniel's life. As much as Daniel has disabilities, he has abilities. He may not function well in society, but he is one of the finest human beings I have ever known.

Email, Nilla to Melissa October 24 (Daniel Age 25)

Dear Melissa, I know what you mean about the First Fridays group being centered on the needs of young children. I feel the same way most meetings, but there are so few parent supports, I felt it was important for me to continue. I'm desperate! I imagine the group may feel the same way we do, in reverse, that our needs are so different from theirs, not only in the ages of our children, but sometimes I sense they are frustrated (maybe even, in a sense, resentful?) that our sons are more high functioning, and maybe they think we can't relate to their children's intensely basic needs?

Sometimes I feel grateful that the autism group "allows" Asperger members, since it's still controversial whether Asperger syndrome is "on the spectrum" as High-Functioning Autism or a separate disorder. Asperger syndrome is so individual; every child is so different; there are almost more differences than there are similarities! If I waited for more commonalities or uniformities, I think we would each be in a group of ONE! —Nilla

Daniel's Answers (Age 29)
[Do you think it's okay for parents to have support groups?]
    "Yeah, I think that is appropriate."

STEP FIVE
MATCHING DETAILS

N illa's Method for Completing a Jigsaw Puzzle
1. First, I turn all the pieces out of the box.
2. I plop the pieces onto the table into a big jumbled pile.
3. Turning over each upside-down piece right-side up, I begin to see what I have.
4. Next is finding edges—pieces with straight edges form the outer border.
5. **I look for matching details like fragments of words, faces or shapes.**

Now we're getting to the fun part! As you spot a salient detail, like a bright color or a facial feature, or as you recognize a fragment of a familiar object—group those pieces together into separate piles. Then, when you are ready to begin fitting pieces together you will have all the bright yellow pieces near each other that will link to become the sun; all the face pieces near each other when you are ready to connect the people pieces.

After Daniel's year of "training," a comprehensive plan was needed to help him establish a healthy and satisfying life on his own. I made one of my famous lists of supports I knew Daniel needed: a stable place to live, a pet companion to give him responsibility, a roommate to subsidize his rent, a job coach to help him navigate employment, a social mentor to encourage leisure activities, a church buddy to accompany him on Sundays, a cooking instructor to advise on menu and nutrition, and a fitness membership to promote exercise.

PIECE 61 — GROUNDED

To prepare for Daniel's moving back home at the end of his year at The Program, Steve and I found a condo for him nearby. The down payment would be paid from what remained of his college fund. I arranged inspector, insurance, mortgage financing, attorney for real estate closing, and so on. Having a place of his own will provide stability to his life. He won't have to face rising rents or deal with the whims of landlords. He doesn't have to move ever again!

Steve and I helped Daniel shop for appliances. He chose the most basic refrigerator/freezer and a washer and dryer for the basement. He refused a vacuum cleaner I brought over for him to borrow. Was it the noise it makes? Was it the cost of electricity? Was it too heavy? He wouldn't say. He simply would not allow it to remain in his house. He was definitely insistent on his wishes, as he confidently wielded the power of owning his own place.

He had strong opinions about furnishings: they had to be minimal, simple, inexpensive, and lightweight. He rejected the oak filing cabinet I found, saying it was too heavy. At the consignment store, I found a wicker dining set with two chairs that nested together; he ruled that acceptable. Only one lamp was permitted in the living room. Everything had to be utilitarian, nothing decorative. He wanted everything visible, in the open. Daniel wanted to remove the kitchen cabinets. I got him to compromise: to remove the cabinet doors only.

Daniel did not want a sofa, a loveseat, or any kind of cushy seating. He wanted office guest chairs. What he chose looked so sterile. I steered Daniel's choice to three Danish style teak wood chairs with golden vinyl seats. Very simple, but sturdy and comfortable. Later, I found one of my favorite quotations from *Walden*, in the chapter on "Visitors" by Henry David Thoreau: "I had three chairs in my house. One for solitude, two for friendship, three for society." I painted one word on the back of each chair: "Solitude," "Friendship," and "Society." Daniel seemed to like the creative addition.

He and Steve turned his bedroom closet into a sleeping nook by building a platform and topping it with a futon. His room became his closet: his "dresser" is made of those connect-it-yourself plastic-coated wire baskets. He created a desk from a discarded door balanced on two folding chairs. He is drilling holes in his books and hanging them from the ceiling on a clothesline. He even drilled holes in books he had borrowed from me which I wanted back. Oh, well.

I cut beautiful pictures of healthy foods out of a yard sale cook book. I drenched decoupage to seal them onto a $3 door from the Habitat for Humanity Re-store. The colorful collage brightens up his tiny kitchen and I hope it will inspire him to improve his eating habits.

We and a few friends and family held a "house-warming" weekend workday. One friend brought essentials: toilet paper, paper towels, and trash bags. Another friend offered to help scrape wallpaper off the kitchen walls—a big, messy project!

Daniel's Answers (Age 29)

[Do you remember why you didn't want a vacuum cleaner?]

"Probably because I don't have a problem with dust."

[What do you think now about your condo? Are you glad you have a stable place to be?]

"In some ways, I wish I didn't have it. I would feel more free to go do some other things or accept a job somewhere else. But it is good to have a little bit of responsibility, like *having* a roommate rather than *being* a roommate, so in that sense, it has been good."

[So, for example, you probably wouldn't have had your heat fixed if it was just you living there, but since you have a roommate, you have to get it fixed?]

"Yeah."

PIECE 62 — COMPANIONSHIP

D aniel wanted a pet of his own. He has always related well to animals, especially dogs and cats. They seem magnetically attracted to him. When we were hiking in Europe, a cat came up to us on a trail in the Swiss Alps and snuggled up to Daniel, rubbing against his ankles. It did not do the same to me. On his travel to Maine, a cat adopted Daniel in the campground.

Even when Daniel seemed awkward around people, he related easily, naturally, warmly, to their pets. He cared for other people's pets when they were out of town, much as he had cared for our Standard Poodle during his teenage years and our King Charles Cavalier Spaniel when he was a boy.

Daniel hasn't had many friends. I have tried to set up random opportunities for friendships to develop. His next door neighbor is an elementary school teacher who works with a student with Asperger syndrome. Often she sits outside on her front porch and plays with her dog and chats with other neighbors. But Daniel will not go outside or even have his front door open.

For a young man with few, if any, friends—no hugs, no kisses, no snuggling, no touch—I suppose the only remotely satisfactory substitute for human companionship is having a pet.

I believed that if Daniel had a dog, he would have some responsibility outside of himself and it might bring him to keep a more regular routine. He would have to let the dog out to pee in the mornings, so he couldn't sleep all day and stay awake all night playing video poker! Having a dog would give Daniel a reason to get outdoors—in the fresh air—and away from his computer. He'd have to at least take a short walk every day.

I had investigated every possibility for a pet. My friend Lisa, Daniel's godmother, who has a heart for animals, and is familiar with Daniel's needs, had recommended a bird, specifically a cockatiel, as being affectionate, easy to care for. "Get a cockatiel! They are low-maintenance and very affectionate. Our cockatiel talks to us and mimics our whistles and gives us kisses."

We tried that idea. We went to an "expert" pet store. It turned out to be a chaotic, nightmarish experience. The birds had been neglected during the holiday season and the temporary staff had no idea what they were doing. Neither Steve nor Daniel would hold or even touch the bird. Naively, I held the bird that the clerk handed over to me. Frantic, it bit my finger and wouldn't let go. It HURT! As soon as I recovered from that pain, it bit again, another finger, this time drawing blood.

Daniel stood there, traumatized by watching this creature attack his mom. Steve walked away in the middle of all the excitement, escaping having to deal with what he had considered a stupid idea anyway. We left the pet store, having given up the idea of a bird for a pet. That ended that, except as a reminder, the wound became infected and I had to nurse it for days. Lesson: *No bird!*

Next, I thought about a cat. Easy to care for—they can use a litter box and can be left home alone for a day or two if necessary with food and water. I remembered that cats have always been very affectionate with Daniel.

We tried the cat option. Daniel told me if he got a cat he would want a little one (a kitten.) We went to the Humane Society. The volunteer advised us to get an adult cat so you can know its personality. One cat kept biting the volunteers, another one scratched me and another hissed at Daniel. As soon as we got to the car, my nose and forehead started itching. I already knew I had allergies, but I was willing to tolerate anything to find a little friend for Daniel.

On the drive to the county animal shelter to look for other cats, Daniel said "I don't think I want a cat. I can never figure cats out. I know what dogs need." That ended that. Lesson: *No cat!*

The new mission: to look for a dog. A quiet one that doesn't bark much; one that doesn't shed. "That is important to me. I don't want a bunch of dog hair everywhere."

"You know, our two dogs don't shed. Poodles and schnauzers are known for having hair, not fur. They don't shed, plus their dander (skin flakes) are hypo-allergenic."

"Yeah, that's the kind of breed we need to look for."

Daniel couldn't afford to pay hundreds of dollars to a breeder for a specific breed of dog. I thought to myself, "Oh, great. We'll never find one of those breeds at the shelter."

PIECE 63 — GETTING JADA

Thursday morning, we set out across the railroad tracks to the dreary county animal shelter. As I pulled the heavy door open, the stench attacked my senses. Concentrate of urine gripped my nose. I hid my nostrils under my shirt collar. We slinked down a tunneled hall of dull concrete block walls, dimly lit, past metal cages containing cats. To get to the dogs, we had to trudge through puddles remaining from hoses spraying the feces-infused dank concrete floors. When I opened this heavy glass barrier, my ears pained from the explosive barking. I raised my hands to cover my ears, resisting the operatic begging.

Cage after cage, we saw shepherd-, Labrador-, Doberman-, and terrier-mix breeds. We needed a dog that wouldn't shed (allergies.) We wanted a dog that wouldn't bark incessantly (apartment life.) We needed a house-trained adult dog, not a puppy. Grimly, we walked past cage after cage. Each step brought us closer to the realization that coming to the shelter was a lost cause.

In the last cage on the right a friendly cocker spaniel wagged its tail, its eyes pleading for release. But, unfortunately, I knew cocker spaniels shed. But, what was that clump of fur lying on the ground behind him? Was that a dog? All we could see was a filthy, tangled mass of black fur, a small blob lying quietly, head resting on its front paws, with its back to us. Oblivious, it ignored the chaos. How could it stand the cacophony of barking? How could it not join in with the others? Was it deaf? The blob even ignored the parade of people—its only hope of rescue, its last chance for survival—which all the other dogs seemed to sense. Had it simply given up? Was it resigned to awaiting its miserable finale?

We asked the shelter volunteer if we could have a closer look. She brought the dog into a room so we could interact with it. The room stunk. It was wet and filthy. The little black furry blob was so overgrown that its limbs were not discernible. Its shape was oval, and I mean from head to toe and all around oval. No front legs, no back legs, no tail, no ears. Felted mats of fur clumped like moccasins below its feet. I guessed it hadn't been groomed in over a year.

Daniel wouldn't touch or pet the dog. I scratched her back and she loved it. She sniffed around, curious enough to allay my worries that she seemed too withdrawn at first. I petted and cooed and stroked the dog and thought she seemed very sweet and calm. I kept asking Daniel if he wanted to hold her or pet her. He shook his head no and stayed standing in the same spot.

"Something is wrong with its eyes."

It was so shaggy I could barely see any features at all. I brushed its fur back and reassured him, "She's probably just dirty from lying in the filth."

Daniel shook his head, "No, it's got a problem."

I looked closer and underneath the clumps the eye was filled with pink mucus, and was swollen partially closed. The volunteer said she didn't know anything about any eye problem. She checked on its records and said it had passed the shelter's medical exam a few days earlier. I still thought the dog had potential, if it could be groomed, removed from this filthy environment, and be treated with antibiotic eye drops. It was quiet. If it was a poodle we wouldn't have allergic reactions. It was small; it was adult; it seemed gentle. She said the dog had been there five days; she was about four years old, but hadn't been spayed.

I asked Daniel if he wanted her.

"That might work."

Knowing that was Daniel's positively affirmative response, I told the shelter volunteer we wanted her. We filled out all the application papers, gave references, wrote checks for adoption fees; then we sat and waited.

A tall, gawky man came out to interview Daniel. The more he grilled Daniel, the more defensive I got. Daniel continued to slump in the chair, sitting like a bump on a log. Daniel did not look at him, did not turn toward him.

"Do you have a job?"

"No."

"Why don't you have a job?"

[No response]

"When are you going to get a job?" "What kind of job would you get?" "Why should someone unemployed be adopting a pet? "How will you pay for her food or shots?"

"I don't know."

I piped up, "Until he gets a job, I will help him pay those expenses."

He asked if Daniel lived at home.

"No."

The tall, dark haired man said they do not allow co-sponsors for pet adoptions. *He refused to allow Daniel to adopt Jada.* I felt shocked. Why? Here was a filthy, diseased, unresponsive, discarded animal on *death row*! Was the man saying that it would be better for the animal to die than to go home with my wonderful son? I understood (logically) that he couldn't know Daniel's character after such a short interview, but how could I convey to him Daniel's good heart—in spite of his awkward mannerisms, his poor body language? How could I make this busy, pre-occupied man understand the importance of this animal to Daniel's life?

The man walked away. Daniel stood up, expressionless, and began to walk to the car. I told him to sit back down, that I needed to think. There had to be a way to make this work out. I put my head in my hands in despair and disbelief. How could this be happening? And what would become of that little dog, lying on a putrid, urine-stained, cold concrete floor? We sat and we sat for minutes that seemed like hours in the hard plastic chairs.

"Daniel, I'm sorry." I was dumbfounded. What could we do? Now that we had finally found a dog that fit our multiple, demanding needs, this awkward man stood between us and all this potential for improvement in Daniel's life! I was angry. I was crying. I was livid. The only problem was that Daniel's autistic behaviors were an opaque screen, once again preventing the world from seeing his true self. Daniel is a tender and gentle person. This wasn't fair, it wasn't right.

I noticed a woman wearing a bright, kelly-green sweater, passing us back and forth. She was busy, going from person to person, into and out of the shelter offices. Apparently she was the volunteer coordinator. I decided to talk to her and tell her the situation. I followed her outside and asked for a few minutes of her time. I explained how important this dog was for Daniel. She stood behind the shelter's decision. She said that her volunteer had told the shelter manager that Daniel had not interacted with Jada, that he had not petted her or talked to her, and that was a concern.

With that, I let loose, explaining Daniel's autism, "He has high-functioning autism and he needs a companion. I will completely back up the adoption and make sure that the dog is well cared for. Our dogs are like family. He is not good with body language or social interactions but he is very good with pets."

By now tears were streaming down my face. My tears were about the dog, but even more, over the fact that *everything* was always so difficult, even adopting a pitiful creature on its last leg of life. If *this* was difficult, compare this trivial effort to the more complex effort of finding a girlfriend, building a marriage, eventually, finding a job, surviving an interview, keeping a job. If Daniel couldn't advocate for himself enough to adopt a scrawny canine, how would he ever do anything in life? No wonder everything seemed impossible for him.

The blonde, kelly-green sweater's compassionate side responded, "Why didn't you say so earlier? I wondered if he might have had a disability, but I wasn't sure. It seemed odd that his mother filled out the application, he doesn't have a job, he owns his own condo—how could that be?" She explained that she had several volunteers who are autistic and agreed that they were very good with the animals. With this understanding, she said she would go back inside to talk to the tall, strange man (later I found out he was the director of the shelter!)

My face was reddened and soaking wet by the time the shelter director came back out and called me into his office. "You should have told me! Why didn't you tell me he had autism?"

I felt stunned. What should I have said? "Excuse me, my son has autism?" How do I explain a lifetime of nuances in two minutes? This is the most maddening aspect of Daniel's condition, that he looks perfectly normal but his behavior, his affect, his responses are different, and usually misinterpreted.

The shelter director explained that he thought Daniel was angry. He reiterated that the volunteer observed that Daniel did not interact with Jada. He said it was unusual that I filled out the paperwork when Daniel was the applicant. In the end, the director was very kind and apologetic. He said he knew how much animals would mean to someone with autism. He made an exception and listed me as the co-applicant. He went back out to the hall and spoke to Daniel. He gave him his business card with all his and the other woman's home numbers printed on the back, telling Daniel "Call either of us if you have any questions. We have a volunteer program here, and if you are ever interested in volunteering with the animals, we would like for you to consider it."

You might think, "Whew!" the end of the story! But no. Not

yet. I asked them to wait a few minutes. I went outside to get my cell phone to call my husband to make sure he would approve. Daniel came outside with me and sat in the car. Steve anxiously asked how we could afford this: "Why couldn't Daniel pay for it—if it is his dog?"

"Daniel doesn't have a job."

"Then he shouldn't get a dog."

"But," I argued, "His having this dog may help him get into a routine so that he can find a job. I'll pay the $92 adoption fee out of my Christmas cash from my dad. And I'll pay any vet bills as well. I consider this to be my Christmas gift to Daniel. You know how impossible it is to find anything for him that he would like. This is important."

One hour later I went back inside the shelter and confirmed that yes, we did want the dog. It was only two days before Christmas and the shelter would not release a dog until it was spayed, but all the vets were closing the next day. I was afraid that if we waited until after the Christmas holiday (the shelter would be closed for 10 days) the dog would have died or gone blind from its eye infection. Miraculously, an appointment at a vet had opened up for the next morning. She would be transported directly there and we would pick her up the next afternoon.

When we finally left the shelter to go home, Daniel turned to me and asked matter-of-factly, "Did you use the autism thing?"

I admitted, "Yes." I had hoped he hadn't heard me making excuses for him, but he is too smart and observant to miss anything. I told him that the shelter director had thought he was angry.

He looked confused and surprised and questioned, "Angry? Why would he think that?"

"Because you didn't look him in the eyes and your answers were so short. It was your body language," I explained.

"Hmmm. I don't think anyone can get angry that fast."

"Well, yes, a lot of people could have been angry, and quickly, if they were already sensitive to being put down for not having a job."

Showing realization, he said, "Oh, yeah, I guess that could be."

The next day, Steve, Daniel and I went to the vet's office to pick her up. Daniel seemed more nervous than the dog did—his hands were shaking as he stood up to take Jada from the vet tech's arms. That is how Jada's life with us began.

Daniel's Answers (Age 29)

"That is not fair that they would judge me like that. My reaction to the dog, I was doing that on purpose. I knew what I was doing. They should know better than anybody. Just like the obedience classes are all about excitement and teaching certain commands, instead of about dog psychology. I mean, if I was going to live with that dog for the rest of its life, I don't need to go 'gaga' over it. I need to observe it."

[Did you think of Jada as "companionship?"]

"I think we get the dog we need, like Cesar Millan says."

[What does that mean?]

"If you get a dog that is excited, you'll have to address that, to figure out how to get it to calm down. It probably means that YOU are too excited. It's like a mirror."

PIECE 64—FINDING JIMMY

September (Daniel Age 24)
Daniel wants a roommate. He has a two bedroom condo. It would help him pay his mortgage. He talked about getting a "room for rent" sign and putting a notice in the newspaper. I told him he has to clean up first, before he does any of that, so he could show it to someone. His eyes widened, like he was surprised, but he didn't say anything.

November

At my Autism Society "First Fridays" Parent Support Group, the president, Sylvia, gave me the name and phone number for Rosie, whose son Jimmy is about Daniel's age. Rosie and I seemed to connect instantly over the phone. We talked for a long time. She has a younger daughter, age 8. Jimmy has his own apartment now, but he hasn't worked steadily for three years, so his parents are still paying the bills. I have a sense (probably unfounded) that Jimmy and Daniel may work out as potential roommates.

December 12

Daniel and I meet Rosie and Jimmy at Borders. We order coffee drinks. Rosie and I sit at one table. The guys sit at another. Both guys are interested in computers. I can't tell if they get along, but I suggest that they put each other's contact information into their cell phones.

December 29

Daniel and Jimmy have met three times (once a week) since our first meeting. I am so grateful. When I talk to Daniel after he and Jimmy have met, the tone of Daniel's voice seems perkier; he sounds more optimistic. I don't know if it's the contagion of Jimmy's nonchalant outlook, or that Daniel's self-esteem is boosted by the concept of having a "friend." Anyway, it seems to be a good combination. Jimmy doesn't drive, so Daniel picks him up to take him to their meeting places (public library, or Biscuitville.) I theorize that it makes Daniel feel good to be useful, to be able to provide a ride for him.

August 17 (Daniel Age 25)

Daniel and Jimmy are making plans toward becoming roommates. Jimmy is slow to make decisions, so it may take a while, but they had a trial weekend and all seemed to go well. Daniel took a lease form to him yesterday. Daniel always seems to be more outgoing/ happy/ confident/ "bubbly" when he is around Jimmy. Jimmy works at Food Market in the evenings, and mornings in the computer lab at Forsyth Tech.

September

Eventually, after nine months of suggestions from both families: "Hey! Guys! You could each lower your costs by sharing living expenses!" and negotiations: "How much rent is fair? How will we divvy up utility costs?" and meetings: "Who will do what chores? How will we get along and work out any disagreements?" Jimmy and Daniel finally became roommates.

To prepare for Jimmy's moving in, Steve and I insisted that Daniel get a small sofa so Jimmy and his girlfriend would have somewhere to sit and talk. We helped Daniel clean up the place. He knew Jimmy was terribly messy, so Daniel wanted to set a good example and start out with a clean place.

January

Jimmy did not wash his dishes. He was constantly leaving his dirty plates, pans, and utensils in the kitchen sink until they became slimy with molding food. Steve and I stopped by the condo to pick up Jada and noticed a checklist by the sink. It had tally marks and a dollar amount totaled at the bottom. We asked Daniel to explain what it was. Apparently, after months of coaxing his roommate to wash his own dishes, Daniel devised a plan: He announced he would wash Jimmy's dishes, but with that service he would fine Jimmy one dollar for every dirty dish or utensil left in the sink.

My first reaction was embarrassment. What if Jimmy's mother came over and saw this list and judged Daniel for being a selfish, greedy money-grubber? But the technique worked. Now whenever I go in their kitchen, I notice the sink is spotless and all dishes are put away in the drawers.

Months later, I think Daniel applied the same psychology to another area that was becoming annoying: providing transportation. Jimmy was able to take the city bus to work, but inevitably, he did not plan his time effectively, so he would miss the bus and ask Daniel for a ride. I guess Daniel got tired of his many last minute requests and began saying no.

If Jimmy didn't get out the door in time to catch the bus, he often called a cab. When Daniel found out Jimmy was paying $8 for the cab, I guess Daniel decided to apply the same rate for his own increasingly requested taxi services. If Jimmy didn't want to take the bus or walk, and didn't have time to call a cab either, Daniel would charge Jimmy $8 for the convenience of a ride in his car. What do you know... the accumulation of natural (financial) consequences worked like magic to get Jimmy to figure out how to make it to the bus on time!

Daniel's Answers (Age 29)
[Tell me some positive stories about Jimmy. I know he's a great guy, but I don't really know what to say.]

"He likes to give money to homeless people. He has done that a couple of times. One time we were helping someone with their computer. They were having trouble with their kid, or didn't have any groceries, so Jimmy wanted us to go out and buy groceries for them. Then he didn't charge them for helping them with their computer. He has helped someone with a brain problem with their computer. He meets people in the school computer lab who need his help. He doesn't like to charge to help them with their computer. Jimmy is really into computers and computer programming. He really likes to talk about them, even if the other person isn't interested."

PIECE 65 — SPINNING ENERGY

Daniel and his roommate are as different as night and day, but the combination is working! Daniel is as quiet as a mouse. Jimmy is talkative and outgoing, and has a loud, rambunctious, infectious laugh!

You know the cartoons where the roadrunner's speed is represented by the animation of its legs as a spinning circle? Jimmy is like the roadrunner: non-stop energy. He moves so quickly from one thing to another, and speaks so quickly that being around him is like trying to keep up with a high-speed video game. The only way to settle him down is to get him in front of a screen, to analyze a computer or become engrossed in an action movie.

Daniel would be represented in that same cartoon as the stone that the coyote hides behind to try to catch the roadrunner. The stone appears solid and impenetrable. Scientists say that even stone has molecules that move, albeit at an imperceptive, slow rate. Daniel is unmovable from his convictions. He is reliably stable and consistent. You can count on the stone to always be there; in the same place it was a few minutes ago. You'll never hear an emotional outburst from a stone! The only way to get movement out of that stone is for the coyote to shove it off a cliff.

Jimmy had a stroke as a newborn baby and has had a lifetime of epileptic seizures. He was recently diagnosed with Asperger syndrome. His wiry frame contradicts the evidence of the massive quantities of food and drink he can consume. It seems he doesn't like to wash his hair or brush his teeth. Either he is too busy to waste his time and mental energy on basic hygiene, or he doesn't like the way the toothbrush feels on his teeth and gums; maybe both.

Two jobs keep him busy. He spends every dime he makes. He doesn't drive, so he walks or takes the bus or calls a cab or gets his mom or stepfather to pick him up. Jimmy is a mess, but I say that with all fondness. You can't help but like Jimmy.

I cooked dinner for Daniel and Jimmy to celebrate their officially becoming roommates. We were all sitting in our dining room at our round glass table. Daniel pointed to the line on the lease where Jimmy needed to sign. He moved the pen so quickly and messily that Steve felt compelled to comment, "Whoa! Your signature is worse than mine!" followed by the stereotypical joke, "It's like illegible doctor's prescription scribble!"

Jimmy scowled and reprimanded Steve, "You shouldn't tease people. I have epilepsy. I've had seizures since I was small and I don't write well."

Steve wasn't used to someone being so direct. He didn't know how to react, so he kept on talking in a humorous tone. "It's not a big deal. Everybody kids about people's handwriting, and about how they can't read doctors' handwriting."

Steve and I were in the Food Market shopping for our groceries last week. We called out, "Hey, Jimmy!" and rolled our cart down the aisle toward him. He was wearing dark sunglasses inside the store.

I pointed to his glasses, "You must be on your way outside to get carts."

Jimmy s-s-s-s-speaks s-s-s-s-so quickly that the words bump into each other, flying past my ears as I try to reassemble the phonemes.

"What?" I asked.

He repeated his sentence at the same lightning speed: "*Thelightbbbbothersmyeyes.*"

"Oh, yeah, it is sunny today! Hot outside, too!"

"No...*thelightsbothermyeyes.*" He pointed toward the ceiling.

"Oh, the florescent lights?"

"Yeah."

Then I remembered that the flickering of florescent bulbs can contribute to epileptic seizures. We carried on with our grocery shopping as Jimmy went whizzing past us, returning misplaced items to their proper places on the shelves. Every time we went down a new aisle we spotted Jimmy flying from one end or the other.

PIECE 66 — "STUFF"

When I call Daniel on the phone, he answers either "Hey!" or "Hey." I say, "Hi, Daniel!" and follow with the commonly-accepted social nicety, "How are you doing?" [Silence.]

"What do you have planned today?"

[Pause.]

"Stuff."

When Daniel says "stuff" it translates to "I don't want to answer you." Or, "I am not going to elaborate." Or, "I don't know." I wonder… if I give him a yes-or-no question, instead of a fill-in-the-blank question, whether I'll get an answer.

"Did you go to work today?"

[Silence.]

"Are you playing tennis tonight?"

[Silence.]

"Where are you?"

[Silence.]

"Are you at home?"

"Uhhuh" or "Mhmm" (or some other guttural sound that doesn't mean either yes or no.)

Now I think… if I provide the answer, maybe I will get a confirmation? "It sounds like there is some noise in the background, like maybe you are at a deli or a bookstore."

[Silence.]

By this point, I give up on the questioning. I just start talking. "I went to work today. Dad is going on a bike ride this evening. This morning I put together a beef stew in the crock pot."

When I finish talking, I wait. If I am patient, Daniel may say something, but usually, it's the end of our conversation: "Seeya."

I repeat "Seeya" and hang up.

Dictionary of Daniel-ese

- "Maybe." or "Maybe so." = Yes
- "Prolly not." = Probably not. = No
- "I'm busy." = No. = Don't ask for further explanation or elaboration.
- "Pretty much." = Affirmative answer.
- "Cool." = Affirmative
- "I don't know." = answers "How are you feeling?"
- "Seeya." = Goodbye
- "Stuff" = means "I don't want to elaborate."

- "Go for it." = Affirmative answer to: "May I make a doctor's appointment for you?"
- "Baby talk." = "Don't make cooing sounds to dogs."
- "Movies are stupid." = Negative to: "Want to go to this movie with us?"
- "Tell me a story about…" = Open-ended conversation starter

Neologisms

Means "the making of new words." Daniel invents his own idiosyncratic vocabulary.

- "poww gooo." = Poor girl. (leaving our female dog home alone)
- "paw, paw pittefuhl." = Poor, poor, pitiful. (even sadder than poww gooo)
- "peeps" = People or = Family
- "lugada" = Look at the…
- "googee" = Good girl (referring to our dog)
- "lurly" (rhymes with girly) = Nickname for our female dog.
- "Sveehaagn" = Nonsense exclamation.
- "Cooger." = Cool.
- "Insane." = Extremely cool.

Minimalism

- Calls his friend "S" short for "Scott" and "Gfa" short for "Grandfather"
- Does not waste his breath on articles such as "the"
- Does not use possessives like "my." He says he is at "Providence" instead of "at your home."

Non-Verbal

Daniel doesn't talk to his dog Jada. Instead of calling her name, or simply saying, "Come," he slaps his leg. He uses all non-verbal commands with her. When it's time to go home, he leans over forward and shakes his hand near the ground as if he has a treat in his fist. That is his command for her to come to him so he can hook her leash to her collar. After watching the TV show "The Dog Whisperer," he now speaks one word, "Hey!" in a firm, deep voice to correct her behavior; or uses Cesar Millan's trademark sharp, whispery "schhht" sound.

Echolalia

Echolalia comes from the same root as the word "echo." Some of Daniel's responses simply echo, or repeat, what was just said. For example: when I ask, "How was tennis?" Daniel answers, "Tennis-y." When I ask, "Was the place you went with Dad good for biking?" Daniel answers, "Bike." Sometimes the repetition is extreme, such as the time Daniel's summer camp counselor wrote that Daniel repeated the word "Grandmother" over and over again until all his cabin-mates were rolling on the floor with laughter.

Abbreviation

Steve wrote on a square yellow Post-it-Note: "Daniel, can you show me how to use ext. hard drive?" He left it on the computer keyboard where Daniel would see it next time he came over.

Instead of asking his dad, "What does this note mean back here? Do you need help installing your hard drive?" or, "Hey, do you want me to install the hard drive for you?" He walked into the room and said: "External hard drive." He didn't even inflect it as a question. He said it like a statement.

Gesture

If I try to hand an object to Daniel, he is reluctant to take it from me. Usually, instead of saying "Will you please put it over there?" he will just point to where he wants me to put it. In the past, out of frustration, I have teased him sarcastically in a robotic voice that he *"Must conserve energy!* You wouldn't want to waste a molecule of effort, or contribute a morsel of energy to touching an object!" That usually brings a smile from him and breaks the tension I feel from his withdrawal.

Here is an example: One day we were in the car. Steve and I were in the front seats. Daniel was in the back seat. He pointed up front. I interpret his point to mean "Give me that."

I said, "What?"

[Again: a point.]

"What do you want? I don't know what you're pointing at. Tell me what you want."

[Closer point: almost touching the object.]

I refused to play his game. Finally, he reached up front and took what he wanted.

Literal Interpretations
Daniel said, "When you said 'If it gets too hot in Florida, you can come visit us,' I didn't know if you meant come stay all summer or fly up every day at noon."

Body Language
Daniel seems uncomfortable looking in my eyes. He communicates more easily if two of us are sitting parallel in the car, riding bikes, or at a baseball game, both looking straight ahead. If we must talk face to face, it is better for him if the lighting is low, so that it is difficult to discern facial features. I suppose that makes a more level playing field, since Daniel doesn't seem to "read" body language and facial expressions. When the light is low, no one can discern facial features clearly.

Slow Processing
All of the areas of Daniel's brain do not function at the same speed. It gets hung up and results in delay and frustration. He takes a moment to gather his thoughts.

Daniel's Answers (Age 29)
[About making up new words:]

"I wonder if other people do the same thing? Or if they won't get it? I assume everyone else does this too? Every family makes up their own words. That's how words catch on. It starts with a group; they make up their own language, and it spreads."

[About being non-verbal with the dog:]

"Silence is compensation for other people using baby talk with their dogs, or singing to them even, which I think is ridiculous! I have to compensate. I have to be overly strict with dogs. I despise having to do that, because I love to give dogs affection, but other people abuse that; they are not strict enough with their dogs. I learned from the Dog Whisperer Cesar Millan 'No touch, no talk, no eye contact. Dogs respond first with their nose. Respect nature the way nature is. Dogs don't talk." [About gesture:] "I would be in the middle of something, and I wondered, why don't you just set it on the table?"

[Oh, so it was like I interrupted you?]

"Yeah. You think you have to make me do something. Why can't I do it on my own time? Like the other night, when Dad was hurrying me to go to the movie, I was ignoring him on purpose. When I know someone is trying to control a situation, I'll do the opposite on purpose. It's like yesterday, when I was taking the mower out of the back of the car, I was just getting it ready to take out, but you had to control the situation."

[I thought you were going to try to take it out by yourself and hurt your back, before I could go in the house to get Dad to help you lift it.]

"It was like you thought the world's going to fall apart if you aren't in both places at once."

PIECE 67 — CIRCLE THE WAGONS

When pioneers traversed the American "Wild West" they arranged their wagons in a circle at night, which created a fortress effect and made it easier to defend themselves against predatory animals or enemies. A month before Daniel returned from his year at The Program, I realized that most of our closest friends and family did not understand what we had been going through. Because we had moved around the country so frequently, and only visited briefly at holidays, most of them remembered spending time with Daniel when he seemed to be a carefree, smiling ten-year-old boy. I wanted to "circle the wagons" by bringing together people who could help us defend Daniel against the difficulties he faced.

I wanted an opportunity to describe to them our intelligent, creative, and wonderful son, who has had trouble with seemingly simple things over the past decade. I wanted to share what I'd learned. I knew we needed their support during this critical transition. The old African proverb, "It takes a village to raise a child" was certainly true in our case.

I had read about other families in our situation which had assembled a group of people to support a disabled individual throughout their lifetime. Some groups called themselves "Circle of Friends." The night before my meeting, I located a consultant, "Ginny," who had created such a group to support her son, an adult on the autism spectrum. She agreed to facilitate our group if needed. She talked to me about how to get started.

I invited a dozen people to a lunch meeting. I explained basic information about Asperger syndrome and how it manifests specifically in Daniel. I described the unevenness: how I don't know what he knows and what he doesn't know. For example, after two years in college, he asked me, "What's registration?" and recently, when we were staying at a hotel and I said I was going downstairs to check out, he asked, "What's check out?"

I explained that because his appearance is normal, his condition is invisible. The downside to that is that sometimes people perceive his awkward mannerisms as rude or think his communication is angry, when it is not.

I asked for their help in making contacts for Daniel to help him find a job. I asked the pastor to find someone to be his "Church Buddy" to pick him up and take him to church on Sundays and to go with him to the young adult fellowship groups. Our neighbors offered to invite Daniel to dinner and to go to movies and play board games with them. My sister agreed to coordinate everyone's efforts. I felt comforted knowing there were other people involved besides me!

Email, Ginny to Nilla May 3

Nilla, You have an amazing group of friends, I must say. I don't know you well enough to understand how you've done it, but you and Steve—and Daniel—have a whole lot of love and dedication represented in that room. You did a wonderful job today, Nilla. I'm in awe! You can be very proud of yourself and your wonderful friends. Best, Ginny

PIECE 68 — SLOW MOTION

Email, Nilla to Evelyn September 8 (Daniel Age 24)
Things are going very well for Daniel, but there are many pitfalls also. The unevenness, I keep remembering. Yesterday, when Daniel came over he seemed so happy and normal, and then all of a sudden, he refused to answer my questions,

and then outright ignored me. Constantly, I have to remind myself of his "condition" so I don't fall into despair.

My "neatnik" son who always kept his room and his things organized, has now let his place become a wreck. I can't even walk in; the floor is covered in paper trash and cluttered items. Instead of filing important documents, he stuffs everything into plastic Wal-Mart bags. Last week I found his passport in one of them. I don't know what to think about this new side of Daniel. Maybe his roommate at the Program infected him with chaos, or maybe Daniel is experimenting with the freedom of having his own place

.   He hasn't been able to find a job. Finally, he met with TEACCH, and their evaluation confirmed he is on the Autism spectrum. Their referral was required to get him in to Vocational Rehabilitation, and now we're waiting for their decision whether to take Daniel on. I have to get used to the slowness of governmental bureaucracy. I have to be patient with non-profit agencies that are maxed out.

Yesterday I got a phone assessment for an intake appointment for Daniel through the local mental health agency. They wouldn't talk to me on the phone since Daniel is an "adult," so he spoke my scripting while I told him every word to say. When he told them he had a "developmental disability" they asked what kind. Again with my prompting, he said, "Asperger syndrome." They said "That's not classified as a developmental disability."

To get services from them, we might have to say he has high functioning autism—which maybe he has, anyway. There is a thin line dividing Asperger syndrome and High Functioning Autism.

The funny part is they told him, "Oh, you have Bill Gates Disease!" We laughed and laughed over that one. I think that made Daniel feel good for the first time about his diagnosis. So from now on I think that's what I'll say.

PIECE 69 — GOOD WILL

I had been begging Daniel for months to get new clothes. He had lost so much weight that his clothes were falling off of him, or he had a belt cinching the fabric into multiple folds. I had offered to take him shopping, to pay for his clothes, to buy clothes for him for Christmas, whatever. Always, his answer was, "No."

One afternoon, Daniel called my cell phone. "If it would work into your plans… I'm at Goodwill. Would you come help me decide which clothes to buy?"

"Sure."

When I arrived a few minutes later, he showed me the shopping cart he had filled over the past few hours—full to overflowing, containing dozens and dozens of khaki slacks and collared shirts. He couldn't decide how to eliminate and how to choose which ones to buy.

He had taken them all off the hangers. He didn't know to leave them ON the hangers until he decided which ones to keep. "Concentrate on what's important here, Nilla," I reminded myself, "This is not the time to instruct him on proper store etiquette. Just be proud of him that he has made it into a store and he is actually choosing new clothes." Temporarily, I had to let go of my ingrained sense of obligation to behave perfectly in public, always considerate of the sales clerks.

I shuffled through the stack, speaking aloud my opinion about each pair, hoping he might learn from my process of elimination. "This one has a spot on it. … This one is too long and would need hemming. … Wow! This is a great pair, from Nordstrom, a fancy, expensive store! … These were custom made. … This fabric is flimsy. ... Put these back. ... These look like new! This one still has the tag on it! I can't believe these only cost $3.75 a pair! ... Great prices!"

The entire wardrobe, consisting of 7 slacks, 5 collared knit shirts, two dress shirts, and a couple of sweaters came to a total of only $72, so I gladly offered to pay for them all.

"Cool!"

PIECE 70 — ODD JOBS

Computer Programmer
From age 17, Daniel worked summers doing computer programming, first for his uncle in Atlanta, then for friends Steve and I knew. In each workplace he was a valuable member of the team. His colleagues were impressed with the code he wrote.

Court Sweeper
I showed Daniel a want-ad in the paper: *Indoor Tennis Center needs part-time attendant to answer phones, take court reservations, to sweep the courts, and keep facility well maintained and clean. $7/hour.* The person who interviewed him realized he was my son. She and I used to play tennis together! Her children had also attended Daniel's private elementary school. He was hired. He worked there until he returned to college.

Pharmacy Deliverer
The job Daniel found delivering prescriptions for a pharmacy (which he loved doing!) lasted only two days. He unintentionally offended the manager with a casual comment made to a co-worker who was training him (which the manager overheard.) Daniel was not able to

"mend" his conversation by explaining to her what he actually meant, so she told him to leave immediately. Daniel is a kind person and *never* says an unkind word about anyone. He was just trying to figure out how to do the job. It was an Asperger-typical, confusing situation. He had not disclosed his disability to the manager when he applied, so I'm sure she assumed he was being rude.

Honey Pourer
One odd job Daniel found on his own, though the Employment Security Commission, involved pouring honey from huge vats. By the end of the day, honey coated Daniel's skin, hair, clothing, and stuck to everything he touched in his car. One day was all he could stand of that.

Screen Printer
Our next door neighbors had a small screen printing business. They had one skilled full-time employee who set up the screens. They hired unskilled temporary part timers to spread the ink on t-shirts and run them through the dryer assembly. Daniel usually worked by himself in a dingy, open warehouse with no heat or air conditioning.

Project Programmer
Daniel's Uncle Kirk is an experienced computer programmer. He was too busy to take on a well-paying assignment, so he passed it along to Daniel. It could be done over the internet, so geography wasn't a factor. Kirk knew Daniel's capabilities; he had seen the programming "code" he had written before. Daniel was very skilled at this kind of work. This job would pay five or six times what Daniel was earning by screen printing or loading cars.

Halfway through the project, Daniel wasn't getting paid as contracted, and the client wasn't returning his phone calls or emails. Steve and I were puzzled. Daniel didn't know what to do about it. Daniel's Aunt Sally volunteered to step in to help him straighten out the communication glitches. Finally, he was paid.

Computer Whisperer

I told Daniel he is like the "Dog Whisperer" in getting people's home computers to behave, so he should print business cards calling himself a "Computer Whisperer."

Lumber Loader

His job coach Erika helped him improve his resume and applications. She applied online for him to Home Supply; he interviewed, and was hired as parking lot attendant. His job was to collect the carts and load heavy items into cars.

The first day he took a training program in their home office. He did not go to the bathroom all day because he didn't know if he was allowed to take a break. No one had told him when he could take a break; no one had shown him the restrooms.

The next week the temperature was in the upper 90s. Daniel wore heavy black denim jeans and got a terrible friction rash from sweating. He could barely walk the rest of the week.

The following week his car was broken into. He had parked it in the side lot, which was more isolated. He had to pay to have his window replaced, which cost more than the money he made all week.

The next day he told his dad he wanted to figure out a route to ride his bike to work so he wouldn't have to drive his car there anymore. Home Supply is located on the busiest, high-traffic, commercial four-lane road in town.

One day Daniel smashed his hand, pinched it in between some lumber and a cart. His hand was still bloody when he arrived at the steak restaurant where our extended family met for dinner. His brother David noticed his hand caked in dried blood; asked him what had happened, and told him he needed to go wash his hands with soap and warm water.

Other than those personal difficulties, Daniel performed well at Home Supply for a number of months until he developed some intestinal problems, which became so severe he had to quit work. Maybe he had bathroom issues there. Maybe he found himself way out in the parking lot when he needed to use the bathroom. Maybe he thinks the strain of heavy lifting caused his anal fissure, even though the doctors told him that would not generally be the cause.

His next job coach arrived just in time to help him deal with this difficulty and helped him negotiate unpaid time off. She helped Daniel communicate with his boss, who was very understanding, until the busy season returned. At that point he advised Daniel that it would be better for him to quit than to be fired.

AmeriCorps

Daniel volunteered through the public library to help seniors with computer basics. He taught them how to use a mouse... one senior was using his mouse like it was a TV remote control, lifting it in his hand and pointing it at the computer!

The volunteer coordinator must have been impressed with him because she recommended him for this annual position with AmeriCorps. Daniel would be paid a small stipend, to cover basic living expenses. We all agreed that this would be a good opportunity for Daniel and a good addition to his resume; plus, a full-time schedule would bring consistency to his life. Daniel was hired and decided to accept. He worked with "One Economy" to help the poor get access to computers and internet through a program called "Resources Unlimited" It was a stretch for him, but gave him increased confidence.

He was sent to Chicago for a week for training. What an amazing accomplishment, that he was able to complete the training. Knowing this was a team-building training, and how difficult social events are for him, I liken it to his surviving a year as a soldier in combat. I am so proud of him.

Daniel called us the night before the "swearing-in" ceremony and said he thought he needed to quit and come home. I "read between the lines" that he didn't feel comfortable making an oath. I sensed that he was taking this more seriously than most people do. Because of their "literal thinking," many people with Asperger syndrome are obsessed with truth; Daniel cannot tell a lie.

I assured him that this was not a life or death declaration. As long as he intended to do his best for the organization, I explained, that was the context. You promise to do the best you can, but it is not like a marriage vow or swearing on the Bible. That seemed to quell his anxiety somewhat.

Steve and I held our breath for 24 hours, wondering if he was on a flight home. But he made it through! That was a miraculous achievement.

The busier, the better: having a consistent routine seems to be wonderful for him. He taught classes one night a week and sometimes taught classes on Saturdays. I couldn't get over the thought that Daniel was TEACHING others!

Work Study

While he took classes toward his Associate's Degree, the Financial Aid office approved 10-20 hours per week at $9/hour for Daniel doing web design, graphic design data entry and content management for the community college.

Tech Supporter

In late December, Daniel resigned from the web development position to accept a temporary (four to six month) job at a national bank. He and 100 others were hired and trained as support techs to fix computer glitches during a huge corporate transition. Daniel would advise un-technical stockbrokers by phone, and would be able to control their desktop remotely over the internet. Unfortunately, the company over-estimated their needs. The majority of computer techs were laid off within the first two months. Daniel was once again out of a job.

Daniel's Answers (Age 29)

[Do you remember what happened with the pharmacy delivery job?]
    "I didn't like that lady!"
    [Oh, then maybe it's good you didn't keep that job.]
    "I don't remember the words I said, but I felt like she totally overreacted to whatever it was. I didn't like being in the pharmacy,

anyway. The part I liked was being out on my own, making the deliveries."

[Do you remember the bathroom issues at Home Supply?]

"It was hard to get an opportunity to use the restroom. It was a *huge* warehouse. It took five minutes to get to the restrooms, way in the back, then five minutes to use the restroom, then five minutes to get back out front, all while they were paging you, 'Daniel Childs, report to loading, Daniel Childs, report to loading.' so there was a lot of pressure."

PIECE 71 — FIRE WALLS

In November, "One Economy" (the agency that is sponsoring Daniel's position this year at AmeriCorps) paid all expenses to send him and two others to California to help communities devastated by the massive wildfires there. Their group of three established five computer labs in five different poverty-stricken communities.

Several weeks before they went, Daniel told us it was a possibility that he would go. We thought Daniel had misunderstood something.

Several days before they went, Daniel told us they were going. He had known for a week, but hadn't told us yet, even though we needed to keep his dog while he was gone, and even though we could have helped him prepare for the trip.

The day he left, *I* was crying and anxious because I didn't know if anyone knew about Daniel's Asperger syndrome. Since AS is an invisible disability, they may have assumed he was fine and failed to give him clear instructions. I imagined the worst. My friend Lisa called the trip leader and explained the situation. The guy did know about Daniel's AS. He had met him in Chicago at the orientation. He asked if there was anything he could do. Lisa just emphasized speaking clearly, making sure Daniel understood, etc. I felt so much better after overhearing her conversation.

I could tell Daniel was nervous about the travel aspect. I offered to drive him to the airport, to which he responded, "Cool."

On the way to the airport, he wanted to listen to an educational CD about physics (instead of talking to me.) I asked him if he planned to listen to the CDs on the plane. He said he didn't have a CD player. I went into the airport gift shop and bought a portable CD player with headphones. He was reluctant for me to spend the money, but I knew it would be worth it to help keep his mind distracted from worry and annoyances of travel. He listened to that CD series the whole way there and back.

Daniel's Answers (Age 29)

"I didn't know you contacted my supervisor. This was like you going behind my back and doing something you didn't have my permission to do. That makes me want to tell you even less, if you are going to do something like that."

[So it makes you trust me less?]

"Yeah."

[I'm sorry.]

PIECE 72 — UNEVEN

We learned that Daniel has cancelled all of his appointments with psychiatrists and psychologists. Also, he abruptly stopped taking his medications for depression and anxiety; although it is essential that all such medicines be tapered off gradually to avoid withdrawal symptoms. He has quit attending his *one* class at our local community college. No luck with a job. He does have a job coach now.

We continue to be on a roller coaster ride of violent ups and downs. Every day is uneven. That is my new title for Daniel's life: Uneven. Uneven-ups and uneven-downs. Buckle up for a wild ride, and keep your hands inside at all times. Do not try to stand up.

Uneven-up: Daniel travelled *on his own* to Washington D.C. for pleasure. He had a free airplane voucher to use before it expired. Steve and I were so proud of his independence and adventurousness. He stayed in a youth hostel for $40/night instead of hotel $200+/night. Good move. He specifically intended to go to a certain art show called "Post Secrets" he had discovered online.

Uneven-down: When he booked his flight (two months ago?) I reminded him to consider the dates/times the exhibit was open. The night before he left, I looked online and found the exhibit would be closed the entire time he was in D.C. I called to tell him that, and he said, "Well then, there's no point in going at all." Steve and I were upset then, discouraged that he would cancel, when there is so much else to see in D.C.! All night, I tossed and turned. All the next day, I assumed he was hiding out in his dark, quiet apartment by himself. I called him several times, with no answer.

Uneven-up: Around 5 p.m. he finally returned my phone call from the airport! He went anyway!

Uneven-down: The whole time he was gone I worried (and family and friends with whom I discussed his trip participated in my anxiety) that he could be mugged, beaten up, that his money could be stolen, etc., in D.C. My imagination went to all four corners of dread.

Uneven-up: He was fine! He survived. He made it to the plane both ways and found the youth hostel on his own! He slept 12 hours each night, 7 p.m. to 7 a.m.

Uneven-down: Next day, he called us 8 a.m. in front of a museum, saying nothing opened until 10 a.m. (Daniel had picked up AAA guidebooks months before his trip and could have figured out opening times, maps, addresses, phone numbers, etc. I would have been glad to go over them with him. Also, the front desk at the international youth hostel is accustomed to guiding foreign young people with all kinds of information. He could have accessed that before walking outside that morning.) He said he was cold and didn't know where to go. This was *December—in below-freezing temperatures!* We tried to think of coffee shops, book stores, etc. Steve used his visual/ spatial skills to remember directions to tell Daniel which way to walk.

Uneven-up: Monday morning, as soon as the "Post Secrets" museum's office opened, I called them (my typical, maternal, co-dependent intervention) and explained the situation, and arranged for a (miraculous, fluke!) special appointment for Daniel to see the exhibit, even though it was closed that day. Someone agreed to meet him there at 2:30 that afternoon.

Uneven-down: I sat anxiously by the phone for hours and hours, minute by minute, hoping and praying he would call me so I could tell him this amazing news: I had secured an appointment to the exhibit he wanted to see! Daniel never called. I couldn't get a message to him. Finally, I had to call the museum and cancel the special favor. Daniel had turned his phone off (he was trying to save battery power, since he didn't take the power cord with him.) He didn't check his voice mail all day, even though I had told him I would try to see if I could work something out with the museum, to try to pull any strings I could. He says the voice mail didn't cycle through—didn't show the voice mail icon on his phone. But, he could have called me anyway, to check in.

Uneven-up: Daniel loved the Smithsonian's Air and Space Museum so much he spent two entire days there.

Uneven-down: Daniel did not take *any* luggage with him. No toothbrush, no deodorant, no extra underwear or socks. He was away for two nights and three days of travel on airplanes and trains, not to mention walking all over the city. The thought was too disgusting for me to imagine. And, it was so cold, Steve and I were thinking how he would have been so much warmer and more comfortable if he could have taken a hot shower at the hostel and warmed up in fresh clothes.

Uneven-up: Without luggage, he was free to move around with no worries about keeping up with heavy gear, or where to store things, or how much earlier to leave for the airport to account for baggage claim, security, etc.

Uneven-down: We felt remotely sorry for his roommates at the youth hostel, who had to tolerate his loud snoring and probably hideous body odor.

Uneven-up: He actually communicated with us when he returned! He said he had a great time and was so glad he went. He told us some things about his trip. He told us one person in his hostel room was from China, one from Spain, one was a university student. This solo journey seemed to boost his confidence.

Daniel's Answers (Age 29)

"When I read 'we felt sorry for his roommates at the hostel' I thought that was weird that you would worry about it, someone you had never met, from across the world. I shouldn't have to tell you this, but I remember taking showers there. I might not have had a change of clothes, but I did shower. You were just imagining things."

PIECE 73 — ARUGULA

Jambalaya (Daniel Age 24)

Daniel and David "cooked" dinner for Steve and me to celebrate our wedding anniversary (at my request/ insistence?) It was the most boring, bland food I've eaten, but delicious because it was the first meal cooked in Daniel's kitchen. They used a boxed mix for Jambalaya (basically spicy rice) and added a can of kidney beans and leftover chicken. They forgot tomato sauce. They heated up bread. Steve kept reminding me (at least a half dozen times) to stay out of the kitchen and let them bring it to us.

Nutritionist

I arranged for a county extension "home economics" agent, wonderful Maxine, to provide weekly nutrition lessons for Daniel over several months. They prepared a few meals together. She showed him the food pyramid and discussed healthy food choices. She took him to the grocery store to review product labels. Daniel asked her how long it was safe to keep foods in the refrigerator or freezer.

Email, Nilla to Evelyn (Daniel Age 25)

Evelyn, You'll like this: the psychiatrist (I'm told he is the best in town... I have informed him about AS... but he still doesn't seem to "get it.") seemed puzzled when I said I still had to help Daniel figure out what to eat, since Daniel couldn't manage.

"Why not?" he asked?

"Because of his autism," I answered.

"What do you mean? What did he do before?"

"Go through the drive through or eat crackers out of boxes."

The psychiatrist shrugged his shoulders, dismissing my concern. "I think Daniel is cognitively able to plan his meals..." and went on to his summary.

I can relate to his confusion, because we were certainly bewildered for years about why/ how this smart young man couldn't / wouldn't fix a sandwich for himself. We thought he was just lazy and wanted someone else to do it for him. Instead of my getting exasperated again by the misunderstanding of professionals, I take a step back and try to realize that they are new to this mystery. I have lived with it for years. All I can do is to figure out new ways of explaining, to try to express the needs... and it helps immensely to have someone like you who understands! —Nilla

Nilla's Diary February 24 (Daniel Age 26)

I bought beets he requested, for him to bake in the oven, like a potato, wrapped in foil. They were delicious!

Nilla's Diary Spring (Daniel Age 26)
Daniel made soft ginger cookies from the recipe his Grandfather had given him. He doubled the recipe. He had never made anything like it. It took him four and a half hours, from 7 p.m. until 11:30 p.m. He followed every instruction exactly. I was available to answer his questions or to find measuring cups or mixing bowls.

Email, Daniel to Nilla April 15 (Daniel Age 26)
I'm glad you told me about frozen bread! This Ezekiel bread is good.

Nilla's Diary Spring (Daniel Age 27)
Daniel is going through a phase now where he is experimenting with foods. He went to the produce department and bought six or eight foods he had never heard of, that have bizarre names... rutabaga, persimmon, arugula, etc. Foods I have never bought or prepared before. He found instructions on the internet on how to prepare them.

Daniel's Answers (Age 29)
[What are you laughing about? The sandwich thing again?]

"It's just your funny interpretation. I mean, bread disguises the flavor of everything else. Like, you could buy deli turkey that cost $12 per pound, and pay $2 for a loaf of bread, and only taste the bread."

[So that's why you eat deli meat plain!]

"It just shows how dogmatic Dad is, that he eats the same kind of sandwich every day, made in the same way, or back when he used to eat at Murphy's Lunch every day. And Jimmy, I look at him funny when we go someplace nice to eat breakfast, and he always gets the same thing, like maybe, bacon and eggs. I mean, why go to some restaurant where you can get all kinds of good stuff?"

[Yes, I know you do like to try new foods.]

"You have to be aware of the lens you are looking at it with. And when you say 'eats crackers out of boxes,' crackers come in boxes, don't they? If you have crackers, eat them. If you don't want them, don't buy them."

PIECE 74 — MOMENTUM

Two things changed Daniel's life substantially for the better: a 12 pound dog named Jada and a skinny 125 pound roommate named Jimmy. Those two would improve Daniel's functioning more than any expensive year-long "treatment program," dozens of hours of therapy, or a job coach.

Email, Nilla to Esther March 3 (Daniel Age 24)

Esther, Thank you for asking. It is such a blessing to hear from you and to know that you are praying for our family faithfully. Thank you, thank you, and thank you. We need your prayers. Other than needing a job (desperately) Daniel is doing so well now. He is building strong positive *momentum*, as you will see in this list of twelve major accomplishments:

1. Daniel has a new dog. Having a creature to take care of gives him a feeling of purpose, I assume.

2. He has a new (only) friend, a young man his age who also has Asperger syndrome. Jimmy is upbeat and enthusiastic. Daniel, who usually has "flat" (blank) facial expressions, seems more "bouncy" after he's been around Jimmy.

3. Daniel's younger brother David has a wonderful influence on him, getting him to recover from failing an accounting test. Daniel didn't return to class after he failed the first test. With David's prodding, Daniel went back to class and even went to talk to the teacher after class (a huge accomplishment) and she agreed to let him re-take the test!

4. Then Daniel went to the disabilities office (another huge accomplishment) to request a tutor. Unfortunately, the (only) accounting tutor was unavailable, so Daniel failed the second

test. Keep in mind; this is a student who used to make mostly "A" grades. I can't understand how he can't understand the material of a basic managerial accounting class.

5. Daniel has been making to-do lists for himself and getting things done... like, taking the ten bags of cans, bottles, etc. piling up in his apt. to the recycling center. He's checking off his list all the annoying things that we avoid when we're paralyzed by depression.

6. Daniel "called a meeting" with me to say he needs help ("Asking for Help" is a huge accomplishment!) He made a list of what he needs help with:
   - planning meals,
   - shopping,
   - cooking,
   - cleaning his apartment,
   - exercising,
   - finding a job, and
   - friendship.

7. Daniel's Job Coach has missed so many appointments, rescheduled, called in sick, or just didn't show up and never called. They've had confusion over meetings. She says it's Daniel who has missed the meetings. He says no. So, anyway, I'm going to meet with both of them this afternoon to make sure they actually do get together.

8. Daniel is willing to go to a Social Group for adult men with Asperger syndrome that meets in Greensboro twice a month. (Friendship)

9. I convinced Daniel to start a "Happy Book:" a journal for himself of all these good things that are happening, to keep so that when times get low again, he can review it and remind himself of natural ups and downs, to encourage him to keep on going. We laughed and laughed over that one.

10. Daniel likes having David's fiancée Andrea around. She and David will be married in June. I had falsely assumed that Daniel

would have felt jealous or lonelier with his brother having a steady girlfriend, but instead it seems to boost Daniel's feeling of being surrounded by more and more people who love him. She is wonderful toward Daniel, too, and can get him into long conversations.

11. Daniel went with our family to a surprise 40th birthday party for our next door neighbor Fred, given by his wife, Jackie. This couple has been particularly supportive of Daniel. It was a very formal, crowded, wonderful party, at Southern Country Club, but a very stressful situation for someone with social phobia and panic attacks to endure. He survived it—well! Daniel was the only one of us to think of getting Fred a birthday gift—a blockbuster gift certificate... they often discuss movies.

12. Daniel went with Steve and me to an artists' potluck gathering where one of the artists was showing slides from their trip to India.

Well, Esther, you can see that there are many positive things happening for Daniel. We are all so proud of him, and I can see that he is proud of himself, too. Thank you again for your prayers. I know you weren't expecting an epistle of a response, but it is cathartic for me to get it down "in writing." So thanks for asking! Nilla

Email, Esther to Nilla March 3 (Daniel Age 24)

Oh, Dear, Nilla, What to say, I can see that my asking has opened up the flood-gates for you, so I'm glad that I asked. Now you can see why I'm grateful that God has given me this very private and quiet ministry. I encourage you to keep being encouraged. You are exactly the mother Daniel needs and he is exactly the child you need. Now, the question is to find out how to glorify God in the process. The best to the both of you! It's worth the battle. It sounds like you are a needed "communicator." That sounds very encouraging, because neither of them, the job coach nor Daniel seems to be able to handle the task of communicating with each other. It seems like Daniel is beginning to understand the need for community. We do shrivel up when we're alone too much. Lovingly, Esther

Daniel's Answers (Age 29)
[Do you still have the "Happy Book?"]
  "Yeah."
    [Do you ever look at it?]
    "Yeah, I look at it occasionally."

PIECE 75 — LEADERSHIP

Email, forwarded from Nilla to Daniel (Daniel Age 26)
The North Carolina Youth Leadership Forum Planning Committee is pleased to announce YLF to be held this July. Anyone who lives in North Carolina, has *any* disability, and is between ages 16-28 is eligible to attend. It will be an intensive four day event focusing on involving young people in the disability community and preparing them to organize locally through advocacy, direct action, and community mobilization.

By incorporating themes of pride, community-based leadership, and accountability, delegates will have the opportunity to develop leadership skills, become equipped with invaluable tools and resources, and expand their identity as well-rounded persons with disabilities.

We will be selecting 40 delegates from all across North Carolina to attend. We are specifically looking for youth with disabilities who have some leadership experience or who show leadership potential. The forum, including lodging, food, and accommodations, will be at no cost for delegates.

Email, Nilla to David
Daniel was *accepted* to the North Carolina Youth Leadership Forum for Students with Disabilities! He is so proud! It will be a great opportunity for him. Yippee!

Email, forwarded from YLF Planning Committee

Hey Daniel, I wanted to know if you mind two other people being in the car with you. You would have a total of 3 people. The two new people have service dogs that will be coming with them. Is that ok with you? If not please let me know. There would be a total of two dogs.

Email, Daniel to Nilla

Can we trade cars for the YLF so I can fit all these people?

Daniel did drive three other people to the conference. He got lost getting to their homes, but figured it out, and arrived a little bit late. He made the most of the conference. He met people with all sorts of disabilities from all over the state. Since then, he has stayed in contact with his group, which has met again to work on the issue they were studying.

Later, he traveled with a group of people with disabilities to the state capital to join a "march" seeking equal rights. The Youth Leadership Forum helped Daniel to develop confidence, and it helped him to get to know other people who are also "different" from "normal" which gave him a sense of community and belonging.

Daniel's Answers (Age 29)

"The real benefit of YLF was not about gaining leadership skills. I think you can get that at any conference. What was unique was to be around people you don't get to be around every day. That was the ONLY advantage to The Program, being around the group. That's why I didn't like college, because everybody is perfect, and I don't like being around perfect people."

[Why don't you like being around perfect people?]

"It's just not fun."

STEP SIX
FITTING TOGETHER

Nilla's Method for Completing a Jigsaw Puzzle
    1.   First, I turn all the pieces out of the box.
    2.   I plop the pieces onto the table into a big jumbled pile.
    3.   Turning over each upside-down piece right-side up, I begin to see what I have.
    4.   Next is finding edges—pieces with straight edges form the outer border.
    5.   I look for matching details like fragments of words, faces or shapes.
    6.   I start fitting together complementary pieces to form the central design.

The puzzling pace picks up as the outer edge is in place, and pieces with similar colors are grouped near each other. It's time to connect pieces! The speed varies. Sometimes it's slow, and sometimes you get "in the zone" and almost without looking, from your peripheral vision, you move a piece into place.

Some jigsaw puzzle pieces are shaped like little people. They almost look like they have a curvy head on top, two curvy arms out by the sides, and two curvy legs below. When you find two pieces that fit together easily, it is almost as satisfying as getting together two people who become friends. You feel responsible for and proud of the connection.

You can also tell when a piece just doesn't fit quite right. At first it might seem to fit, but if you are honest, you can tell something is off. Better to remove it now and wait until you find the exact right spot for it later.

PIECE 76 — BROKEN HEARTED

Daniel's roommate Jimmy had been trying to get things together so he could ask his girlfriend Lauren to marry him. Lauren's family took them out for dinner regularly. Lauren often gave Jimmy rides to work. They enjoyed their time together; they were close, close friends.

Late one afternoon as I was driving home from work, I passed Daniel's roommate Jimmy out walking. I assumed he was on his way to work at the Food Market. I stopped to ask him if he needed a ride. He looked dazed, confused. Tears were streaming down his face.

"What's wrong, Jimmy?"

Once he got in the car, I turned into a parking lot and pulled the car over so I could listen to him. "mliuom… bildw… .mlkndel… mnrftu…." He was crying so hard I couldn't understand what he was saying.

"What did you say?"

"Lauren broke up with me."

"Oh, honey, I am so sorry." He sobbed some more. I rubbed his back, trying to offer some kind of comfort.

"I was going to marry that girl."

"I know you were, honey, I know."

[Silence]

"Here you go." I handed him a tissue. "David and Andrea and

their dog Finnegan are coming over tonight. Daniel and Jada are coming over too. I'm cooking. Would you like to come over and hang out? You are welcome to be by yourself if you want to be quiet, or watch TV in the den, or join us, whatever you feel up to. You don't have to talk about it unless you want to."

"Yeah, that would be good."

I turned the car around and drove home, passing their apartment a mile before our house.

Jimmy sat in the living room. I brought him a glass of water and a few cookies, a box of Kleenex, and a throw blanket. "Make yourself at home. Is there anything else you need?"

"I don't think so."

"Do you want to borrow my cell phone? You can call your stepfather and tell him you are over here, so that when your mom gets home, she will know where you are and she can call you here on my cell phone." Jimmy didn't have a cell phone because in the past he had run up bills from impulsively using online features. I knew when his mother returned she would be calling his land line at their apartment and not getting any answer and then she would worry about him.

David and Andrea pulled up. I went out to the car to explain what was going on. They understood the impact that would have on Jimmy. They went in and consoled him, "Hi, Jimmy. I am so sorry to hear about Lauren. I know you must be heart-broken."

"Thanks, yeah. It's really hard."

Steve drove home from work. I went out to prepare him as well. He came in and sat down in the living room. "Hey, Jimmy. I'm sorry to hear about Lauren. Yeah, that's really tough. I had the same thing happen to me when I was your age. I moved all the way across the country with my girlfriend freshman year in college. As a matter of fact, her name was also 'Lauren.' She broke up with me the day we arrived. There I was, 3000 miles from home, and I didn't know a soul. I know from experience that it really hurts."

Dinner was almost ready when Daniel walked Jada up the sidewalk on her leash. Steve went out to let Daniel know what had happened to Jimmy so he would know why Jimmy was sitting in the living room, and to suggest that he go in and comfort Jimmy.

Daniel wouldn't go in the same room as Jimmy. He walked through the front door, past the living room, and stood fixed in the kitchen. He didn't speak to Jimmy. He seemed not to have heard what Steve said. I turned from the carrots I was peeling for the salad, and reiterated to Daniel, "Lauren broke up with Jimmy today. Why don't you go in there and tell him you are sorry to hear that?"

[No response.]

The timer dinged, letting me know the corn was fully boiled. Steve went outside to bring the steaks in from the grill. Minutes later, Jimmy walked in from the living room.

"Hey." Daniel said to Jimmy.

"Hey." Jimmy replied.

We all fixed our plates and went into the dining room to sit down together.

Daniel's Answers (Age 29)

[Why didn't you tell Jimmy you were sorry?]

"Most people don't personalize telling someone they are sorry for a hurt. They don't personalize it. I think of friendship as being ongoing, about actions. It's about sticking around; and being a part of someone's life. It's not about just a couple of words like, 'I'm sorry.' It's more about what you do. For me personally, if I've gone through something, the last thing I want is to walk into a room and be bombarded by people walking up to talk to you. I try to put myself in their shoes. How would I like to be treated? I thought, if I didn't like it, maybe he wouldn't either. It's like Cesar Millan, the Dog Whisperer, says, 'No touch, no talk, no eye contact. Just keep moving.' When people walk into his pack, he instructs them to act like they don't see them. You need to act confident. It's all about your energy. Once you've established an understanding, then you can do the other thing, like give dogs affection. I'd rather take a dog on a walk than to give them affection. I think that's the best thing for them."

PIECE 77 — SILENCE

How can I possibly use words, the antithesis of silence, to express the depth of the silence I experience regularly from the son I love more than life itself?

If my child were deaf, at least we could communicate through gestures or lip reading or sign language.

But the silence is nothingness.

The non-response is a void, like the matter-less vacuum of outer space.

Look at this blank page

for the same amount of time

that you would spend

reading a page full of words.

That is how long the silence lasts.

I ask a question, and the pause is

one,

    two,

        three,

            four,

                five,

                    six,

                        sometimes seven

                          seconds long,

                        or longer,

and that is only the times when he intends to answer my question. It simply takes him a while to process what I have asked him, then a while for him to process what he thinks, and then a few more seconds to form what he wants to say.

Daniel saves his words. He doles them out sparingly. He conserves energy, not exerting any unnecessary expenditure. Why use two words if one word will suffice? Why speak at all if a head nod will do? Why nod if silence will result in inevitable action?

His face gives no clues. He has no expression on his face. Psychologists call that blankness a "flat affect."

His eyes are not turned toward me, so I cannot look into them, searching for human existence in their depth.

His body guards him, as if he is a statue, no, a plain stone, not even carved as a statue is, because a statue has been shaped by human hands. This rock is untouched, unaffected. It is solid, hard, and cold. It never moves. His body is like a wall, concrete, flat, smooth enough so that nothing sticks to it; it provides no footholds.

Daniel's Answers (Age 29)

"I realized I could go without saying anything. I learned I could get by without responding. In school, you are trained that way, in class, you are trained to sit and listen to a lecture for an hour, and asking questions is seen as an interruption. The way I remember it, in most places, it would always be like us as a family. Somebody would always monopolize the conversation. Even if someone would ask me a question, Dad would take over from there. It was like Dad just asks me a specific question if he needs help with his story, like, 'Daniel, what was the name of that...' or 'what was that website...' and that was the only way he would acknowledge me, was to help him to remember the name of something. It was like Dad and Rich would be talking the whole time and go on like I wasn't really there."

PIECE 78 — GREAT OUTDOORS

One of the finest gifts Steve has given to me and our family is the gift of the great outdoors. It is truly the way he restores the life in me. Even though I love being outside, I usually remain indoors, immobilized by the faulty thinking that I have important things I have to do. For some reason, maybe I have "threshold paralysis," but I just don't do what I love most: go outside.

Once I am outdoors, I have no trouble noticing the beauty all around me. I breathe deeply the fresh air my stale lungs need so much. I admire every detail I see: purple flowers contrasting the deep green color of spring grass, varieties of bark and leaves, squirrels darting tree to tree. Naturally, I appreciate the glorious sunshine and I am awed by dramatic clouds at sunset. I love to feel myself moving along with the world, whether it is one foot in front of the other, or gliding down a hill balanced on a bike, feeling the breeze stroking my cheeks.

Steve is my initiator. He arranges for us to go outside and do things together, whether it is to take the dogs on a walk, ride bikes, or to go snow skiing. He is the one who makes an appointment I cannot cancel with any flimsy excuse. He gets all the equipment together. He pumps up the bike tires, adjusts the brakes, and puts the bikes in the car with our helmets. He tells me what the weather is so I know whether to wear a jacket or long sleeves. He schedules weekend hikes in the mountains and overnight camping trips, suggesting his favorite destinations and routes. He gets together all the backpacks, cooking paraphernalia, tents, sleeping bags, and plans and packs the food. He gets everything in the car, ready to go. What a gift!

Baby Backpack

When Daniel was old enough to walk, Steve gave him a tiny backpack big enough to hold his own diaper and took the three of us hiking to see a mountain waterfall.

Summer Camping

Once David was old enough, Steve and his brother Kirk planned campouts each summer for all the cousins, along with a couple of other fathers and their children. They hiked in to a location with a top-secret swimming hole in the North Carolina mountains where they jumped off rocks and splashed around in the creek on a hot summer day. They carved sticks to roast marshmallows over the campfire at night.

Autumn Beauty

One gorgeous Saturday when Daniel was nine and David was six, Steve loaded our four bikes on our car rack. We headed for the Virginia foothills to ride along old railroad tracks that followed alongside a river. The gravel trail was a perfect surface for the boys because it was level. It was a golden October day with leaves of all colors falling across the trail. A day we would all remember forever.

September Wonder

When we lived out west, Steve and I surprised the boys one Friday when they came home from school. "Put away your book bags. We're going camping this weekend! We've packed everything for you—yes, even your pocketknives." We found a campsite near Jenny Lake at the foot of the Tetons. Soon we were off to explore trails around the lake and the rocky banks of the Snake River. I sat on a boulder and peeled apples for our dinner cobbler. Steve gathered firewood for the campfire. Daniel and David hopped from rock to rock.

Ten year old Daniel described what happened after dinner, after nightfall: "We went out to that big boulder by the river. Dad said, 'Get ready to look for shooting stars.' About 20 seconds later, I was lying down with my hands behind my head and I looked up and I saw a shooting star and it was as big as the moon! It was green and blue and red and lit up the whole sky. And then I kept yelling, 'Were those fireworks? Were those fireworks?' And Dad said it must have been lightning, because he was turned the other way and missed it. But I said it was REAL big. You could see the tail and a ball at the end. A half second after you saw it, it exploded into all these little dots. The ball was the size of the moon and when it shattered it was even bigger."

The man from the next campsite came running up, "Did you see that? It was a meteor! It was the brightest I've ever seen, and I've been looking at them my whole life. I've never seen one as bright as that!" We wondered if we would find a crater in the earth in the morning. Gradually, the exhilaration of that sighting mellowed as sleep began to take over. Our lullaby was the eerie, part screech, part melodious cry of the elk, called bugling, the resonant sound the male elk make during mating season.

Annual Adventures
The older the boys got, the more elaborate the camping trips became. First they explored areas in the Southeast, and then they traveled to the Colorado Rockies, the Idaho Sawtooths, and southern Idaho, where Steve pulled them up onto a big boulder when a momma moose approached.

Deep Powder
Our first family ski adventure was to Grand Targhee in Wyoming during Christmas vacation. The weather was so bitterly cold that we had to wear face masks to ward off the frostbite.

Later, when we lived out west, the guys developed an addiction to the fresh, dry, powdery snow that Utah ski resorts are known to deliver. When the weather predicted snowfall, Steve would start looking for special deals on lift tickets. The guys skied through the trees, swooshing down the mountain, as smoothly as if they were dolphins gliding through water. As they followed each other downhill, they whooped yelps of joy like wild animals.

Naturally Healing

Nature is the great equalizer. Indoors, Daniel is obligated to perform appropriate eye contact, just-firm-enough handshakes, and proper conversational techniques. David, who in a school classroom displays classic symptoms of attention deficit hyperactivity disorder, thrives outdoors. In nature, the focus is taken off of minor human interactions and is expanded to enjoying the fullness of God's creation. Social expectations are null and void. Outdoors, Daniel does not have any disability. His only disability is within culturally defined human interactions of communication and relationship. Nature is God's greatest healer.

PIECE 79 — ATTACKED

March 26 (Daniel Age 25) Daniel's little poodle Jada was attacked by a larger dog Saturday afternoon while he was alone walking in the park. The other dog was also on a leash, but the two young girls around 9 years old (no parents anywhere in sight) couldn't control it. It was traumatic. The attacker was a Brittany Spaniel, a hunting dog, and held Jada in her jaws up in the air like she was a chicken; and wouldn't let go until Daniel had kicked the dog three or four times.

When the other dog finally released her, Jada ran, spinning in circles, squealing in pain. Jada's intestines were bulging out from both sides of her belly. Daniel had to run through the woods with her in his arm to the car (a quarter of a mile?) while he called me on his cell phone asking me what to do. "Jada was attacked by a dog. It's real bad. What should I do?"

Miraculously, I was already out in my car (thank you, God!) near him, and was able to rush to pick him up and race them to the emergency vet. Jada was screaming and writhing and biting Daniel instinctively from the pain. Daniel had a small cut on his finger. He was covered in her blood.

Jada had two hours of surgery that night. They had to cut her belly open from the front and work on her "from the inside out." Thank God, her organs were spared; just serious bruising but no cuts to her major organs like intestines or kidneys. Her abdominal muscles are basically shredded from one side over her back to the other side. She is doing well, considering the extent of the damage. Hooray for modern technology and skilled veterinary surgeons.

Daniel had the foresight during the crisis to get the phone number of the dog's owners. We met with them late Saturday and they offered to pay the vet bills, but yesterday, when they found out how expensive they are, they hesitated. I pray they will do what is right and pay the bills. The financial is only a fraction of the trauma we will endure over the next two or three weeks. She is doing well, considering the extent of the damage.

Daniel still wanted to go to church with me yesterday. I was able to find Pastor Milner to pray with Daniel. Last night we waited in the emergency clinic for two hours to see Jada. When Daniel saw her, he seemed about to faint.

I am so proud of Daniel for handling this crisis. And... just when we thought we couldn't love Jada any more than we already did... we are forever proud of our brave little "angel" doggie.

March 27

The family did pay all the vet bills; they already gave us a check. We are grateful that we can forget about that part of the burden. Jada is getting a little bit better each day. We brought her home Monday night and she slept and slept. Tuesday they removed the large red bandage that wrapped her entire abdomen (the techs had decorated it with a cute bunny and Easter egg.) She has gruesome drains; she looks like a tiny Frankenstein's monster. It is very difficult to see her like this.

March 28

Jada is badly injured. But, amazingly, every day she is better than the day before. Today when she woke up her little tail was wagging to see me. Daniel is handling it better than could be expected. She is an angel of a dog. I can't tell you how much she has meant in Daniel's life. She is my brave tiny canine hero.

March 29

The vet removed the drains today. She is moving around more. Yesterday when she saw Daniel she gave him kisses on the face for several minutes without stopping. It made him so happy; he said, "She's Jada again!"

April 1

Daniel went to church with me. I asked several people from our fellowship group to pray for him. Finally, Daniel was able to release tears for the first time since the attack.

April 24

Jada is doing very well. For the past week, she has been back living with Daniel and Jimmy. Her wounds are healed and she seems to have the same energy back again; just a little vulnerable to startle.

Daniel's Answers (Age 29)

"I wonder what I would have done if you hadn't been available to take us to the vet? I guess I would have made it to my car, but it was far away. I wouldn't have known where to go. I knew it was an emergency, but I don't think I knew there were emergency vets, and I didn't know where it was."

[You probably would have found someone to ask for help.]

"There really wasn't anyone around to help."

[The girls were too young to help you.]

PIECE 80 — WEDDING PARTY

July (Daniel Age 24)

David and Andrea are engaged. Daniel has been home from The Program and living in his own condominium for about a month. I know David will want his brother Daniel to participate in his wedding, but I cannot imagine Daniel standing up at the front of a church in front of a crowd of people. Andrea says they will ask Daniel to be a groomsman, and then they will leave it up to him to decide what he is comfortable doing.

May (Daniel Age 25)

Daniel agrees to be a groomsman in David's wedding. He is fitted for a tuxedo.

June (Daniel Age 25)

Steve is scanning childhood photos of Andrea and David. Daniel will "produce" a DVD for the rehearsal dinner. Our friends kindly agreed (arms twisted gently behind their backs) to record our voices as Steve and I read our script. The A/V project has been the finest way possible to involve Daniel and Steve. They have come to life working on this together. It seems to have given them a focus, a purpose, a reason to concentrate on this ritual called wedding.

Wedding Weekend

Daniel rode with Steve to pick up the tuxedos from the formal shop at the mall. At the Rehearsal Dinner, Daniel helped set up the projection equipment for the DVD photo show. He monitored the music and the transmission of a Skype call from David's best friend who is living in Venezuela.

Arachnophobia
David has a fear of spiders in a bad way. After a perfect evening of wedding rehearsal, dinner, and a fun "after-party" playing shuffleboard by the pool, David settled down for some much-needed rest. In the room that the two brothers shared at the mountain lodge, David spotted a spider crawling across his pillow! The groom-to-be jumped up in terror, ran screaming from the room, down the hall, and pounded on our door, shaking and trembling. Steve and I heard his pleas for help and leapt out of bed to see what was wrong. Within seconds, as we arrived to contain the emergency, Daniel calmly picked up the pillow, walked out of the room, and nonchalantly brushed the spider off the edge of the balcony. We cheered Daniel's heroics and then tended to the shuddering groom.

Wedding Day
Daniel dressed in his tux along with all the rest of the groomsmen. When it was time for him to be an usher, I showed him which arm to use to lead the woman and how to put his arm out for her to hold on to, and told him the man would follow behind them. I must have forgotten to tell him to seat the groom's family and friends on the right side of the chapel and the bride's family and friends on the left side, because in our wedding photos I noticed that my aunt and uncle (escorted by Daniel) were seated on the wrong side. But it didn't matter. I was beaming with pride not only for the precious groom and bride (my new daughter-to-be!) but also for my courageous son, the usher, who braved his social phobia, determined to stand at his brother's side!

June 22 (Daniel Age 25)
When we got home from the wedding festivities, Steve found a Post-it Note from Daniel on the front door wishing him a "Happy Father's Day to a great father!" Daniel had unpacked the car we had stuffed to the brim with luggage so we could fit the couple's wedding gifts in our car. He had unloaded Steve's bike and bike rack and even mowed the yard before we got home!

Steve dropped me off to shower and so I could go to bed early while he and Daniel drove the gifts over to Greensboro to David's apartment.

Later that week, while David and Andrea were on their honeymoon, Daniel asked me to help him wash their car. We sprayed and scrubbed and vacuumed and wiped windshields and detailed every speck of dust from their car. It was Daniel's gift of love to his brother and his new sister-in-law.

Daniel's Answers (Age 29)

"The spider story makes me realize how little I really know David. I didn't know he had that kind of issue."

[Even after you scraped the spider off the pillow for him?]

"No, not until I read it here."

[When they were first engaged, I didn't know if you would be able to be a groomsman, with your social phobia.]

"I probably had conflicting feelings. It was good to have a project to work on, a way to be involved."

PIECE 81 — PAPER CUT

Whenever I get a paper cut, I am surprised that an inanimate, flimsy leaf of paper pulp could cause such invisible agony. A microscopic slice on the finger is one thing, but a pain located in a place you don't want to think about, much less talk about, is humiliating.

December 31

Daniel has been in excruciating pain all weekend. My dad, a retired physician, called a friend, a surgeon, who was willing to meet us at his office, even though it was a holiday. Dr. Watkins told us it's an anal fissure.

January 5
Daniel has been living with us the past ten days; out of work for two weeks. He hasn't left the house once. The intense pain is motivating him to learn about proper diet rather than subsisting on crackers, cookies, and fast food.

January 17
At my suggestion, Daniel has been recording in a little notebook everything he eats, and every time he takes meds or supplements. I had him start by recording his pain levels, ranking them from 1-10, next to the time of day. That little notebook has helped him to remember and to figure out what has helped.

January 18
I went to Daniel's appointment with him and tried to help him describe what was going on to the gastroenterologist. I started with his medical history: "As a child, Daniel had surgery for Hirshsprung's disease."

"Oh, so he had a pull-through?"

"Yes: three surgeries by age one. He has also more recently been diagnosed with Asperger syndrome, which I have read, is often associated with gastro-intestinal problems."

"What?"

"Asperger syndrome." His face still looked blank, as his pen was poised over his notepad, so I spelled it out, "A-S-P-E-R-G-E-R," twice, so he could get it written down. Then I explained, "It is a developmental disorder. That is why I am in here with Daniel, because the Asperger syndrome makes it hard for him to explain his situation; and it makes it hard for him to remember what doctors say. I'll step outside while you examine him."

When I came back in from the hall, the young doctor, who appeared to be about the same age as Daniel, summarized the exam, "That's nothing compared to what I usually see."

I protested, "But how can it be that he is in such severe pain?"

"I don't know. I would describe it as similar to a paper cut."

Later that evening, I told Steve, "The doctor seemed like he wasn't paying attention. I felt like I was asking a car mechanic to build us a house. It was a completely useless visit."

January 24

Daniel is shivering, trembling, and wincing from pain. His ears are red. His whole body seems to go into contractions every five minutes. He even began "flapping" his hands (looking very autistic for the first time in his life.)

January 29

Daniel says, "I think it's healing." Steve and I did a celebration dance! I am happy and full of energy all day.

February 2

Daniel was "angry" (that is my interpretation of his mood) with me (he rarely expresses this kind of objection) when he overheard my explanation to the doctor's office about Asperger syndrome, Daniel asserted emphatically to me that he "Does NOT feel pain DIFFERENTLY."

February 9

Our family doctor examined Daniel and said the anal fissure is completely healed up. When the doctor told us that, we must have had puzzled expressions, because Daniel is still wincing and cringing in pain from spasms every five minutes or so.

Daniel's Answers (Age 29)

"It makes me mad all over again to read about people saying it wasn't real pain, that it was in my head. It makes no sense. Just like all the sensory stuff at The Program was so stupid."

PIECE 82 — MOTHER'S DAY

May 11 (Daniel Age 27)
Sunday afternoon. Daniel phoned. "Shouldn't we do something tonight?"

I wondered what he meant. Hmmm… it was Mother's Day—maybe he was hinting at that? "Sure, why don't you come over for dinner? We have salmon and leftover hamburgers. All we need are hamburger buns. Could you bring that?"

"Yeah. What else?"

"That's all. Just hamburger buns. When do you get back?"

"I'm already back."

"Oh, how was your trip?"

"I'll tell you tonight."

"Can you just give me a summary?"

"Later."

"When do you want to come over?"

"Hmmm…. Seven?"

"That's great. See you then."

7:00 p.m. Daniel walked in the front door and into the kitchen where I was preparing the salmon. He took the bag of buns out of the plastic grocery bag and plopped them down. As he walked past me and toward the side door, he handed me a folded piece of paper. My hands were sticky with fish slime. I couldn't take it from him, so he laid it on the counter. He tried to hide a little grin, but I saw it anyway. "What? What is it?"

He slapped his thigh—his signal to his dog to follow him outside.

I glimpsed the initials YLF on the piece of paper and called after him, "Did you get accepted? What does it say? I need my glasses!"

I turned to my husband, gesturing with my dripping hands, "Steve, come here, look, what does it say?" I was impatient. "He wouldn't show it to me if he weren't accepted, would he?"

Sighing, Steve shrugged off to find his reading glasses.

"Quick! What does it say? Did he get accepted?"

"If you'll be quiet, I'll read it to you. Quiet!"

[Pause.]

"Congratulations...."

"Oh! Yea!" I interrupted, "He got in! That's great!"

"Got in to what?"

"Youth Leadership Forum"

"What's that?"

I huffed and rolled my eyes. "Don't you remember?"

"Is this that thing he applied for, down in the eastern part of the state?"

"Yes. Remember? He applied for this position for the Youth Leadership Forum for Students with Disabilities. All housing and meals are covered for free. Mentors are coming from all over the country. It's a great honor. They only accepted forty students ages 18-28 from all across the state. It has been two or three weeks since he applied, so I was worried that maybe he didn't get accepted."

"Yea! He got in! That's awesome!" I shouted to the ceiling. "Daniel—Congratulations!" I yelled outside, through the closed door. "Keep reading!" I insisted to Steve.

"Congratulations. You have been chosen to participate in the first annual Youth Leadership Forum..."

I opened the door. Daniel was sitting on the concrete stoop, watching his dog sniff around in the grass for rabbit droppings.

"Way to go, hon!"

He just sat there, his back toward me.

"Are you happy about it?" I stared at the back of his head. He was motionless. I recognized that outline, that familiar head shape, with the same two distinctive ears and the same hair sworl at the top.

[No response. No turn of the head, no smile, no verbal reply.]

Steve deadpanned, "Of course he's happy, can't you tell?"

I closed the door and went back to preparing dinner, humming this time.

Later, Daniel came in the kitchen, opened the refrigerator, pulled the burgers out of their foil wrapper, and warmed them in the toaster oven. He took several buns out of their packaging, split them and added them to the toaster. He pulled three plates out of the cabinet.

Later, I asked him, "Are you glad you were accepted?"

"Yep."

8:00 p.m. He turned on his favorite TV show: The Simpsons. I heard him cackling with raucous laughter at the irreverent cartoon as I walked to my sitting room to watch a sappy movie on the Hallmark channel.

9:00 p.m. He walked in to my sitting room, where I sat in my blue recliner, surrounded by feminine, floral print fabrics covering all surfaces: the love seat, pillows, and curtains.

"Happy Mother's Day. Good Night." And he slapped his thigh, signaling his dog to follow him outside to the car.

Daniel's Answers (Age 29)

[How could it be that I was so excited for you and you just ignored us?]

"This is a good example of different ways you and Dad respond to things. Dad shows no emotion. You are over the top. This is a good contrast. It's like with dogs, with equal and opposite reaction."

[What does that mean?]

"Like, if you pull on a dog, it will pull back in the opposite direction. Or, if you push down on a dog's rear to try to get them to sit down, they will resist even more. They do the opposite."

PIECE 83 — LOSING FINNEGAN

Nilla's Diary March (Daniel Age 26)

David and Andrea's precious one year old "Labra-Doodle" dog Finnegan became sick from leukemia and died within a week. They had been out of town when she got sick. They had spent the past five days living out of suitcases, back and forth to the emergency vet clinic.

David and Andrea were devastated, grieving the loss of their adorable canine companion. This dog had been like a child to them. They stopped by our house on their way home. Their faces were pale and splotchy, with dark circles under their reddened eyes. Steve and I gave them both long hugs and tried uselessly to rub away the pain from their shoulders.

Later, I relayed to Daniel that Finnegan had died, and I described how David and Andrea must be feeling. Daniel's face remained blank. He did not seem to be sympathetic. He listened to my description of their experience and my explanation of the depth of their emotions, but he did not ask questions. He did not comment when I shared that I felt sad on their behalf. Daniel did not call them to console them, even to say that one little word "sorry." It seemed he did not care about them or share in their grief.

From the emptiness of his body language and facial expression, I could never have guessed the depth of feeling deep within him.

Several days later he casually mentioned, "I thought about giving Jada to David and Andrea, but then I realized they probably wouldn't want her."

When I repeated this story to Andrea, tears welled up in her eyes. She could not imagine such a sacrifice, that he would give up his own beloved companion.

Daniel's Answers (Age 29)
[Why didn't you tell David and Andrea that you were sorry when Finnegan died?]

"They're hearing it from fifty different people. One more saying it won't make a difference. I'd rather think of some other way of doing it. Like, in high school, if someone had a cast on their leg, they would hear it from fifty people, the same question, 'What happened?' and they would have to explain it so many times. Like, if you wore a certain shirt, it would get so old, having everybody say the same thing over and over again."

PIECE 84 — DIAMOND WORDS

January 27 (Daniel Age 26)
Daniel called. "I had lunch at Roly Poly."

"What's that?"

"Restaurant near the mall. Jimmy and I went. I had a buy-one-get-one-free coupon. They're these wrap kind of sandwiches. You can get anything on it you want. I had a tuna fish with apple butter and spinach and pecans and carrots. They didn't even look at me funny. It was awesome. You've got to try it."

"I've heard of that place, but I hate the name. Roly-poly is what we used to call those ugly caterpillar-like bugs with a million legs—when we were kids."

He laughed. Then he continued to talk on and on, for maybe 10 or 15 minutes. That long of a conversation is a once-a-year event, so I totally stopped what I was doing and listened and savored it.

"How was tennis?" I asked.

"Good."

"Who did you play?"

"Mike. I may have some computer work. His sister-in-law needs help with Microsoft Windows and will pay me for it."

"Oh, that's great! How is Jada feeling? Is she getting her medicine?"

"Yes."

"She missed three doses while she was staying here. Give me several in a baggie next time you come over so I will have them for just in case. Has she seemed weak?"

"No, she seems normal."

"Kevin has to have hip surgery again."

"You only have one hip!" he said defiantly, as if I was trying to fool him.

"No, you have two hips." I corrected.

"You do?"

"Yeah, like…" I tried to explain, "…if you put your hands on your waist, you have one on the left and one on the right."

"Oh."

"Well, I'll talk to you later."

"Seeya."

After we hung up, Steve said, "That sounded like David, talking on and on. That couldn't have been Daniel." He hesitated. Then he went on: "You might not be ready for this. I have two things to tell you, but after I tell you the second one, you won't remember the first one, so you'd better write this one down. The first is: I don't think we should ask Bob to bring his slide show of his trip when we invite him for dinner." We discussed that further.

"The second: I don't know if you can take this."

I wasn't sure if this was going to be good news or bad. And he was right. After he told me the second thing, I did forget the first.

"You are a wonderful mother. Listening to you talk to Daniel just now, you seemed to enjoy talking to him. You took time to listen and be excited for him. I realized you are like that all the time. I realize I never tell you this, but you're the best mother to both our sons. You're patient. You treat even the mundane things they tell you as if it's the most exciting accomplishment. You have spent your life doing this for years and years, sacrificially giving your time and energy, instead of doing things you might have wanted to do. You have been consumed by trying to figure out what Daniel needed, getting what he needed.

If it was just me, I wouldn't have known what to do. I wouldn't have even known there was anything wrong. You are aware. You figure things out. You are a mother bear, protecting your cubs. If you ever think your life is worthless, it is not. If you ever doubt whether we should have moved to this city or not, or you should have left this job or not, or whatever, just remember: You are a great mother. You have done such a great job."

I could hardly contain my joy. My smile became a double-wide. I was trying to absorb this moment fully, hoping I would never forget it. I leaned into Steve for a hug.

"You've been a good mother to both our sons. But let's just talk about Daniel right now. Look at the progress he has made in the last three or four years. If it hadn't been so yechhy, it wouldn't be so satisfying now. What if you had died or not been around four years ago? What would I have done? I wouldn't have known what to do. You have figured things out and stuck with them. You are a really good mother."

I leaned my face deeper into Steve's chest, "Thanks for saying that. That is better than any diamond ring."

The phone rang again. It was Daniel, calling back. This was sure turning out to be a red-letter day. Not only did he call me once, he called back again? That had never happened before. "Oh, yeah, I meant to tell you thanks for dinner last night. It was awesome!" (I had taken leftovers to his condominium and left them in his refrigerator.)

"I made up the recipe myself."

"Gyaww!"

"I just squeezed lemon juice on the chicken and sprinkled lemon pepper on it and baked it. I'm glad you liked it! Dad and I had a good dinner tonight too."

"Coupon?"

"Yep, we went to Moe's."

(Steve piped up in the background, "It was so good I want some MO…! Ha, ha," he laughed at his own joke.)

"So thanks for pointing out the coupon to your dad."

"Seeya."

"He called back!" I shouted to Steve, who was still standing right next to me. We were both amazed. I couldn't contain the joy. I had just had a long conversation with my monosyllabic son, and as a bonus to that once-a-year-event, he even called back again to thank me! And my husband had just told me I was a wonderful mother. My only goal in life! It was a JOY crisis. I was nearly bursting with joy.

PIECE 85 — CANINE CUSTODY

May 16 (Daniel Age 27)
It was Friday, the night before David's graduation. Andrea's whole family drove across the state to celebrate with us all weekend. I invited them all over for dinner. There was someone new to meet, Andrea's brother's girlfriend.

Daniel jogged over from his apartment. He met everyone in the kitchen. Then he stayed away the rest of the night. He looked through my scrapbooks. He didn't eat at the dining table with the rest of us. After everyone else had eaten, he put his food on a tray and went in the den to watch TV.

The group of seven went out to get ice cream. I stayed home to finish up the dishes. When his TV show ended, Daniel stood up and walked to the front door. He slapped his thigh to signal Jada to "Come."

At the threshold, he leaned down to clip the leash on Jada's collar. I followed them outside and stood barefoot in the damp grass. While Jada "did her business," I looked up at the stars and tried to find the planet Mercury. "Let's see, it's supposed to be in the southwest part of the sky." I realized he wasn't looking where I was pointing, so I asked, "Are you interested?"

He said "No." Then, in a matter-of-fact way, "I want her [Jada] to be with you or with me. I don't want her to be in both places. Do you have a preference?"

I was stunned. I had been keeping my "grand-dog" Jada in the afternoons, since Daniel was at work nine hours a day, from 10 a.m. to 7 p.m. weekdays. The dog is one of our only real connections. She is our jester, our comical distraction. She serves as a common character we can laugh about and share stories about.

This was out of the blue. I wondered what could have brought this on. Had I done something wrong with the dog? He had asked me a few weeks ago not to give her bits of carrots as treats (which the vet recommends as healthy treats), because she had had a few days of vomiting spells. I didn't know. Was Daniel angry at me? He had just been watching an episode of "Dog Whisperer with Cesar Millan." Did he extrapolate something from that show about how his dog should be managed? Earlier that evening, I had put the dog in the bedroom so she could eat her food without interruption from David's dog, a huge rambunctious puppy who was visiting. Daniel was critical of that choice. Was he punishing me?

I wanted to ask "Why?" I wanted a discussion, an explanation. But I have learned that is futile. I tried to answer his question as directly as he had asked it. But quick, what would I say? I love that little dog. She brings me so much joy with her tippy-tappy tiny toenails clicking down the hardwood hallway. Her black puff-ball poodle tail wags every time she sees me, even if we have only been separated a few minutes. I love it when she snuggles in my lap and her mere twelve pounds of fur keeps me warm in my rocking chair as I settle down for the night.

Was he jealous that the dog loved me too? Was Daniel feeling down about being the only "single" person tonight? Now even his sister-in-law's baby brother had a girlfriend. Was Daniel depressed that his three-years-younger brother graduated from four year college today, while Daniel had just graduated with a two year degree? And even if he had any of these emotions, was he even aware of them?

But no matter what my personal attachment to the cute little canine, her whole purpose and angel-hood revolved around being like a "therapy dog" for Daniel, and also, now, for his roommate Jimmy. I knew what I had to say, even though it would hurt my heart to acquiesce to this black-and-white, all-or-nothing dictate.

"Well… I guess… with you."

"Okay. Seeya." He led her to the car and drove away.

Email, Nilla to Daniel May 16
Hey. Jada is your dog. Did I do something wrong with Jada to make you want to keep her away from me? I would like to understand why you want it to be all or nothing. Is it 'cause I'm getting in the way of your life and your independence? Or 'cause I was bringing her home too late? If you don't mind, it would help me to know a little bit more about what you're thinking. Is she a burden to you? Thanks, Mom
Email, Daniel to Nilla May 17
I need to establish independence. **Email, Nilla to Daniel May 21**
Thanks for telling me. If I communicate the least I can possibly stand, and you communicate the most you can possibly stand, it should end up being just about right! :-) Love, Mom

June 15
Jada was sitting in urine soaked bedding. Their apartment smelled like urine every time I opened the door. Both her beds were drenched, both upstairs and down. I had come by to take her to the vet for her regularly scheduled vaccinations. While I was there, I asked the vet (I truly wanted her objective opinion…) if it was OK for her to be constantly in wet bedding.

She said "No. Jada could get urinary tract infections. Her fur/skin could be burned by the acid in the urine. Also, it's just not sanitary, for the dog or the humans."

I drove back to Daniel's apt and picked up the bedding to take it home to wash. I called him and left a message what the vet said, and I told him that I took Jada home with me, to give her a bath. I told him his apartment reeked of urine.

He called back and said "You can take her."

I said I wanted to discuss this with him to make sure it was all right with him.

He said "We just did talk about it."

I cried when I couldn't have the dog a month ago, and now I was crying because he said I could have her—crying both ways. But I still didn't know if he meant I could have her for today or have her permanently.

Email, Nilla to Daniel June 19
Daniel, will you please give Jada to me? Let me know what you think. I want to be sure it is really OK with you. Love, Mom
Email, Daniel to Nilla June 20
keep her

Several weeks later I asked, "So, are you sad without Jada?"

"Nope."

"'Cause I was sad without her, so I thought you might be sad, too."

"Nope."

"Is it kind of a relief to you...?"

"Yep."

"...that you don't have to worry about going home to let her out..."

"Yep."

"That's good."

PIECE 86—LETTING GO

Your children are not your children.
They are the sons and daughters of Life's longing for itself.
They come through you but not from you,
And though they are with you yet they belong not to you.

You may give them your love but not your thoughts,
For they have their own thoughts.
You may house their bodies but not their souls,
For their souls dwell in the house of tomorrow,
    which you cannot visit, not even in your dreams.

You may strive to be like them, but seek not to make them like you.
For life goes not backward nor tarries with yesterday.
You are the bows from which your children
    as living arrows are sent forth.

The archer sees the mark upon the path of the infinite,
    and He bends you with His might
    that His arrows may go swift and far.

Let your bending in the archer's hand be for gladness;
For even as He loves the arrow that flies,
    so He loves also the bow that is stable.

—*The Prophet* by Kahlil Gibran

Starving for Attention

When my boys were nine and 12 years old, they both begged for a pet. I had a demanding full-time job and a long daily commute, so I relied on Steve to be the stay-at-home dad and take care of the home front. Steve took them to the pet store to pick out a hamster. I was not at all involved in selecting the hamster or what it needed. I assumed Steve had figured it out. There couldn't be much complexity in providing for a tiny hamster. How hard could it be?

Before long, the poor little creature went crazy insane. It seemed to be shaking like it had a neurological problem. Somehow, it escaped its metal cage and died. When I was cleaning out its cage and paraphernalia, I couldn't find any food. I searched and searched, then came to the horrifying conclusion that Steve had chosen a box of snacks instead of food, so it never had any real nourishment. The pitiful furry being had starved to death.

This trivial example about a relatively insignificant hamster has stayed with me as a metaphor that seems to validate my fears. When I depend on others, I am often disappointed. I am afraid to let go of control because I envision bad things happening as a result.

Email, Nilla to Evelyn (Daniel Age 26)

We made an appt. with Daniel's psychiatrist (Daniel hasn't been to see him for a year and a half) but Daniel wouldn't go. Steve and I went to his appointment anyway. Steve told the psychiatrist that **I** was the one having trouble separating from Daniel, and not the other way around. Ha, ha! So once again, it's my fault!?

Email, Nilla to Esther, June 13 (Daniel Age 27)

Our son Daniel finished his two-year Associates Degree in May. Daniel was accepted to the Youth Leadership Forum for Disabilities at State college for a week in July. His AmeriCorps job ends in August. He will need another job.

Daniel is separating from me, a healthy phase for him, but it is painful to me, mostly because of zero communication. Of course I want him to be independent, but he doesn't have many other links, so I worry about "what if..." all the time. Though he is age 27 in chronological years, he is socially/emotionally more like 18 years old.

Daniel is getting lots of exercise, tennis, bicycling. He is very healthy and fit, but now I worry that he is losing TOO much weight. He is looking very thin. He has gone from one extreme to another over the past six years or so in his weight, up and down, up and down.

His roommate Jimmy bought a bike a few months ago, and they've been taking long rides. I worry about them because they are often out late at night (weekends) on busy roads (Mall Blvd.) Please pray for angels to protect them from harm, and to make them visible to drivers.

Email, Esther to Nilla, June 14

Separation is harder on the mother than on the child. Let's hope he finds a happy medium.

Email from Nilla to Group List January 23 (Daniel Age 27)

Dear Friends and Family,

If you don't already know, we had to put Jada (our toy poodle) to sleep this week. We miss her. This Monday night, we are having a brief prayer service (somewhat following the format of the "Rainbow Bridge" ceremony) and will light three candles in Jada's memory. If you would like to join us at that time, in whatever place in the world you are, please do. If you would like to see Jada's photo/tribute, look on the third page [link]. Thanks, Nilla

Daniel's Answers (Age 29)

"This is a good example of too much worry. I think of the Dog Whisperer saying that's what messes up the dogs so much is when the owners are totally anxious. It's like an energy transfer. Even though the owners think they're doing a good thing, they're actually creating a problem. It's the same thing if kids hear the same vocabulary over and over when they are a kid, like 'worried,' they pick up on that."

PIECE 87—INTERSECTION

Daniel and Jimmy were riding their bicycles all over the place; in town, out of town, across the county, to lakes, and up mountains. Their bicycles provided them pride, inexpensive practical transportation, leisurely entertainment, as well as vigorous aerobic exercise.

With this new-found confidence, one night after dinner, Daniel announced to the family he planned to sell his car, since he didn't need it any more. We tried to dissuade him—what about inclement weather, rain, cold? What about transporting heavy objects? He wasn't listening to reason. He had made up his mind. After he had gone home, I told Steve we should buy Daniel's car from him so we could return it to him when he eventually realized he needed it again. I prayed myself to sleep that night.

Later that week, as I was watching the TV game show "Wheel of Fortune," Daniel called and calmly asked, "Can you give me a ride home?"

"Sure, where are you?"

"Baptist Hospital."

"What? You're at the hospital?" I tried to hide the alarm in my voice, but the high pitch probably gave it away. "What happened?"

"I had a bike wreck."

"Oh, honey, I'm so sorry. Are you all right?"

"Yeah."

I knew not to ask him many questions, only the information I had to know: "Where are you in the hospital?"

"I don't know."

"Is there a nurse around? See if you can ask someone where we should pick you up. Are you in the emergency room?"

249

He turned to ask a nurse where he was. "Yes, the emergency room. She says come to the front."

"We'll be right there, hon."

I hung up the phone and screamed to the other end of the house, allowing my strained voice the freedom to panic, "Steve! *STEVE*! **HURRY!** Come here right now! Daniel has had an accident—a bike wreck! He is in the emergency room. Grab your keys and come on, hurry!"

I was confused. Why hadn't Daniel called sooner? Why had no one from the hospital called us, his nearest relatives? He probably didn't ask anyone to call us. Either he was severely injured and in shock and could not speak, or he had some warped idea of wanting to be grown up and independent, or he just didn't want his anxious mother around, or all of the above. I was angry that we had been just sitting around, idly eating dinner and watching television, when we could have been at the hospital helping him.

Steve and I raced to the hospital, only a few miles away, to pick him up. He was waiting for us at the emergency room entrance, not in a wheelchair. No one was with him. He had a sheet of paper in his hand with discharge notes, but he could not explain anything that he was supposed to do.

While Steve collected the bike parts leaning against the brick wall, I went inside to ask for more instructions, but the doctor who had treated Daniel was not available. The attendant suggested that I phone the contact name printed on the discharge sheet.

Steve found Daniel's cell phone and wallet tucked inside his backpack along with his school books. The policeman had apparently collected Daniel's belongings and put them safely away, along with the policeman's business card. Steve called the officer to see if he could provide any information for us, as Daniel was in shock and could not remember what had happened.

I looked at the diagram the officer had drawn on a grid to illustrate the accident. I was horrified to realize my son could have been killed or paralyzed. I couldn't believe that he did not even break a bone. His shoulder was extremely sore, and he was badly bruised and his skin was badly scraped down one side, on his left shoulder, knee and ankle. His bike helmet had literally saved his life. The helmet had cracked, protecting his skull from cracking, as it hit the pavement multiple times at great force.

The police report listed several witnesses and their phone numbers. I called one of them. They were relieved to hear from us and were amazed to learn that Daniel was alive and safe, with only minor injuries. They explained how the timing was miraculous, because had it been a second later, the traffic light would have changed, and they would not have seen Daniel and their car would have struck or run over him. They said his bike flipped forward several times, and that the left side of his body and his head hit the pavement with each rotation.

The witnesses explained that as soon as Daniel landed, people jumped from their cars and a group of people surrounded him until the police and ambulance arrived. The accident occurred only a few hundred yards from the hospital. This couple had just left the hospital after visiting a sick relative. Several other people who came to Daniel's aid were nurses, who had just left their shift and were on their way home.

Hearing this story from these witnesses, and piecing together all that happened in my absence helped me to realize that although I cannot be everywhere all the time to protect my son, there are kind people in this world who will help a stranger in a crisis, like I would.

I realized that God must have sent His angels to surround Daniel as his bike tumbled, and as he lay in the middle of the road. This story, this image has helped me to visualize that I can "let go," and reminds me that I am not ultimately in control of the universe.

Daniel's Answers (Age 29)

"I don't know why you said I was warped."

[Warped? I don't remember saying you were warped. Where? Oh, yeah, I did use that word.]

"You say it's warped. I don't see it as warped. I chose not to call for a reason.

[Was it because you didn't want me getting worried about you?]

"If I'm in the hospital, I'm being taken care of, so that was enough."

PIECE 88 — "JACKPOT"

Steve spent two years achieving his life-long dream of creating a documentary film. Finally, the world premiere took place. Daniel, David, and Andrea stayed with us until the award ceremony was held, late at night, long after the rest of our friends and family had to leave to drive home, several hours away. The film festival announced that Steve's film won the "Audience Choice" award! This was a great achievement, a satisfying cherry on top of the already delicious ice cream sundae, drenched in rich, steaming hot fudge, under a fluffy tower of whipped cream.

Everyone in the room was congratulating Steve on this great accomplishment. Steve made a speech to the audience that remained. David and Andrea and I were hugging Steve, rubbing his back, saying "Way to go," smiling back at the beaming novice director. It was nearing midnight, so the five of us piled into our minivan and drove back to the hotel together, as Steve phoned his film crew and supporters to share the great news.

I had seen the film a half-dozen times, in its many generations. David and Andrea had seen it two or three times at various stages. Although Daniel had set up the film's website for Steve, Daniel had not yet seen any part of the film over the past year of development.

We dropped off David and Andrea at the hotel. Daniel went on up in the elevator too, to the room he would share with Steve and myself that night. Steve and I had to drive back to the festival location to pick up a forgotten poster.

In the car, I asked Steve if Daniel had said anything to him about the film.

"No, he hasn't. You know, I am more interested in what he has to say about the film than in what just about anyone else thinks. I value his opinion, and I'm dying to know his reaction, but I'm not about to ask him, because I have learned that doesn't work."

I nodded my head in the dark, and agreed, "Uh, huh."

When we got back to the hotel and walked into the room, Daniel said one word, without looking up: "Jackpot," he said nonchalantly, monotonously, with zero intonation. I wasn't sure if he was talking to Steve or if he had reached some new level in an online game he was playing on his iPhone.

When Steve went into the bathroom to brush his teeth, I considered whether to let Daniel in on the confidence Steve had in him. I wanted him to know how important his opinion was to his dad. But I didn't say a word. Shortly, we were all asleep, Daniel lying flat on his back in one queen-sized bed, and Steve and me in the other bed. Steve had his earplugs in, and a portable fan blowing white noise next to his head to drown out my obnoxious snoring.

The next day we ate the continental breakfast together and hit the road. David and Andrea left earlier, in their car, and we all met up on the drive home at IKEA for lunch and to browse the huge Scandinavian furniture warehouse. We discussed the Swedish meatballs, the almond cake, the Sunday crowds, the weather, the news, politics, Facebook, and the wide selection of furniture. We must have talked about everything but Steve's movie. Daniel didn't mention the movie during the remaining two hours' drive home.

Once home, I curled up in bed for an afternoon nap. Steve and Daniel went on a twenty-five mile bike ride around the lake.

Later that night, Steve told me that half-way into the bike ride Daniel, unprompted, said, "About your film..." and shared long, insightful, deep, critical and complimentary opinions, such as, "I liked how you..." and "That was cool when..." This revelation occurred almost twenty hours after the film premiere concluded, although there had been many intervening opportunities for such a conversation.

The praise and acknowledgement from his son Daniel may have been an even greater award to Steve than the official, public, "Audience Choice" award. Daniel may not celebrate with the masses. He may not applaud in the same timing or in the same manner that others do, but with enough time, and an unpressured setting, the depth of his thoughts and the significance of his feelings of loyalty and pride eventually surface, almost always in unexpected ways.

Daniel's Answers (Age 29)
[Any reaction to this?]

"I think if I recognize certain social expectations, sometimes I'll try to do the opposite. Anyway, even if people say 'congratulations,' it's not necessarily genuine."

PIECE 89 — BRILLIANT

rilliant Smile
Daniel radiates a beautiful smile, as bright as the powerful beam from a lighthouse—bright enough to shine across a great expanse of land and sea. When he smiles at you, you feel like you've won the lottery, or the jackpot on a Las Vegas slot machine, as if all his straight white teeth, lined up in a row, are like the three symbols that match to announce you a winner.

Just as the light in the lighthouse circles around, waving its beam far into night's darkness to direct ships to shore, Daniel's light is either ON or it is OFF. When Daniel is not smiling, when the lighthouse beam is turned away, Daniel has no expression. It is as dark as night.

Brilliant Character
Daniel has wonderful, enduring qualities, the kind of traits that count. Notice, I didn't say "endearing" qualities, which you might use to

refer to someone who is more charming, or naturally more socially appealing. Daniel has the finest, deepest, most important, character qualities. He is:

- Honest. Daniel absolutely cannot make himself tell a lie. He is unable to be manipulative.
- Genuine. He is the real thing. He doesn't wear masks, he is not artificial.
- Principled. Daniel believes in what is right and will do what is right no matter what.
- Loyal. Daniel is devoted to his family, friends and pets.
- Thoughtful. He wrote his mom a note "Congratulations on your tennis win," and he gave his dad a gift for Christmas, an original work of art, listing "the things I admire about you."
- Spartan. Daniel lives simply. He is frugal. He doesn't spend money unless it is a necessity.
- Generous. For instance, he delivered groceries for Meals on Wheels and helped the Medical Health Center manage their computer database.
- Persistent. **Email, Nilla to Daniel, Age 26**: Congratulations on your perseverance getting the wallpaper scraped (five and a half hours!?!?!) and bathroom walls painted. They look great! I'm so proud of you! Love, Mom

Brilliant Athlete

At 18 months Daniel could whack a baseball with an oversized bat on every toss. Home movies show him pitching an oversized ball to Steve, and then catching Steve's return toss with his little glove. He imitated the professionals he had seen on TV, because before each pitch, Daniel ritualistically stomped each foot, like a pitcher would have done in his wind up on the pitcher's mound.

Around age two we took him to the county fair. He wanted to try the game where you throw the football through a hanging tire. His dad (who had played semi-pro football for a time) tried it and couldn't do it, but Daniel wanted to do it anyway. We gave the fair worker his dollar, and since Daniel was shorter than the railing, he told us to let Daniel stand on top of the railing, making him about the same height as an average adult. Daniel nailed the ball in a spiral, right straight through the center of the tire and won the big prize!

As a child, Daniel took tennis lessons and clinics. Summer evenings, Steve and I frequently hit tennis while Daniel and David knocked the ball around on the next court. When they were a bit older, our little family of four became a perfect doubles match. One summer, Daniel took a daily tennis clinic from a good local coach. Daniel competed in juniors tennis tournaments around the state. He still has a beautiful, strong ground stroke and a powerful serve. Daniel plays tennis several times a week, playing very, very well. The main person Daniel plays with was in a tennis clinic with me a year ago and I got them connected to play. The other player is someone whose number I saw posted on a tennis court, and I called Daniel to give him the number. Recently, Daniel beat Eddie, who is a 4.5 to 5.0 USTA rank (an excellent player!) Daniel is good at all racket sports. His squash opponent predicted Daniel will become one of the best squash players in town.

Daniel is now going to the YMCA regularly and working out on weights. Two years ago, he wouldn't even go to the Y. Eventually he went reluctantly, *only* if someone (Steve, David or I) drove him there and stayed with him the entire time. After months and months, he was willing to meet Steve at the entrance of the Y. Gradually he agreed to meet Steve *inside* the Y at the swimming pool. Later, he was willing to go on his own, but only if he had a swimming lesson scheduled. So, little by little, inch by inch, he was willing to go on his own. Now he hangs out in the lobby and works the jigsaw puzzles they have set out on a table. He plays pick-up games on their new ping pong table. My friend, who is a swim instructor, met Daniel and offered to give him swim lessons in exchange for him helping with her computer. She says he is one of the better swimmers at the pool now. She laments that he wasn't on a swim team in his youth, saying he would have excelled competitively.

Watching Daniel snow skiing downhill takes my breath away;

it's like watching a fluid, graceful curve, flowing down the mountain, as if he naturally belongs to the powdery white slopes; as if he is one with the snow. Daniel is still an amazing athlete.

Brilliant Mind

Daniel helped me figure out how to invent a gadget to illustrate a point in a talk I was giving. He can easily envision ways to solve problems. The way he is resourceful, finding everyday objects to fix unusual challenges, reminds me of his favorite TV hero, MacGyver.

Daniel is a natural with computers. He is a web designer and developer. He taught himself HTML. He knows the computer languages Visual Basic, C++, Pascal, and Linux. The summer he was seventeen he interned with his Uncle Kirk's company and helped debug programming for major airlines. He initiated and wrote a program to track employee locations; the company still uses the coding he created.

Chess, an intellectual game with more potential configurations than there are molecules in the universe, sufficiently challenges Daniel's mind, which can envision multiple future moves as ever-dividing branches on a tree.

PIECE 90—BROTHERS

Rescue

The two summers that we leased a cabin in Maggie Valley, North Carolina, Daniel and David enjoyed being mountain men together: shooting cans with BB guns, finding snakes to handle, hiking to drench themselves under waterfalls, and tracking animal paw prints. They built a fire ring out of rocks and cut tree stumps for seats in a circle. To cook dinner, they wrapped corn on the cob, potatoes, and apples in foil and roasted them on a big campfire, along with the standard hot dogs and marshmallows.

One hot summer afternoon, the boys were at the cabin by themselves. Steve and I were at home, several hours away. David was 15, Daniel was 18. David was stung multiple times on the arm by yellow-jackets. David tried to cool the stings with a shower, but he remembers the itch creeping under his skin, almost like it was moving through his veins, all over his body. When his legs started swelling, he knew it was serious. Daniel drove David down the bumpy gravel mountain road as fast as he could, racing his brother to the hospital emergency room over ten miles away. Aloud, he muttered, "I'd better turn on my flashers." As soon as David arrived, they gave him a shot of epinephrine, and the swelling decreased. Now David knows he is allergic to bees and he has to carry an Epi-pen with him at all times. Daniel was the hero of the day, rescuing his brother from a life-or-death emergency.

Purple Cubes

The year after Daniel and I toured Europe, David convinced me to treat him for his 16th birthday to a special, all-inclusive, travel bargain deal for his spring break. We flew to the tropics: Cancun, Mexico. We snorkeled through reefs and jet-skied canals. David filled up on virgin strawberry daiquiris. We toured Chichén Itza during their festival celebrating the Spring Equinox, when a serpentine shadow winds down the stairs of the main pyramid.

The day we left home, a cold front moved in. At the Atlanta airport, we had to wait outside for a shuttle bus. Neither of us had brought a winter coat—we were headed for the tropics! We didn't even have a sweater or light jacket. He and I were both in short sleeves. I was shivering, miserable, grabbing my arms, wrapping myself in a hug, desperate to generate warmth. David just stood there, as if oblivious to the cold. "How can you just stand there? Aren't you *freezing*?"

"No, I'm fine."

"It's *cold*! I don't understand how you can take it. You're not even shivering. How can you not feel cold?"

"Purple cubes."

"What?"

"Purple cubes. I imagine purple cubes are bouncing around in my head. Friction generates warmth, so it makes me feel warm."

I shook my head in amazement, as I felt a gust brush my bare arms.

Starbursts

I drove our Ford Explorer, stuffed with David's belongings, umpteen hours to help him move in to an apartment, where he was a freshman in college. He drove his sleek, sporty car, accompanied by his new puppy Zuka, a miniature schnauzer. We arrived, unpacked, and walked the tiny dog, carrying her up the stairs because her legs were too little to reach from step to step. We assembled Zuka's crate, so at least she had a place to sleep. David began arranging for utilities to be connected. I set out to find a few furnishings to complete the set-up. He still needed a bed, mattress, and dining table.

When I returned from shopping, I walked in the door and almost stumbled over Starburst candies strewn across the carpet. "Oh, yum, reds are my favorites. You can keep the greens and oranges for yourself."

"No, wait!" he shouted, "Don't touch them!"

"What? Why? You have plenty here. I want something sweet."

"That's my new phone number."

"What? What are you talking about?"

"That's my new phone number. I didn't have any paper or even a pen to write on my hand, so I grabbed this bag of Starbursts and arranged them in patterns so I could remember the number."

I glanced down at the floor, recognizing: seven candies in a little pile, then three, then five, followed by four more digits represented by clusters of square, colorfully wrapped confections. I burst out laughing, "Ha! Great system! You are hilarious!" I pulled ever-present paper and pen out of my purse and wrote down the number for him, before I snatched up the last few digits (reds and pinks!) to pop into my watering mouth.

Advisor

When Daniel first moved into his condominium, David came over and made sure Daniel knew how to pay his bills. He helped him establish a budgeting system using cash envelopes: one for groceries, one for gasoline, etc. David advises Daniel about his finances. He helped him figure out if he could afford his living expenses on the stipend he received from AmeriCorps. David said yes, as long as Daniel also looked for supplementary income, like helping individuals fix their home computers, or like mowing grass, dog sitting, etc. Each year, David helps Daniel to file his annual income tax return.

Ticketed

A policeman pulled over and ticketed Daniel a few days after the tags on his license plate had expired. If Daniel had accepted and paid the fine, Steve's and my automobile insurance would have doubled for the next three years. Daniel wanted to go to court by himself to defend it. He did not want my help or Steve's. He did not want us to call a lawyer to defend him.

Daniel called his brother, who had been through a similar experience. David "walked him through" what would happen. Daniel brought his tags up to date immediately and appeared in court on the proper date. The judge did give him a "P.J.C." (Prayer for Judgment, Continued) which was good news, because it meant he did not have to pay the fine, and the infraction wasn't reported to insurance—as long as he didn't commit another offense over the next 12 months, which he didn't.

Influential

David is a logical thinker, rational, practical, and realistic. He speaks what is on his mind, even if it comes across as blunt. His style is just what Daniel needs. David has been an important influence in Daniel's life, in all of our lives. David has been willing and eager to provide financial counseling for our whole family. He encouraged us to get out of debt and set up emergency funds. Daniel must be tired of hearing his mom's and dad's nagging, but he doesn't seem tired of hearing from David. He loves his brother and respects his advice. Whenever there is something critical happening in Daniel's life, I usually try to step back, and defer to Daniel's little brother to step in. It seems backwards and upside down that the youngest of all of us is the wisest counsel, in many ways.

Saying Goodbye
We knew Jada had a heart problem. The vet had warned us a year ago and put her on daily medication. During the coldest winter week one January, she was obviously very sick. She shivered and coughed horribly. She couldn't get warm, even though I held her curled in my lap, wrapped in a fleece blanket. Jada didn't want to go outside because it was so cold. Saturday morning I woke to find she had wandered out of my bedroom. I saw piles of diarrhea all over the front hall and living room. She wouldn't eat anything, not even her favorite: scrambled eggs. Steve and David were on a ski trip out west and I didn't know what to do. This was too big a decision for me to make on my own. The vet's office was closed for the weekend. I called Daniel and asked him to come over to observe Jada and help me figure out what to do for her. He didn't come over.

Late Sunday, I couldn't stand seeing Jada like that any longer. Something had to be done. I drove her to the emergency vet. I called Steve, who was still out of state, and we discussed what we should do. I could tell it was the end of Jada's life, and we had to do something to help the poor angel out of her misery. I talked with our vet, who agreed. But I didn't know how to handle this situation with Daniel. Jada was actually his dog, and I wanted him to be able to see her again before she was gone, if that is what he wanted. I couldn't imagine making a permanent decision like this without his input, but I wasn't getting any response from him.

I called David to ask him to call Daniel; to let him know what was happening, and to find out if he would like to be involved or not. David called me right back and told me Daniel didn't think he could handle seeing Jada in that condition. So now I knew what I had to do. I asked the emergency vet to put Jada to sleep. Meanwhile, David

called back. He had just flown in an hour ago. He said that he and
Andrea wanted to drive over from Greensboro to be with me if
that's what I wanted, but they wouldn't come if I preferred to be
alone. I didn't want to be alone, but I knew how tired he was from
the long day of travel. It was so late, it was snowing, and he had to be
at work early the next morning. They came, despite it being 11:00 on
a Sunday night, and the roads were icy. Andrea said a last good-bye
to Jada, and went out to the waiting room. David stayed in the room
with me and stroked Jada's little head as I held Jada in my arms and
kissed her and thanked her for her bravery and service to Daniel and
told her how much we all loved her.

STEP SEVEN
LINKING BACKGROUND

Nilla's Method for Completing a Jigsaw Puzzle
1.   First, I turn all the pieces out of the box.
2.   I plop the pieces onto the table into a big jumbled pile.
3.   Turning over each upside-down piece right-side up, I begin to see what I have.
4.   Next is finding edges—pieces with straight edges form the outer border.
5.   I look for matching details like fragments of words, faces or shapes.
6.   I start fitting together complementary pieces to form the central design.
7.   **Nearing the end, I focus on solidly colored pieces, linking background.**

By this stage, the central design of the jigsaw puzzle is evident. The rest of the process is filling in the background. The remaining pieces are probably all the same color, solid, with no design elements, so you have to shift your attention to only the shapes of the pieces.

Learning about Asperger syndrome, I read every book I could find, until they all ran together in my mind. I attended training workshops and conferences. I read magazine articles and searched internet sites. I talked to other parents. I joined support groups, comforted somewhat by similar situations, but more often puzzled by our many differences. Nothing held the complete solution.

As I wondered what all of this meant for me, for our son, for our family, I turned to metaphor, analogy, charts and diagrams to illustrate at a deeper level, to digest fully what I had learned.

PIECE 91 — DSM-IV 299.80

When I first heard the word "Asperger" I thought it was a naughty word, the equivalent of a grilled patty of "donkey" meat. In the English language, "Asperger" is an ugly word; an awkward name for an awkward syndrome. When I searched the dictionary for words similar in sound to "Asperger" I realized why I have a negative connotation for the word. "Asperity" means harsh or rough. "Asperse" means to attack or slander. "Aspersion" means slander or criticism.

Austrian pediatrician Dr. Hans Asperger wasn't self-conscious about his name, because everyone else around him was speaking German, and all those consonants—the "esses" and "pees" and "errs"—fit right in. The name Asperger was probably as common in German as Smith or Jones in English.

Even though Dr. Asperger brilliantly identified a cluster of symptoms in a number of his young patients, he published his findings in 1944, during the worst of World War II in the most devastated of all possible places, central Europe. People were concerned about surviving bombings and extinction. No one could pay attention to one pediatrician's observations in the midst of such chaos.

Forty years later, the term Asperger syndrome was popularized in the west by Dr. Lorna Wing, in 1981 (coincidentally, the same year Daniel was born.)

Another decade passed until the American Psychiatric Association published section 299.80, the criteria for Asperger's Disorder, in the *DSM-IV (Diagnostic and Statistical Manual of Mental Disorders, 4th edition, 1994.)* By that time, Daniel was thirteen years old, so it would have been impossible for any of his childhood psychologists or counselors to have diagnosed a condition that did not yet exist in their field's official handbook.

In simpler language, the diagnostic criteria for DSM-IV 299.80 Asperger's Disorder (which means confusion or disturbance) lists:

1) Impaired social interaction, such as:
   a. poor eye contact, facial expression, body language
   b. few friends
   c. not sharing interests with others (showing, pointing)
   d. lack of social or emotional give-and-take
2) Restricted patterns of interests:
   a. abnormal intensity
   b. not flexible; prefer sameness
   c. repetitive movements (flapping, twisting)
   d. focus on parts, details
3) Significant impairment in social, occupational functioning
4) No delay in communication (single words by age 2, phrases by age 3)
5) No delay in cognitive development, self-help skills, curiosity. I prefer the term "syndrome" because it means a "cluster of symptoms" rather than the term "disorder" which, while technically accurate, seems to me to have a more negative connotation.

Daniel's Answers (Age 29)

"I think a diagnosis can be helpful, but it loses its effectiveness if it's too general. I think it is a trend now, like ADHD was, when any kid bored in class who wanted to go out on the playground and didn't want to listen to a lecture for 8 hours straight, they would pull out and diagnose and give medicine to. I think of [Asperger syndrome] in the same light. It's a generalization that could fit a lot of people."

PIECE 92 — DIAGNOSIS

The word diagnosis comes from the Greek meaning "split apart... knowledge." Diagnosis is the process where professionals use their experience and skill to analyze information they gather through observation or examination. Diagnosis is like a descriptive opinion, based on facts, such as calling something yellow, red or blue, large or small.

Steve is a rebel. He can't stand to be labeled. He hates it when I try to guess which one of sixteen personality categories he would fit into. His eyes glaze over when I talk about my fascination with personality styles, such as are described in the Myers-Briggs inventory of preferences to:

Introversion/Extraversion,
Intuitive/Sensing,
Thinking/Feeling,
Perceptive/Judging.

Steve changes the subject when I discuss the four psychological temperaments of Phlegmatic, Choleric, Sanguine, and Melancholic. He doesn't want to hear about the nine classifications of the ancient Enneagram personality typing system.

I like identifying bird species by the colors of their feathers, their beak shape, their behavior and song. I enjoy identifying trees by their leaves and bark. I feel satisfied when I know the names of shells I find on the beach. Knowing how to identify snakes by their colorful patterns is useful, because if I come upon a copperhead, I know to leave it alone and move away. If I see a black rat snake or a green garden snake, I can walk up closer to it to admire it. I know I can pick it up and feel how smooth it is.

Steve does not want to be grouped in any way. He thinks psychological diagnoses make people seem pathological, rather than just normal variations of being human. He says categorizing mental function is ridiculous, because every human brain is unique. Steve says labels don't help him, because he acts the same way no matter what.

Having information about someone helps me to know how to approach them. If I know someone is grieving a recent death, then I know not to run up to them and tell them a silly joke. If I know someone doesn't like to be touched, then I know not to hug them.

After twenty-three years of getting to know my son, I still couldn't understand how to help him grow up. I was puzzled. What did he need? What motivated him? He wouldn't communicate much, so how could I understand him better? I had collected lots of information over the years. I had his school records, medical records, my diaries, and stories. I pulled it all together into one notebook. But I didn't know where to go to get someone to evaluate him and the information.

I called every mental health office in the yellow pages. No one specialized in Asperger syndrome. Finally, someone referred me to the local center for studying epilepsy. I never would have thought to call them, because Daniel certainly did NOT have seizures, but what did make sense is that they study the brain. I scheduled a neuropsychological evaluation for Daniel.

Ten hours of testing over a three day period included:
* Diagnostic Interview
* Wechsler Adult Intelligence Scale—III
* Rorschach Inkblot Test
* Wechsler Memory Scale—III
* Stroop Color and Word Test
* Personality Assessment Inventory
* Peabody Picture Vocabulary Test

* Brown Attention Deficit Disorder Scale
* Expressive Vocabulary Test
* Fisher Auditory Problem Checklist
* Personality Assessment Screener
* Conners' Continuous Performance Test II
* Gilliam Autism Rating Scale
* Gilliam Asperger's Disorder Scale
* EEG (Electroencephalogram)
* Halstead-Reitan Neuropsych. Battery
* Woodcock-Johnson Psychoeducational Battery Tests of Achievement

In addition, to screen us as parents for issues in providing consistency, emotional support, and structure required by a child with special needs, Steve and I both took Personality Assessment Screener and ACOA Checklist.

One month after the testing concluded, we re-convened for a conference to discuss the findings. We were given a six page written report, which gave an overview, itemized test results, summarized findings, and recommendations. The tests did show a profile consistent with Asperger's Disorder. It described Daniel as a very bright young man with excellent memory and solid academic skills, who has difficulty with social interactions and relationships, and who is uncomfortable asserting his needs or wishes.

Was it helpful to get a neuropsychological diagnosis for Daniel? Steve would say no. I would say yes, because it:

1) Assured us all that the problem is not physical (such as brain damage.)

2) Condensed a mountain of paper to only six pages.

3) Not only gave a broad "label" but it described particular features—such as slow language processing—that helped us zero in on specific issues.

4) Gave us an official "label" we could show agencies that Daniel does need their support—such as Vocational Rehabilitation so they would provide a job coach.

Daniel's Answers (Age 29)

[What do you think about getting the diagnosis? I thought it was helpful, Dad thought it was not.]

"I was more on the side of it not being helpful. I just thought it was stupid. It was more like an IQ test."

[Do you accept the Asperger syndrome diagnosis now?]

"No, not unless everyone has some of it."

PIECE 93 — TWO-THIRDS

I call this my "Two-Thirds Rule of Developmental Delay." To estimate the social maturity of someone with Asperger syndrome, divide their chronological age by two thirds.

When Daniel was three years old, he acted socially like he was two. When he was six years old, he acted like he was four. When he was 12 years old, he acted like he was eight. Around teen years is when the disparity becomes evident. Three year olds, two year olds, four year olds, often mingle and play together. But once teen years begin, it becomes more obvious which children are mature and which are immature.

When Daniel started driving with a learner's permit at 15, socially, he behaved like a ten year old. Imagine—the audacity—of a ten year old driving a car! When Daniel went to college at age 18, it was like sending a 12 year old off to live on his own with no supervision. Now that Daniel is 27 years old, he has probably finally attained the social maturity of the average 18 year old college freshman. Now—this year—not nine years ago—would be the best time for him to begin college.

The good news to keep in mind is that a developmental delay means he will most likely catch up socially to his peers. Reaching adulthood, there is not as dramatic a contrast between ages. For example, in the workplace people of all ages work together, whether they are in their twenties or forties or sixties. It is socially acceptable for people of different ages to be in romantic relationships.

Once a person has reached adulthood, whether that is considered age 18 to vote, age 21 to purchase alcohol, or age 25 to rent a car, most adults function at the same relative social maturity level. Of course, the older, the wiser, but I am speaking of a generally accepted social maturity, not the more subtle characteristics gained from life experience. There is less distinction between adults aged 18-24 or 27-36; as there are obvious differences in abilities and independence between four-six year olds or 12-18 year olds.

So that gives me hope... until I remember that when David was a teenager, he was bitterly rude as he was "separating" from us, his parents, and establishing his independence. I sense, from a few thoughtless comments I'm getting from Daniel lately, that this is the same phase we are entering next. Oh, dear! At least I can remind myself that even if I am the victim or the recipient of snide remarks, at least it is evidence of Daniel's growing confidence and development.

Daniel's Answers (Age 29)

"I think it would be the other way around. I was always spending time around people older than me. I was more comfortable with adults. I was more interested in things grownups were interested in. People my age were interested in things like, music, or going to a concert, well, that could be just about a personal preference. But whatever it was, they were into it, and didn't understand why I wasn't into it."

[So maybe I should put another line on the chart, say, a 'four thirds' line showing that you were more mature than neuro-typicals in a certain way, for example, what would the word be—morally?]

"I don't know. I just know if you extrapolate, there was a disconnect with people your own age."

PIECE 94 — CARERS + NEEDERS

When I began to understand why Daniel is the way he is; it helped me to understand Steve. Daniel has been diagnosed with Asperger syndrome, but Steve has not. Steve seems to me to have some similar characteristics, but what do I know? I do believe he has perfected elaborate coping skills to deal with any possible "shadow" symptoms.

Experts say that people with AS seem to attract two kinds of people into their lives: bullies, sadly, on the one hand, but on the other hand, they tend to draw out maternal impulses in women who are natural "carers," often found in caring professions such as nursing, teaching, counseling, and social work.

This combination works great for the "needers," as they get their needs met. This combination also works in the short term for the "carers," who need to be needed. However, "carers" soon use up all their own resources fixing bottomless pits of needs until they themselves become burned out.

"Carers" can imagine what the "needers" need and usually know how to provide it. "Needers" do not naturally imagine what the "carers" need. Even if they begin to realize the existence of others' needs, the "needers" have to learn how to help the "carers."

The two use different languages: carers use emotional, relational language; needers use factual, logical language.

Email, Nilla to Marilyn February 16 (Daniel Age 25)
I have had a rough couple of months. Daniel has been sick and out of work since Christmas. It's hard for me to figure out the balance between helping him with serious life problems... and helping him to

separate from me and to learn to cope on his own. The Asperger syndrome throws a wrench into the mix.

I went to Florida for a month and stayed with my aunt and uncle. I "got back in shape" playing tennis and swimming and bicycling. I lost 35 pounds. I'm still exercising regularly and feeling so much more energy!

I'm benefitting from attending "Codependents Anonymous" and Twelve Step Meetings to help me remember to live my own life and to let go of living other people's lives. I've been such a caretaker all my life, so I'm working on new patterns... of taking care of myself for a change!

And I know you will recognize the craziness of my having to get Steve on board to help with Daniel, when Steve is so much like Daniel. I am purposely trying to get Steve involved with Daniel in every way possible, both for my own relief (though often it takes just as much "work" to bring Steve in... like trying to teach a young child to do housework... would be easier and quicker to fold the laundry yourself than to teach a child to do it) and especially because Daniel responds better to him than to me. It seems Daniel craves his dad's attention, but his dad does everything he can to stay out of it (It's not that he doesn't love Daniel, but maybe that he's very self-involved, and his primary modus operandi is *always* to "stay out of it.")

Truly, it is harder for Steve to do the things that Daniel needs most. For example, Steve is not as naturally skilled in "executive functioning," tasks, so those usually fall to me.

I am trying to work myself out of my job of living Daniel's life for him! I am trying to change jobs... to the one of living my own life! It won't be a smooth or rapid transition, but I'm taking baby steps in that direction. It's a convoluted balancing job, isn't it? Helping these guys grow up? Thanks for letting me vent. Therapeutic journaling, if nothing else!

My husband is mostly still just as clueless about Daniel. I still feel totally alone in "raising" Daniel. I wish my father, too, would step in and be more involved with his grandson, but I think he doesn't know what to do either. He and his wife have thirteen grandchildren between them, so they keep busy with their myriad sports activities, school performances, and celebrations.

I am doing OK. I am worn out from caring for so many other people for so, so many years. I have a hard time taking care of myself. I am worn out from my marriage as well. It is especially difficult because so many of the traits that I am trying to help Daniel with are echoed in Steve too, and that is what wears me down. It seems that the "doubling up" is more than I can handle.

I long for the day when I can share with Steve something about Daniel that Daniel needs help with—and Steve can share the burden—instead of uselessly explaining it away, like "He's 24 years old, he's old enough to do that by himself," or instead of Steve being overwhelmed in the same way that Daniel is overwhelmed. I feel like a single mother with three children instead of a protected, cared-for wife with emotional resources and mutual support to parent (together) two adult sons.

Sometimes everything seems wonderful, and other times, it feels just the opposite.

Steve explained to me recently, "I can't shut off my creative brain. It fills so much of my mind that there's not much room for other stuff. When I'm fixing my lunch, I'm not fully in the present. That's why I have my routines. That's why I can't have people talking to me when I'm cooking, or I won't know how many times I've added a cup of rice to the pot of water."

"Like just now, I was imagining something I was interested in editing on the computer, and I wasn't even aware that I was in the middle of taking a shower. That's why sometimes I can't remember if I have brushed my teeth. I tend to live in the future. I'm not really aware of what I am doing in the moment. That's why I use sticky notes, because if you ask me to do something and I don't get up right that minute to do it, I won't remember it again unless I write it down."

PIECE 95 — THREE THIEVES

Blame
Everyone looking for help seems to be pointing their finger somewhere else, demanding that someone else do something. The government needs to fund.... The schools need to provide.... The mental health agency should.... Vocational Rehab ought to.... Some parents are eaten up with anger, targeting external sources—such as vaccines or food additives or chemicals in the environment—for their child's condition. Of course it is important, collectively, to continue to pursue and to eradicate what causes harmful damage; just as it is critical that we fight cancer and that we work to eliminate injustices such as domestic violence. But if we, personally, dwell on blame day after day, our lives are wasted. If we constantly obsess over the negative and deny the positive aspects of our child's situation, we have missed the opportunity for joy and peace.

You have read my stories that point the finger of blame at physicians and psychologists who missed properly diagnosing my son. I blamed The Program for not performing up to my standards; I blamed my husband for not stepping in early enough. I remember that saying, "When you point a finger at someone else, three fingers point back at you." Try it. Point your index finger at an imaginary villain. Look down at your hand. It's true! Much of the responsibility for our problems belongs with our selves—but that doesn't mean we should blame ourselves either. Find ways to solve problems. Action is much more efficient and effective than wallowing in blame!

Guilt

Some parents are eaten up by guilt, regretting they didn't identify their child's disability sooner. I used to feel that way. How could I, his mother, not have recognized the signs? I used to imagine that if my mother had lived longer than 51 years, she would have spotted this. If she had been around as Daniel grew up, past his age of five when she died, she would have known that something was not quite right. Having raised four children, she would have noticed that Daniel's development was not on the typical timeline.

Grief

How would you choose to have your grief served to you if it came on a platter? All at once in massive quantity, as it must seem when experiencing a sudden, violent accident or tragic death? Or would you prefer your grief dribbled and trickled daily, regularly, in smaller portions, kind of like making a dribble sand castle... dribble... dribble... drip... drip... drip... dribble...? Fresh wounds constantly re-opened, so the scab never seems to heal over.

Some people need status in the community or financial wealth to feel secure. My currency is emotion. My bills are printed on the paper of love with the ink of affection; my coins are stamped in denominations of smiles and hugs. As a writer, I love words. I interact with life through the beauty of language. I am sensitive to people around me. I understand people by interpreting their facial expressions, by anticipating the meaning in their posture. My life, the very essence of my being, is centered on relationships, interdependence, and interactions among caring people.

Daniel's currency is logic and silence. He restricts his energy expenditure. What he is comfortable offering socially is so minimal that it is a rare commodity. It is scarce, and therefore expensive, so he hoards it, protects it, guarding his expression like a Brinks driver would his payload. He isolates himself; he is rigid, stoic, pulled away from people.

My fluent verbosity contrasts starkly against Daniel's paucity of words. The silence is the worst of withdrawals to me. When I am lost in the middle of the desert of his silence, I thirst for one drop of liquid language to quench my despair. I wish he would yell at me, scream at me, and curse me. I long for him to slam doors at me in anger. I would take any kind of reaction, other than nothingness, the emptiness, the vacuum.

As intensely as Daniel avoids interaction, I need it for my survival. I feel so limited by his rationing, that I feel starved emotionally. I crave give-and-take the way I imagine the WW II generation felt deprived of sugar, or the way drinkers during the prohibition era must have been desperate for alcohol.

Each individual family member needs to process their own sense of loss on their own timetable. Even though we think our grief is resolved, it may sneak back in and surprise us when least expected.

These three thieves: Blame, Guilt, and Grief, are real. They exist. Be prepared for their assault. Acknowledge their presence. To pretend they are not there gives them permission to steal everything you value most. Defend yourself against their destruction. Be encouraged. Keep on. Let go, but never, never, never, never give up.

I am not a poet; but I tried to arrange words to express my grief:

GRIEF

The pain, the grief, the loss...

of having a child not speak,

not look me in the eyes, never give me a hug,

nor acknowledge my existence, except, maybe, a slight nod...

no "Hi, Mom,"

no conversation, no interaction,

no transaction in my verbal currency of love and affection...

no payoff in my primary language of relationship...

on   ly

lone   ly

se   pa   ra   tion

i   so   la   tion

dis   tance

dis   con   nec tion

g r i e f .

PIECE 96 — HIGH SOCIETY

S teve had said, "Meeting your family was like going to the moon."As I wondered what he meant, I envisioned the night sky, full moon rising. The phrase "High Society" popped into my mind.

High Society... Hmmm. I began ruminating on *society* as the "macro" aspect of the world: the bigness of the universe, the height, the width. The sky is visible (on clear nights) for anyone and everyone to see. Society is about observing and participating in relationships, just as distance, power and importance of planets, moons, and stars influence each other in space.

My father loves books and learning. His broad, intellectual knowledge—it seems he knows something about everything—means he can converse with interest about almost any topic.

Every day, my mother made connections between people, introducing someone she just met to another of the myriads of people she already knew, for their mutual benefit. The value of my parents' abilities was visible and socially acceptable. They fit easily into the "Who's Who" of "High Society."

My husband Steve did not fit into that world. For him, visiting my family and participating in the social world was like traveling into distant space, which required of him as much energy as a rocket blast; skills he didn't have, like technical equipment needed for a risky space-walk.

Steve had said he "lived in his own world." I would portray him as living in a "micro" world, the smallness of the universe, down to the cells, the DNA, the atoms, the infinitely tiny, most basic elements.

I am *not* saying Steve's life is insignificant. I am saying the opposite. As science has discovered through the microscope, and as inventions such as nanotechnology in the computer field are revealing, the "micro" world is as infinite in its depth as the stars are in their breadth.

The main difference between the two types is that the "macro" is visible to anyone and everyone. The "micro" is invisible without a tool such as a magnifying glass or a microscope. Its invisibility makes it prone to doubt and confusion.

My husband's gift for painting; his novel presentation of visual perspectives; my son's talents in programming a computer—are all evidence of their rich depth. Their character qualities are deep, basic, grounded, solid, and as stable as the earth itself.

Maybe Steve and Daniel aren't at ease in "High Society." Their essence may be less accessible to the outside world, but if you are patient and skilled enough to look inside, you would be amazed by the unfathomable treasure. Maybe their essence could be called "Deep Individuality."

I find myself in the position of intermediary; the "go-between" person; the translator. I speak the language of both ends of the spectrum, near and far. I am the interpreter between depth and breadth, but sometimes my flexibility is stretched to the breaking point as I attempt the nearly impossible.

PIECE 97—CASSANDRA

...Yet, mad with zeal, and blinded with our fate,
We haul along the horse in solemn state;
Then place the dire portent within the tow'r.
Cassandra cried and curs'd th' unhappy hour;
Foretold our fate; but, by the god's decree,
All heard, and none believ'd the prophecy.

—Virgil's *Aeneid.* 2.323, Dryden translation

Remember the classical story of the Trojan Horse? In Greek mythology, Cassandra was known as the most beautiful daughter of King Priam of Troy. The god Apollo fell in love with Cassandra and gave her the gift of prophecy. When she didn't return his affections, Apollo twisted her gift with a curse that no one would ever believe her. In this story about the Trojan War, Cassandra warns her father not to accept the giant statue, but he disregards what she says. He orders the gift horse brought inside the fortification. In the night, enemy soldiers hidden within the horse climb out and kill them.

Many times in my life I have felt like Cassandra, in instances ranging from the petty to the consequential. Like when I was a little girl and I told my dad he should tie down the fragile baby cradle he had loosely set inside his car trunk. I knew how much this family heirloom meant to my mother. Quietly, I offered, "Dad, it's going to fall out." He was in a hurry and couldn't be bothered. He scolded me, "It will be fine. We're only going a few miles. Get back in the car." A few turns later, the fine piece of furniture, handmade of cherry wood, lay splintered across the road. My dad huffed out of the car, picked up the fragments, and tossed them into the trunk in angry silence.

I felt like Cassandra when the pediatrician wouldn't acknowledge my concerns about my newborn baby, that his stomach was bloated, that he was constipated, that he seemed lethargic, that something just wasn't right. The pediatrician smiled patronizingly, gently patting my shoulder, "Hmmm. It is probably indigestion. Many babies are colicky." After five weeks of my complaining continually on my baby's behalf, Daniel was diagnosed with a life-threatening condition. His bowels were not functioning. He needed immediate surgery and a colostomy.

I felt like Cassandra when I told my husband that 11 year old Daniel shouldn't be on the computer hour after hour after hour, day after day, that there was more to life than computers, and that he should be interacting more with people. I told Steve that Daniel should be making his own friends instead of always falling back on Steve as his only "playmate." Steve's answer was always, "I was just like him when I was younger. He will be fine."

I felt like Cassandra when my 18 year old son purchased chicken from a street vendor who handled money, meat and dirty rags with the same unwashed hands, when I told my son to wash his hands after a full day of sightseeing before eating that same chicken with his bare hands, when he spent the next day vomiting from the food poisoning and that night in the hospital getting intravenous fluids.

I felt like Cassandra when I asked Daniel's high school counselor to evaluate him for depression, to refer him to a professional psychologist, and the counselor emailed me "to allay my concerns" and that "Daniel said he was fine," and that he was "smiling and looked great."

On the outside, Daniel did look great; kind of like the big, mysterious horse appeared attractive to the Trojans. I, like Cassandra, was the only one shouting warnings. I believed there were conditions hidden within my son that should not have ever been ignored.

Daniel's Answers (Age 29)
"This is just a fancy way of saying, 'I told you so.'"

PIECE 98—WIZARD OF ODDS

"Somewhere, over the rainbow, way up high…" the tune popped into my mind and circled around a while, repeating over and over. I hummed along as though I could see the notes writing themselves on sheet music, moving up and down on the musical scales in front of my eyes.

Somewhere inside these lyrics there was an explanation for my life. Somewhere someone knows how I came to where I am today. It seems that I have been in another world for years. It seems at some point, my life took a bizarre detour, which became both disorienting and lovely.

Just like Dorothy's character in the *Wizard of Oz* movie, I thought I was living a normal life with my mother and father, doing normal things like going to school and helping out with chores at home, like Dorothy on the Kansas farm.

Then, like Dorothy in the cyclone, during my teenage years I was swept up in confusion, trying to figure out who I was. The world swirling by outside my window revealed that my parents weren't as perfect as I thought they were. I was searching for the ultimate meaning of the universe.

As my childhood crashed into the Land of Odds, I met all these strange people, foreigners, who called themselves Christians. Still dazed from the hormones of puberty, I tip-toed amongst these cheery, helpful folk and realized I liked this colorful new place and I wanted to belong here.

When I asked for direction, they told me to follow. A spirit appeared, like Glenda, who told me the evil one, like the evil Wicked

Witch of the East, had been destroyed. She said I must never remove or give away what I had been given, like the ruby slippers.

On my journey, I met the love of my life in a corn field, of all places, with his arms outstretched, a flimsy looking fellow who said he didn't have a brain but he wanted one. He said he would join me. He stayed with me, loyal until the very end, in spite of mortal danger.

Together, the two of us came upon a figure who couldn't move on his own and was in need of "surgical" intervention. He said he wanted a heart. He came along with us and later saved our lives, only because he was not vulnerable to our weaknesses, like the Tin Man in the poppy field.

The three of us were startled by the appearance of a cuddly figure, who admitted that in spite of his fierce reputation, he was afraid of a lot of things. He completed our odd foursome and used his outspoken courage to help us find our way.

In spite of many terribly frightening ordeals, I finally learned to "throw cold water on" the worst evils, then pick myself up, only hanging on to what is useful, like the broom, and keep on going.

My cute, perky little dog has been a comforting companion, proving to me that conversation is not essential to love and devotion, in either direction of giving or receiving.

We discovered some practical assistance and resources, like in the Emerald City. We encountered some ridiculous situations and pitiful people, most of whom meant well, but who were misinformed or exaggerated their power, like the Wizard.

Through this adventure, against all odds, each of us discovered that we already possessed what we desired. The Scarecrow, brilliantly intelligent, used his genius to enlighten the world. The Tin Man had the biggest of hearts and was full of love and empathy and caring— freely available to anyone who will look past his metallic exterior. Every day the Lion faced his fears, knocking down wrongs with confidence and moral strength, constantly guarding the innocent.

Dorothy still wears the ruby slippers, symbolic of her earthly essence, encased, protected by and belonging to the most permanent and perfect of homes. Now she understands that all she has to do, no matter where she lives, no matter what the odds of the situation she finds herself in, is to close her eyes and *ask*.

As simple as clicking her heels three times, when she acknowledges the *truth*, "There's no place like home. There's no place like home. There's no place like home," she is immediately transported to a state where she is loved, where she is safe, and where she belongs.

Dorothy does know for sure now that she could not have survived and made it through on her own. Yes, she was incredibly brave. She was persistent. She never gave up. Eventually, she found her way home. But meanwhile, many others were caring for her, each in their own way.

Something seemed familiar, dream-like, or from another world... about the family and farm hands standing around looking at her. Oddly enough, one looked like the Scarecrow, one looked like the Tin Man, and one looked like the Lion. Now they are all part of her story.

Daniel's Answers (Age 29)
[Dad said this was his favorite "chapter." What did you think of it?]
"I lost the ability to follow along around the fourth or fifth paragraph."

PIECE 99—NO MAN'S LAND

The term "no man's land" originated in traditional war, where each army lined up to battle and the "no man's land" was the area between them. No man wanted to be in this vulnerable position because there was no defense and a high probability of death.

On a tennis court, there is an area between the service line and the base line called "no man's land" where it is more difficult to return the ball. Tennis players strategically avoid remaining in this rectangular area in the middle of the court. When they are in "no man's land," they are at a disadvantage; their opponent can hit the ball at their feet, where it is difficult to return the ball.

Ideally, tennis players position themselves either behind the baseline, in a strong position to return deep ground strokes, or they approach the net so they are in a strong position to return volleys at sharp angles out of their opponent's reach.

My son Daniel is a fantastic tennis player. His athleticism makes him quick on his feet, with a beautiful, smooth stroke. He can place the ball where he wants it to go. He has had years of lessons and practice and playing. He knows where to position himself on the court.

But in the game of life, he is often stuck in "no man's land." He struggles with communication, executive function, and socialization. He is developmentally delayed. In life, he should be playing "mini-tennis" on a half-court like young children do when they are learning the game.

He is so slow to comprehend what someone is saying that it is like he is in no-man's land, where awareness of body language lands at his feet as the words go whizzing past his racket. When it is his turn to hit a conversational ball, it lands in the net, as he doesn't say anything at all.

In tennis, everyone is an individual with their own specific strengths and weaknesses. Some people are physically fit, able to sprint up the court to return a dinky drop shot. Some have good hand-eye coordination, which gives them an advantage connecting the sweet spot of the racket with the little yellow ball. Some tennis players taught themselves to play; others have had lessons. Some practice on the backboard or with a ball machine, day after day, perfecting their strokes. Some play in competitive tournaments; others play only a few times a year.

Just like on the tennis court, in the game of life there is a wide range of abilities among people, including a large variation within the autism "spectrum." High-achieving "neuro-typicals," if compared to skilled tennis players, usually prefer the familiarity of being surrounded by other "neuro-typicals." Skilled tennis players usually do not want to play with a beginner; they want their match to be competitive. If they do agree to hit with a beginner, they have to summon all their patience—or be paid for their tolerance, such as teaching professionals do.

Some improvement in tennis comes with lessons and practice. There are some social skills Daniel can learn, and others he can practice over and over again until they become familiar. But he will never be a "natural" at socializing or communicating like a natural athlete can pick up any sport with ease—Daniel will always have to work hard at social skills.

My son Daniel is fully alive. He is made just the way God created him to be. He is a wonderful person in so many important ways. In the game of life, with his huge heart, he does know how to "serve" others. He is accomplishing his goals; but so slowly; with so much difficulty! It is as if he is stuck in life's "no man's land," where he is constantly on the defensive, barely surviving the point, and usually losing the point.

Staying on My Side of the Net
Sometimes while I am playing singles tennis, the game becomes a living metaphor that teaches me about my life. I realize that the net represents a line I must not cross, symbolic of keeping good psychological boundaries. It is important for me to stay on *my side* of the net. I can't live other people's lives for them. They must live their own lives, suffer their own losses, and celebrate their own wins. I can't hit the ball for them. I can't run over to the other side of the net and return the ball for them.

I remember to focus on my own racket. I can only play the ball that falls on my side of the court. If I reach over the net to hit a ball, if I even touch the net, I lose the point. Playing *my game* —and not my opponent's game—is a way for me to practice lessons I've learned about co-dependence. The best way for me to improve my game is to be in good physical shape, able to run quickly from side to side.

Singles vs. Doubles

When I hear Daniel has trouble I *know* I should stand back and let him feel his own feelings and find his own solutions, but I *feel* like redoubling my efforts and rushing in to rescue him. There is another tennis metaphor! If Daniel is playing singles, I am not allowed on his side of the court. All I can do is cheer from the sidelines, as a spectator.

If he has invited me to be his partner in playing tennis doubles, then he and I work as a team, backing each other up, compensating for the other's weakness, and suggesting winning strategies.

Daniel's Answers (Age 29)

[Do you acknowledge you have struggles?]

"Oh, yes."

PIECE 100 — SERPENTINE BELT

Steve *hates* to put together jigsaw puzzles. His only pleasure is in hiding one piece in his pocket, so when the puzzle is almost complete, everyone becomes frustrated by the missing piece.

Steve smirks to watch heads bob under the table, searching the floor for a misplaced fragment, as others blame the manufacturer and look for a toll free number so they can complain.

Finally, with great fanfare, Steve produces the missing piece and dramatically fits it in place. It is his way of being sure that he is the winner. The rest of us didn't know we were entered in a competition. We thought we were working together in a cooperative project! Steve learned this trick from my father, whose puzzling tradition has been fooling us for generations.

In the same way, Steve waited until I finished writing this book to produce the final piece to complete the puzzle. Ta-da! Dramatic flourish! Drum roll!

Steve and I were out walking the dogs. I heard an odd noise made by the motor of a passing car. I asked Steve what caused such a squeaking. "What's making that noise? The fan belt?"

"Yeah, probably the fan belt, or possibly the serpentine belt."

"The serpentine belt? I've never heard of that. What is it?"

"Cars used to only have one belt, which operated a fan, which blew air on the engine to keep it cool. In today's more complex engines, the serpentine belt connects all the different systems, like the air conditioning, water pump, alternator, and power steering. It is very difficult to replace because it winds around, you know, like a snake, looped this way and that, all through the engine."

Later that day, Steve came to me, all excited, "You've got to put serpentine belt in your book!"

Me: "Huh?" My eyebrows tensed into a puzzled expression. "Why?" I giggled at his enthusiasm. I could tell he wanted to participate in this creation of mine. How could I politely express my appreciation, while still keeping his wacky ideas out? Carefully, I defended, "But I had never heard of a serpentine belt before today—how could I put it in my book?" I tried to dismiss him gently, "Anyway, I don't think most people know what it is."

Determined, he continued, "You are just like the serpentine belt in a car. Our family couldn't operate without you. Look here." He showed me a more detailed explanation from Wikipedia on his laptop:

"A serpentine belt is a single, continuous belt used to drive multiple peripheral devices in an automotive engine. It is *more efficient* than the older multiple belt system. By using a single, wider belt instead of multiple, thinner belts, the belt *may be put under increased tension* without stretching. *Higher tension reduces slip*, which *increases belt life and mechanical efficiency*. Reduced slip can allow the use of lower-ratio pulleys; this *reduces the load on the engine, increasing fuel economy and available power."*

I agreed, "Yeah, I can definitely relate to the 'increased tension' part."

Steve read on, in his usual, stumbling reading voice: "The drawback of this single belt is *that if the belt breaks, the vehicle loses all of its peripheral devices;"* Steve bravely lunged ahead, one word at a time, like a first-grader terrified of reading aloud in class. "... however, the belt *typically gives ample visual warning of impending failure,* sometimes even *totally shedding several grooves (ribs) while still continuing to function normally."*

I felt touched by Steve's persistence and enthusiasm. "I admit my stress has definitely been giving ample warnings of impending failure. And I do feel like I've been wearing thin, although still functioning. Don't know about the 'normal' part."

He clicked a few more keys and read from another automotive website, "Making sure your serpentine belt is working correctly is *essential for any motorized vehicle to continue moving."*

"See what I mean?" he complimented me, "It says if the serpentine belt breaks, the car can't run! Our family couldn't have survived without you."

Steve did it! He came up with the final piece to the puzzle! I am honoring his competitive spirit by allowing him to fit the last piece of this book in place.

Here is a loving letter I've saved from ten years ago:

Letter, Steve to Nilla March 19 (Steve, Age 42, Nilla Age 40)
Dear Nilla,

I want to Thank you for many Things but for a few specific Things. Thanks for being so sweet to me and loving. You are so special and I am blessed to be married to you. Thank you for your respect and affection That you so dearly give me. Thank you for your honesty and genuiness (I can't spell). And Thank you for putting up with my "brain lapses". I love it when you are sweet to me as you have been These past few months. It helps me to make it Through stressful days.

Also Thanks for conviencing me to start learning the cello. I have thought about it for maybe 10 yrs. I never would have started had you not pursued me and gotten me in to the music store that day. It seems so much of my life has been that way. I would never have realized most of my dreams if I had never met you. You bring out the best in me. I only hope I do the same for you. I love you. Steve

STEP EIGHT
SEEING THE BIG PICTURE

Nilla's Method for Completing a Jigsaw Puzzle
1.   First, I turn all the pieces out of the box.
2.   I plop the pieces onto the table into a big jumbled pile.
3.   Turning over each upside-down piece right-side up, I begin to see what I have.
4.   Next is finding edges—pieces with straight edges form the outer border.
5.   I look for matching details like fragments of words, faces or shapes.
6.   I start fitting together complementary pieces to form the central design.
7.   Nearing the end, I focus on solidly colored pieces, linking background.
8.   **Seeing the completed image, I admire my work and pat myself on the back.**

The puzzle is finished. There is nothing more to do. I like to sit for a while and look at it, from all different angles. I run my hand over the puzzle, satisfied by the smoothness of the surface, simultaneously aware of the ridged textures formed where the pieces connect.

I might leave the puzzle assembled for a few days, and walk past it frequently, to reinforce my relief that it is complete.

After a few hours or a few days, or when I am ready to use my dining table again, I return the puzzle to the box. I separate the pieces carefully, knowing the next time someone opens the box, pours the pieces out on to the table, turns them over, finds the edges, matches the details, fits them together, links the background, and sees the big picture, the puzzling will become as much of a challenge once again.

CONCLUSION—PEACE BY PEACE

Piece by piece, I have examined my life from childhood. I married a quirky man who hugged me before we met. I smothered two amazingly gifted sons to adulthood. David finished college and a professional degree, landed a responsible job managing finances, and married a beautiful woman. Daniel still struggles with everyday coping skills and the basics of communication and social relationships.

Whether Daniel arrived at birth genetically molded to portray Asperger syndrome, or whether his symptoms developed due to poor digestion, head trauma, or chemical toxins, or whether his defenses resulted from a harsh cultural environment that judged and bullied anyone who appeared different, or whether his personality boiled over from the stress that bubbled around two anxious and peculiar parents—Daniel is the way he is.

What puzzles me is that *no one* identified Daniel's disability. Not parents, grandparents, aunts, uncles, friends, teachers, school counselors, boarding school guidance counselors, college counselors, pediatricians, physicians, psychologists, psychiatrists. *No one,* over a lifetime, over a generation, over more than two decades, *no one,* over 1, 2, 3, 4, 5, 6, 7, 8, 9, 10, 11, 12, 13, 14, 15, 16, 17, 18, 19, 20, 21, 22, 23 years containing 365 ¼ days each, recognized Daniel's gaping needs. Oh, some guessed behavioral problems or anxiety, or later maybe depression. Others supposed maybe he was just shy, or that he had a hard time making friends because of moving around so much as a teenager, or that he was going through an awkward phase and would grow out of it. It is true that Asperger syndrome wasn't officially designated as a diagnosis until Daniel was 13, but that still left a 10 year vacuum. Maybe Daniel's strengths overwhelmed the visibility of his disability. Maybe my motherly meddling suffocated any evidence of Daniel's needs.

The solution to the puzzle sprouted modestly from black soy-based ink printed on a flimsy piece of slick paper. When I first read the article in the popular weekly magazine I didn't give it much attention, but a seed was planted. The idea lay dormant, buried under layers of papers shoveled into a darkened closet. The idea germinated quietly over the winter months.

When spring arrived I found out that the church counselor whom I had entrusted to shepherd Daniel had abruptly told him to "never contact her again." I couldn't believe this wise woman had misread my gentle son. In the midst of my bewilderment I remembered the hidden story. I dug around in my cluttered closet until I unearthed the pages that held the hint that Daniel might have a form of autism.

The answer to Daniel's struggles originated from an impersonal, inanimate piece of printed material. No human recognized the problem. No human relationship made the connection with Daniel. On the still relatively new World Wide Web I searched "autism" and "Asperger syndrome." I printed off the diagnostic list of symptoms to analyze. How appropriate that the confirmation of Daniel's condition came through cyberspace, communicated through electronic bits of zeros and ones. How ironic that the implement that absorbed Daniel into its world and pulled him away from human social interaction would be the instrument that saved him. Through "Google" I found links to worldwide experts and I discovered a new treatment center for college-aged guys. Without the internet, no progress would have been made in finding help for Daniel.

Of course, if I hadn't been an obsessed mother, the ultimate connection between the printed pages to the stage of taking action would never have occurred. If I hadn't been a compulsive researcher, if I hadn't been so fiercely, stubbornly, obnoxiously determined to **never, never, never, never** give up on my son, Daniel probably would have continued to flounder on his own for years and years.

Life hasn't been as easy as I had expected. Raising Daniel has seemed like assembling a jigsaw puzzle while referring to the wrong picture for clues.

As I have reviewed my life piece by piece, I realized that whatever my circumstances, regardless of how I was raised, whether or not I had fallen in love with a man more similar to me in educational, social, economic status, and no matter what my children's mental, physical, or developmental abilities, no matter what financial or professional resources were available to me, my persistent personal nature would still have tended toward depression, obsession, and compulsive control. I am who I am.

Thanks to my loyal husband who is as stable as a granite wall, many lifelong friends who listen well, years of prayer, counseling, medication, and support from twelve-step meetings, I am finally learning to take responsibility for my own life one day at a time, and to let other people manage their own lives. Every day I recite the Serenity Prayer and every day I find new meaning in these 27 significantly simple words: "God, grant me the serenity to accept the things I cannot change, the courage to change the things I can, and the wisdom to know the difference."

I am learning that the only way to peace is through peace. The only way I can experience a sense of peace in my life is by accepting God's peace, by resting in Him. I cannot attain peace by force or control. I cannot achieve piece by solving life's puzzles. Having a definitive diagnosis of Daniel's condition hasn't brought peace. A full year of expensive residential therapy hasn't brought peace. Learning my own self-help diagnoses such as "co-dependent" or "enabler" helped me to get a handle on my behavior to try to avoid anxiety, but the labels themselves haven't brought peace. Complete "healing" from autism or co-dependence would be miraculous, but still wouldn't bring complete peace.

The only way to peace is through the peace of letting go. I dedicated my life to God when I was 17 years old. Now I remind myself every morning that I am not the one in control. I am finished assembling my 30 year puzzle. I have returned the 100 pieces to the box, closed the lid, and put the puzzle away. That doesn't mean God is done. He continues to teach me to trust Him through the chaos and craziness of life.

Finishing the puzzle doesn't mean I have given up on my son; only that I have given up doing what does *not* work—my addiction to caretaking, my needing to feel needed. At first, when I was letting go of directing Daniel's life, it *felt* to me like I was abandoning him, but I wasn't. I merely had to adjust to new and healthier patterns.

With practice and prayer, instead of constantly worrying about Daniel's growth I simply enjoy being with my son while we go to a movie or walk the dogs. I look for chances to ask him for advice. Instead of pleading for him to join me at my hurried pace, I try to enter his world on his terms. I put aside my agenda so that we can wander around the local farmers' market. Passively, I follow his lead and stop only when he stops. Now I see more than the fresh flowers and vegetables within my rehearsed focus. Daniel opens my eyes to the funky homemade chocolate lollipops.

I still grieve for the hugs I miss and the conversations I crave. My sadness for my loss continues to sting, but I turn my focus to appreciating the treasure of his character, even if it is rarely shared.

I take a deep breath so I can accept the uncomfortably long periods of silence. Grateful for any opportunity to be together, I am willing to sit with him in the dark in his apartment instead of asking him to turn on the lights. Oddly enough, my eyes are adjusting. I now see more clearly how to allow Daniel to live his own life while I go about living mine.

ACKNOWLEDGEMENTS

Puzzled was born in 2008 as a creative project assigned by leaders Janet Fox and Tim Binkley during a workshop based on Julia Cameron's books *The Artist's Way* and *Walking in This World*. My "creative champions" Melrose Buchanan, Nadine Buckinger, Grace Ellis, Janet Fox, Amy Sanders and Hilda Spain stoked me with positive, honest critiques through the years.

A lifetime of appreciation to my father, Joe Dudley, for drenching my childhood in language and surrounding me with his infectious love of books. My college English professor Dr. Floyd Watkins is gone now, but his impossibly high standards still echo through every edit.

How would I have made it through the tears of those critical years without kind listeners Rick Downs, Margaret Harrison, Linda McCoy, Lisa Miller, Jim Morgan, Shannon Rainey, Vivian Turnau and Louise Walpin?

My gratitude goes to manuscript reviewers Dudley Bell, Ashley Bickerstaff, Jane and Julie Bremer, Kirk and Sharon Childs, Ann Covington, Eustacia Cutler, Clyde Godwin, Julia Ann and Ted Goins, Beth and Brian Haskell, Jeanne Lenham, Ella Long, Sandra McGee, Rich Montgomery, Annette and Elise Morgan, Katherine Stoyer, Janice Weiss, Peggy Whalen-Levitt, Allie Wilmot, Jeanie Snow Wilson and Amelia Wong; and to Kim Shufran, founder of the fabulous organization The iCan House; and to copy editors, sharp-eyed Ginny Evans and my wise friend Ruthie Kirk.

My heart belongs to my husband Steve, for his unconditional love, constant encouragement and visual eye. Thanks to my son David, for his "coaching" and advice.

Most of all, thanks to Daniel, for contributing his valuable perspective in response to *Puzzled*'s "pieces" and especially for bravely consenting to allow his life to be examined as if under a microscope and then shared to help others. He is an amazing person and I am so proud to be his mother.

ABOUT THE AUTHOR

Nilla Dudley Childs lives in Winston-Salem, North Carolina in a one-story stucco cottage with her husband Steve. Nilla has been a mother (her most important career) for thirty years. While smothering her two sons Daniel and David with maternal attention, she helped her husband Steve market his fine-art paintings, portraits and films. In the 1990s, Nilla directed art museum education in Logan, Utah and at the High Museum of Art in Atlanta, Georgia, then flourished as Creative Product Editor with Hallmark Cards in Kansas City. Nilla attended Mount Holyoke College; she holds a B.A. in Liberal Studies from Emory University and a M.A. in American Studies from Utah State. Great-granddaughter of George Palmer Putnam of G. P. Putnam's Sons Publishing, Nilla naturally inherited a strong love of writing and books. Growing up, she adopted the persistent, can-do attitude of her great-grandfather's wife, Amelia Earhart.

Made in the USA
Charleston, SC
19 February 2012